D0098983

English, French, German and Italian Techniques of Singing:

A Study in National Tonal Preferences and How They Relate to Functional Efficiency

by

RICHARD MILLER

The Scarecrow Press, Inc.
Metuchen, N.J.   1977

Plates 1 and 7 (see page viii) are used by permission of the Williams & Wilkins Co., Baltimore, from Cunningham's Text-Book of Anatomy, 5th ed., ed. by Arthur Robinson (New York: William Wood and Co., 1919).

Plates 2, 14, 17, and 18 are used by permission from Atlas of Human Anatomy, vol. II, by Johannes Sobotta and J. Playfair McMurrich (New York: G. E. Stechert and Co., 1928).

Plates 3, 10, 13, 15, and 16 are used by permission from Gray's Anatomy, 35th British ed., ed. by Robert Warwick and Peter Williams (London: Longmans, 1973).

Plates 4, 5, and 9 are from Human Anatomy, ed. by Henry Morris (Philadelphia: P. Blakiston, Son & Co., 1893).

Plates 6 and 8 are used by permission from Integrated Anatomy and Physiology, 3d ed., by Carl C. Francis and Gordon L. Farrell (St. Louis: C. V. Mosby Co., 1957).

Plates 11 and 12 are from Hand-Atlas of Human Anatomy, 5th ed., by Werner Spalteholz (Philadelphia: J. B. Lippincott Co., n.d.).

Library of Congress Cataloging in Publication Data

Miller, Richard, 1926-
    English, French, German and Italian techniques of singing.

    Bibliography: p.
    Includes index.
    1. Singing--Instruction and study--History and criticism. I. Title.
MT823.M55   784.9'32   76-58554
ISBN 0-8108-1020-4

This study is dedicated to the many theater colleagues who over the years have discussed national approaches in singing with me, and to
those numerous English, French, German and
Italian teachers of singing who so generously
shared their studios and their methods with me.
To some extent, I am but their amanuensis.

TABLE OF CONTENTS

ACKNOWLEDGMENTS

It is not possible to mention the vast number of persons who have helped shape this book by supplying practical, empirical knowledge about techniques of singing. On the other hand, I can be very precise in acknowledging the assistance I have received from a number of sources with regard to physical function in singing. I owe a very real debt to several authors, some of whom are quoted in this work. Others have contributed in a more general way through their published research, among them especially Richard Luchsinger, David Brewer, Peter Ladefoged, Godfrey Arnold, Knud Faaborg-Andersen, Paul Moore, J. van den Berg, Ralph Appleman and William Vennard.

I wish to acknowledge the inclusion, by kind permission, of certain extracts from The Respiratory Muscles, 2d ed. (London: Lloyd-Luke [Medical Books], 1970), by Professor E. J. M. Campbell, M.D., et al. I wish to thank Professor Harvey Ringel, editor of the NATS Bulletin (put out by the National Association of Teachers of Singing) and Professor Homer Ulrich, editor of the American Music Teacher, for their kind permission to make use of material from those publications--the former, for portions of John Large's "Towards an Integrated Physiologic-Acoustic Theory of Vocal Registers," vol. 28, no. 3 (Feb./March 1972), and of Michael Smith's "The Effect of Straight-Tone Feedback on the Vibrato," vol. 28, no. 4 (May/June 1972); the latter for portions of Elizabeth Rado's "Breath Crisis in Relation to Breath and Resonance Control: I," vol. 23, no. 5 (April/May 1974). The Editorial Board of the Emporia State Research Studies kindly permitted quotation from Professor Robert Taylor's Acoustics for the Singer, which is vol. 6, no. 4 (June 1958) of that series.

Permission by his publishers, Faber and Faber Ltd., London, to quote from Arnold Rose's The Singer and the Voice (2d ed., 1971) was greatly appreciated. I am much indebted

to G. & C. Merriam Company for their permission to quote
from the "Guide to Pronunciation" in Webster's New International Dictionary, Second Edition, © 1959 by G. & C. Merriam Co.

To Oxford University Press go my thanks for permitting me
to use certain passages from Herman Klein's The Bel Canto
(London: Humphrey Milford, Oxford University Press, 1923).
William Heinemann Medical Books Ltd., London, kindly permitted quotation from a work by V. E. Negus, The Comparative Anatomy and Physiology of the Larynx (London: Hafner
Pub. Co., 1962 reprinting). David D. Slater's Vocal Physiology and the Teaching of Singing (London: J. H. Larway,
n.d.) has been quoted with the kind permission of Edwin
Ashdown Ltd.

Permission to use material from W. A. Aiken's The Voice;
An Introduction to Practical Phonology (London: Longmans,
Green & Co., 1963 printing) and from W. J. Henderson's
Early History of Singing (London: Longmans, Green & Co.,
1921) was granted by Longman Group Limited.

Especial thanks is due to Churchill Livingstone, the Medical
Division of Longman Group Limited, for permission to use
both quotations and illustrated material from Gray's Anatomy,
35th British ed. (1973), edited by William Warwick and Peter
Williams.

To the C. V. Mosby Co. of St. Louis, Mo., I am indebted
for the illustrations from Carl C. Francis and Gordon L.
Farrell's Integrated anatomy and physiology, 3d ed. (1957),
I must also extend thanks to the publishing firm of Urban &
Schwarzenberg, Munich, for the use of plates from Atlas
of Human Anatomy, vol. II by Johannes Sobotta and J. Playfair McMurrich (New York: G. E. Stechert and Co., 1928).
Thanks also go to the Williams & Wilkins Co., Baltimore,
for permission to use plates from Cunningham's Text-Book of
Anatomy, 5th ed., ed. by Arthur Robinson (New York: Wil-
liam Wood and Co., 1919).

I am grateful also for plates used from Henry Morris, ed.,
Human Anatomy (Philadelphia: P. Blakiston, Son & Co.,
1893), and from Werner Spalteholz's Hand-Atlas of Human
Anatomy, 5th ed. (Philadelphia: J. B. Lippincott Co., n.d.).

A more direct and personal acknowledgment must go to Lawrence C. Meredith, M.D., otolaryngologist, who kindly spent

tedious hours reading many portions of this work which deal with physical function; although he is in no way responsible for the accuracy of the ideas presented, he is to be thanked for helping to clarify for me some aspects of vocal mechanics.

I am also grateful to Robert Stillwell and to Daniel Messaros, photographers, for their very ready help with the illustrations in this book.

Last and most especially, I must acknowledge the generosity of the Research Status Program of Oberlin College which made possible released time to pursue and complete this project of many years. I have greatly appreciated the help and encouragement given me by various administrative officers and colleagues.

Richard Miller

INTRODUCTION

This study is based upon the premise that the character of vocalized sound is in part determined by tonal ideals which vary in some respects from one national school to another, and further, that the national schools of singing found in England, France, Germany and Italy, and in those neighboring countries with whom they respectively share a common cultural background, have developed technical means for achieving vocal sounds which accord with those ideals. These technical devices are clearly recognizable as distinct pedagogical positions.

Although historically these techniques are to be encountered predominantly within certain national or cultural boundaries, they have been exported as well, and are now to be found wherever the art of singing flourishes. Even in new locales they retain an allegiance to a set of aesthetic principles which indicate their cultural origins.

Multiplicity of Tonal Ideals

Surely it need not be argued that diversity with regard to the technical aspects of tone production exists among singers. It must be equally apparent that the technical means expressed within various pedagogies have developed in response to specific aesthetic goals. Of considerable interest is the extent to which variants in aesthetic and pedagogical goals relate to national propensities. In the process of comparatively examining these national tendencies, those areas which form the basis of vocal pedagogy must be investigated; such comparative investigation comprises the body of this study.

Often a young singer, trained in one pedagogical tradition, has little knowledge of how colleagues may approach the production of vocalized sound. Regardless of method, singers who are natively endowed with fine vocal instruments,

musicianly ears and communicative powers may find themselves in performance circumstances surrounded by a variety
of vocal techniques some of which are foreign to them.   A
singer soon discovers that a wide spectrum of vocal sound
is found to be acceptable, even desirable, to conductors, to
the Intendanten who hire singers, to the critics who evaluate
them, and to the often less than discriminating public which
applauds them.   The wider the singer's performance world
expands, the more evident it becomes that not all artists
(therefore, not all teachers who teach them) are looking for
the same tonal ideals.

    Observing the performance of colleagues, a singer may
well speculate as to how a particular vocal instrument might
sound if certain limitations or excesses built in by a given
pedagogy were removed.   He or she, on the other hand, may
observe the ease and control with which a colleague handles
an area of the voice which for that singer is still problematic.   Technical conflicts between one's own vocal production
and those of other singers may begin to give the young singer
pause.

    At first, such a singer might assume that there are
as many tonal ideals, and technical systems for achieving
them, as there are vocal pedagogues or singers (a favorite
assumption on the part of people who are superficially involved with singers).   On the contrary, any vocal method
can be classified fairly specifically on any single technical
matter.   Even those highly individualistic methods which one
encounters from time to time generally turn out upon closer
examination to be idiosyncratic variations, or compounds,
of several common pedagogical premises dealing with the
physical coordination involved in the production of the singing
voice.   The singer will also discover how totally without
foundation is the comment often heard from teachers of singing, who in spite of ample evidence to the contrary like to
maintain that "we are all after the same thing. "

    Only a naive singer, or one fanatically wedded to cer-
tain technical precepts, will close ears and mind to the existence of techniques other than his or her own.   In all
probability, the individual singer's technical approach is com-
prised of those elements which identify with one of the national schools of singing, even though the singer may be geographically remote from that school.

Purpose of This Study

It is the purpose of this study to examine in what ways
national preferences produce specific technical approaches and
to examine those techniques in relation to physical function.
In those cases where physical function must be violated in
order to produce a tone in keeping with a particular national
aesthetic ideal, the singer may wish to re-examine the sound
produced and look for some more efficient method of production. Without some knowledge of existing techniques a singer
is hardly in a position to assume that the peculiar technique
encountered by mere chance or physical location is unquestionably the superior one.

Areas of Pedagogical Controversy

It can be substantiated that various methods of breath
application make use of opposing physical actions, and that
registration principles differ widely. It is also observable
that there exist diametrically opposed attitudes toward resonance, vowel formation and modification, vocal coloration,
"cover," "placement," laryngeal positioning, buccal and
pharyngeal postures, the attack, vibrato rate, vocal classification, and the uses of falsetto. The most basic kinds of
muscular balance thought to induce proper coordination in
singing admittedly are variable from one technique to another.

National approaches to these areas of vocal technique
frequently stand in opposition to each other. It is the in-
tention of this study not only to identify these technical processes as they are found within specific national schools,
but when possible to describe the physical involvement which
produces them. Further, some critical evaluation as to their
functional efficiency is offered. This critical appraisal is
essential if the work is to serve its intended purpose of
assisting the singer to improve his or her own technical facility in singing.

Information Regarding This Study

Material contained in this study is partly the outgrowth of a number of years spent in Europe in direct association with many singers having backgrounds in specific national schools, partly the result of the accumulation of data
pertinent to the subject acquired over more than twenty-

five years, and in part the result of visits made to thirty-
six conservatories, academies, colleges and schools of music geographically and culturally related to the English,
French, German and Italian national schools. (See Appendix I.)

During the course of this study, more than 700 voice
lessons have been observed and analyzed from over 165 vocal
studios. Additionally, many teachers of singing have been
interviewed at some length on the subject of vocal pedagogy
with special reference to nationalism in singing.

It was, of course, always understood that anonymity
would prevail in any written report, so that no list of individual performers or teachers and no attribution of individual positions on pedagogy can be appended. The vocal techniques examined in this study were widely encountered among
a number of teachers and professional singers within a given
school.

Alternately, such a study could have been made with
the assistance of mechanical devices for collecting pertinent
data, supplemented by statistical survey. The present study
makes no attempt to present laboratory proof for the existence
of obvious, audible vocal phenomena within the four national
schools, but rather to describe and compare them.

For example, even the mildly discriminating lay ear
does not need to subject a singing voice to electromyography
in order to recognize a generally acceptable vibrato rate
(which falls within six to seven frequencies per second for
most listeners not conditioned otherwise), or conversely, to
hear an undesirably rapid tremolo. It may not be possible
to recognize the exact temporal rate of the vibrato, nor
know the contributing causes, but even the average non-pro-
fessional musical ear will detect the sound of a desirable
vibrato or any aberrations therefrom. Therefore, no attempt
has been made in this study to prove the existence of diverse
vibrato rates but rather to suggest what probable aesthetic
and technical factors may contribute to them. A similar approach is taken with most of the topics covered in this study.

If the lack of hard scientific data seems regrettable,
it should be noted that even in the most rigidly controlled
scientific investigations on vocal function, most conclusions
must ultimately be based upon subjective evaluation of the
"quality" of the sound, ranging from such categories as "best
to poorest quality," or described by such non-scientific terms

as "metallic," "pinched," "mellow," "soft," "ringing," etc.
Any aspect of singing which has to do with vocal timbre finally must be assessed by descriptions which remain somewhat
subjective. This study assuredly does not escape that kind
of subjectivism, no matter how objective its intent.

When interviewed on the subject of national tendencies
in the production of vocal sound, some individual singers and
teachers were extremely chauvinistic, demonstrating what they
felt to be the merits of their own national school and the deficiencies of another, not infrequently through the use of quite
recognizable parodistic means. The Italian will quickly demonstrate the excesses of the low-breath and distended abdominal posture of the German School; the German, in turn, will
display the higher chest position of the Italian singer. Both
demonstrations are given in evidence of excessive breath tension on the part of the other national school. The English
singer readily imitates what is considered to be the undesirable spread-smile position of the Italian singer, while the unkind parody of the English dropped jaw can be easily encountered anywhere on the Continent, but especially in France and
Italy. Many teachers in the non-French schools find the
French vocal sound to be characterized by a bright, thin,
nasal quality which they believe can be mimicked easily. (It
might be noted that the imitative powers of teachers of singing must be an earmark of the profession.)

Of further interest for this study is the extent to which
some teachers, geographically associated with a national
school, often point out its deficiencies with razor-sharp criticism, citing specific national tendencies against which they
themselves work. This is more specifically the case in Germany and England, and to a lesser degree in France, while
almost never occurring in Italy.

It would be false to assume that all teachers within a
national school can be uniformly associated with it, or that
any given teacher embraces all of the tendencies of a school
which may be here indicated. These qualifying considerations
will be given occasional mention within the body of the work,
but will be kept in mind constantly. The word typical sees
much service in this study.

With some frequency, teachers of singing who offered
opinions on the subject of national tendencies versus internationalism in singing, felt that the higher the perfection
achieved by the singing artist, the less apparent were the

vestiges of national approaches to vocal sound. Almost all agreed that a knowledgeable listener seldom mistakes any internationally accepted singer as having been trained in any school other than that from which the singer has emerged. Frequently, this kind of sentiment was remarked: "Of course you would never mistake 'so and so' as being anything but Italian-trained (or German, French or English), although he or she doesn't sound really typically so."

Certainly, a significant fact emerges: there is a nearly universal conviction among teachers of singing and among performers that vocal pedagogy does divide in many respects along lines of national tonal ideals. Surprisingly, little examination of those divisions has taken place, nor have they been subjected to comparative studies. This study is devoted to such an examination.

The decision to restrict this survey to the English, French, German and Italian Schools was made chiefly for practical reasons of time and the dictates of personal history. In any event, it seems probable that the four major national schools treated in this study have been the chief contributors to the history of vocalism in the Western world. However, there is sufficient evidence of distinctive pedagogical concepts in other national or regional Western cultures to indicate that some interesting variations in tonal aesthetics and in vocal techniques might be encountered outside the four major schools.

A number of European teachers and singers firmly believe that a Russian School of singing is identifiable, based on clearly differentiated technical emphases, and that distinctly individualistic tendencies exist in that part of middle-eastern Europe comprising much of what was formerly the Austro-Hungarian Empire. Still others feel that Scandinavia and Spain respectively offer interesting technical variations on the Germanic and Italianate schools. For the present, however, these schools lie outside the survey.

While this work intends to treat a number of vocal subjects in as logical sequence as possible, it has also been devised so that each chapter topic is more or less complete in itself. If a particular reader has specific interests, it is appropriate to go directly to the section dealing with them.

Chapter I

THE ATTACK

Skilfully coordinating the pressure of the breath with
the proper degree of tension within the vocal valve produces
the clean, crisp, initial sound which characterizes the good
attack.   Conflicting attitudes toward the production of a good
attack can be identified among schools of singing, differentiated to a large extent by national preferences for specific
kinds of vocal sound.

The Physical Action

In phonation, there is a split-second preparatory action during which time an adduction process reduces the
glottis to a linear chink.   This fissure (the glottis) between
the vocal folds changes its shape in response to action by the
muscles of the larynx.   (See Plate 1.)   The internal laryngeal
muscles, cricothyroid, cricoarytenoid and thyroarytenoid, are
engaged in complicated patterns of movement, during which
varying degrees of tension and relaxation are achieved.   In
addition, the vocal cords themselves play a role, being capable of degrees of resistance or passivity to the breath
pressure which strikes them, and to some extent, to the
longitudinal pull (stretching action) exercised by the cricothyroid muscles, as well as to the adduction activities of the lateral and posterior cricoarytenoid muscles.   (See Plates 2 and 3.)

The muscular action which takes place in approximat-
ing the vocal folds is too complex to submit to voluntary control of individual muscle groups, yet the conceptual ideal of
the attack has a direct bearing upon that muscular coordination.   In some pedagogies even the word attack is avoided as
being too suggestive of muscular activity, and some such
word as onset replaces it.

1

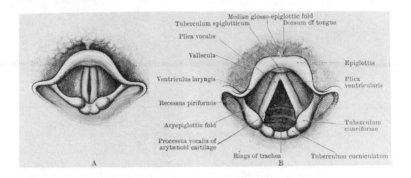

Plate 1. Cavity of the larynx as seen by means of the laryngoscope. A. Rima glottidis is closed. B. Rima glottidis is widely opened.

Garcia and Three Views on Attack

All national schools of singing concern themselves with
the most favorable action for the attack. Controversy arises
as to whether the breath-flow should audibly precede glottal
closure or whether there should be a recognizable commencing
of cordal approximation.

In seeking answers to this technical dilemma, much
speculation centers upon Manuel Garcia's perception of the
glottal plosive, represented by the phoneme (?), and expressed
in several languages as il colpo della glottide, coup de glotte,
and der harte Einsatz (also known as der Sprengeinsatz).
Some teachers of singing believe that Garcia advocated the
hard attack as opposed to the soft attack; others believe he was
attempting to describe yet a third sound which occurs when glottal closure and flow of breath coordinate nearly perfectly. [1]

There are indeed three recognizable kinds of sound
possible in the sung attack. Regardless of Garcia's exact
meaning, one such sound has become associated in many
minds with Garcia's term. This sound (?) has certain functional relationships to a light cough, being the result of audible breath pressure against the closed glottis. [1] The second
kind of sound is produced by introducing the aspirate (h), so
that a loosening of the valve takes place immediately prior to
phonation. A third approach attempts to avoid both the hard
and the soft attack, striving to achieve the exact balance of

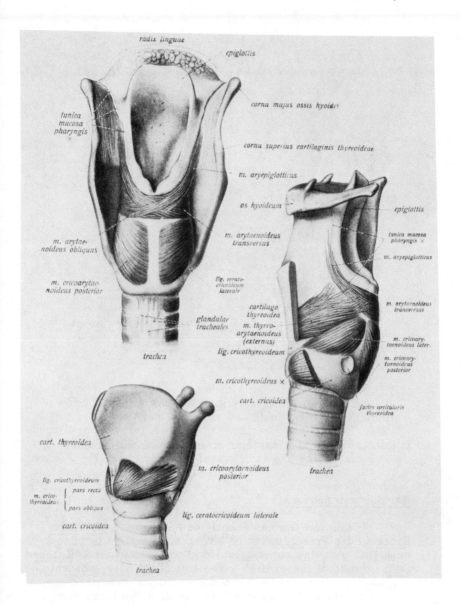

Plate 2.   Muscles of the larynx.   Top, the muscles of the
posterior surface of the larynx.   Right, the cricothyroid
muscle viewed from the left side and somewhat in front.
Bottom, the muscles of the larynx viewed from the left side.

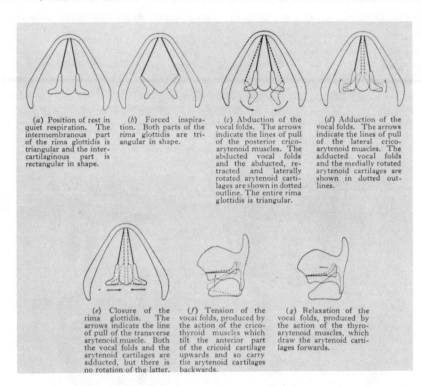

Plate 3. A series of diagrams to show different positions of the vocal folds and arytenoid cartilages.

breath pressure and muscular tension which will produce neither the (h) nor the exaggerated valvular click (ʔ).

The German School

Within the German School the hard attack (der harte Einsatz, der Sprengeinsatz of singer terminology) is often described as being an exaggerated Glottisschlag (also, Knacklaut: stroke of the glottis). The soft attack (der gehauchte Einsatz) is expressed by the phoneme (h) and describes the aspirated attack. In the German School, a third approach which results from a precise balance of cordal approximation and breath-flow, eliminating both glottal click and aspirate, has a minority group of advocates who term this phenomenon der Stelleinsatz.

Surprisingly, the characteristic attack of the German School is not the hard attack one might expect to emerge from linguistic events encountered in the German language, but rather the soft attack (der gehauchte Einsatz).

The vocal mechanics of the soft attack are similar to those which take place in the act of whispering, during which the arytenoid muscles somewhat relax so that the glottis remains parted to a greater extent than in normal speech. A voiceless stream of breath as in (h) may be initiated before any vowel sound and will serve to influence the resultant attack. This glottal fricative is in direct opposition to an attack which utilizes the more distinctively percussive glottal plosive. Essentially, (h) is noise, not tone, the result of escaping, unvocalized breath. Actual phonation does not occur until the glottis is allowed to close (an action determined largely by vowel and pitch).

Although the extent of the initial breath used to commence the aspirated attack may vary among German teachers, most are committed to some form of the soft attack. We will later see that it plays a role in stimulating the Kopfstimme (head voice) quality and in developing the piano dynamic.

Because of their interpretation of Garcia's description of the attack as a light cough, and because of his association with the historic Italian School, many German-schooled teachers assume that the Italians prefer the hard attack. Sometimes German teachers take the position that the Italian physique will tolerate strenuous cordal approximation, but that northerners cannot risk such activity. Given the existence of the Glottisschlag as a frequent phonic occurrence in the German language (while being absent in the Latin languages), this argument appears particularly contradictory. Furthermore, the avoidance of the stroke of the glottis in singing an attack in the German School seems incompatible with the introduction of the Glottisschlag for enunciative purposes during the course of the sung phrase.

Only among adherents of Stauprinzip (breath damming) (see Chapter III, Breath Management Techniques of the German School) and related heroic techniques of the German School is the hard attack recommended. Teachers who present this technique sometimes claim it stems from the old Italian School and often cite Caruso as a prime practitioner of the Sprengeinsatz.

The French and Italian Schools

The ideal attacco of the Italian School avoids both the audible aspirate and the exaggerated glottal click. However, there is present in the commencement of tone a subtle, audible beginning. It should be remarked that this onset is by no means the kind of stroke associated with the heavier Sprengeinsatz of the heroic German School. The sound is also less distinct than the colpo di glottide, yet firmer than the aspirated attack. The Italians term this sound simply l'attacco del suono (attack of the sound) or l'attacco della voce (attack of the voice). They believe it to be the sound which results when proper breath application and adequate valvular impingement conjoin. Most Italian teachers of singing are convinced that Garcia was intending to describe this third approach with his colpo della glottide.

This coordinated attacco del suono is advocated in principle within the French School as well as in the Italian. French singers seldom interpret coup de glotte as representing a heavy glottal stroke. Indeed, a general tendency toward a relatively low rate of energization among French-trained singers often produces a less precise attack than that found within the Italian School.

The English School

Among singers trained in the English School, two distinct approaches to the vocal attack can be identified. Greater use is made of the soft, aspirated attack in that part of the school which adheres to the oratorio-choral literature; the crisp attack of the Italian School is more frequently to be found among voices of operatic background.

Stylistic Demands and the Attack

At least to some extent then, the stylistic demands of the literature influence the approach to the attack, particularly in the English School. However, it should not be concluded that the same singer will use the soft attack in oratorio and the more Italianate attacco in opera; the singer is generally conditioned to one or the other. Additionally, it should be noted that most German singers use the soft attack, whether singing Bach or Puccini. One may well conclude that preferences within schools are dictated more by pedagogical attitudes than by considerations of literature and style.

Chapter II

THE MECHANICS OF BREATH MANAGEMENT

Conceptual Perception

The quality of cultivated vocal sound is largely determined by the manner in which breath is turned into tone by
the vocal bands as a result of the coordination of groups of
muscles within and around the larynx. The singer's conceptual perception of breath management determines the kind of
muscular balance, not just within the laryngeal mechanism
itself but throughout the entire instrument (the body), influencing the character of vocal quality. Direct correspondence
exists between the tonal ideal of any national school of singing and the mode of breath application which it advocates.

Before examining breath support theories as they are
found among the four national schools, some attention must
be directed toward the actual mechanics of breathing. Any
evaluation of the merits of breath management as practiced
within a particular school can be properly undertaken only in
light of such information. This sort of critical evaluation
will be attempted in the subsequent chapters.

The Respiratory Apparatus

THE LUNGS. Although the lungs are the primary
organs of respiration, their movement is largely determined
by the kinds of pressure brought upon them by the neighboring musculature and by the action of the thoracic cage.
Each lung is enclosed by a membranous sac called the pleura,
and although attached to both the heart and the trachea by its
root, lies freely within its respective pleural cavity. (See
Plate 4.) In substance, the lung is of a spongy, porous tex-
ture possessing great elasticity.

THE THORACIC CAGE. The chest cage (thorax) is

7

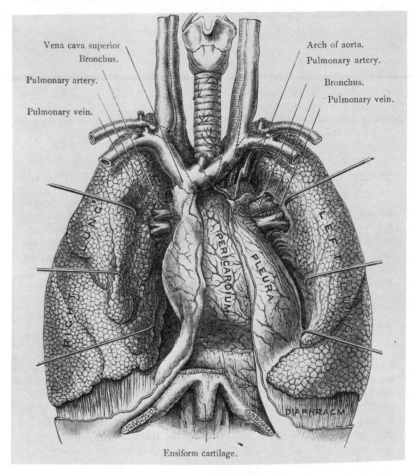

Plate 4. Anterior view of the lungs.

constructed of cartilages and bones and it houses the lungs. It is composed of the sternum, twelve ribs on each side, and posteriorly the thoracic vertebrae. (See Plate 5.)

THE INTERCOSTAL MUSCLES. It is inevitable that methods of breath management in singing should direct considerable attention to the muscular actions which take place within the thoracic cage. Much of this attention has centered upon the intercostal muscles, divided into internal and external groups of eleven on each side. They are thin layers of muscle and tendinous fibres which occupy the intercostal spaces. (See Plate 6.)

The contribution of the internal and external intercostal muscles and their exact relationship to rib action continue to be debated by scientists.

Opinions concerning the actions of the intercostals are not unanimous and at various times the following views have been maintained: that both the internal and external groups act as elevators of the ribs, that the external intercostals are elevators and the internal intercostals depressors of the ribs, that the intracartilaginous parts of the internal intercostals act with the external intercostals in inspiration and that both intercostals form strong elastic supports which prevent the contents of the intercostal spaces being drawn in or bulged out during inspiration. [1]

Having thus summed up the controversy, the same source later adds, "it is possible that the type and extent of activity in the intercostals varies with the depth of respiration. "[2]

Scientists Campbell and Newsom Davis, outlining briefly some of the roles ascribed to the intercostal muscles, conclude that

The mechanical action of the individual intercostal muscles has not yet been definitely established. The most acceptable theory is that the external intercostals and intercartilaginous internal intercostals raise the ribs, and the interosseus internal intercostals depress the ribs. [3]

THE DIAPHRAGM. The diaphragm is a large dome-shaped muscle which divides the thoracic cavity from the abdominal cavity. (See Plate 7.) It is the chief muscle of inspiration, participating in the rhythmic movements of respiration. The central tendon of the diaphragm, through a downward and forward movement, presses on the abdominal viscera; the abdomen, as a result of that action, swells out upon inspiration. "When the limit of this descent is reached the abdominal viscera provide a fixed point for the central tendon of the diaphragm from which the muscle fibres elevate the lower ribs. "[4]

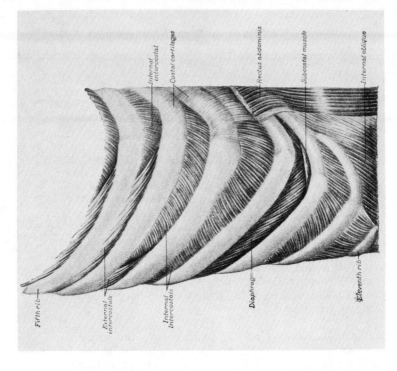

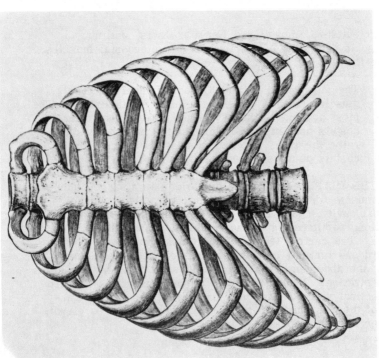

Left: Plate 5. Bony thorax, anterior aspect. Right: Plate 6. Intercostal muscles of the right chest wall.

Each respiratory cycle consists of an inspiratory and an expiratory phase. When the body is at rest the former is about 1 second and the latter about 3 seconds duration. The increased thoracic capacity in inspiration reduces the intrapleural pressure with consequent expansion of the lung, decreasing intrapulmonary pressure and drawing in air through the respiratory passages. The expiratory phase is largely a passive act, the recoil of the chest wall and lungs raising the intrapulmonary and intrathoracic pressure and expelling air. [5]

Regarding the relationship of the ribs to the diaphragm, Agostoni and Sant'Ambrogio offer this comment:

The contraction of the diaphragm decreases the intrathoracic pressure, increases the lung volume, and increases the abdominal pressure. It is easy to understand that these effects are produced by the lowering of the diaphragmatic dome, which may be demonstrated fluoroscopically in man. On the other hand it is difficult to assess whether these effects are favoured or hindered by the direct action of the diaphragm on the ribs. [6]

In a volume which reports research into the nervous control of breathing, A. A. Viljanen presents interesting information regarding the relationship of the regulatory system of the diaphragm and the intercostal muscles:

Although the diaphragm and intercostal muscles are controlled by the same regulatory system, it seems that they are at least partly separately regulated. The idea of this separate control is supported by the observation that the activity of the intercostal muscles, compared to that of the diaphragm, decreased with increasing depth of anaesthesia.... Further, we found in our human studies that the relationship between the electrical activities of the diaphragm and the external intercostal muscles can be changed voluntarily. [7]

Several methods for the attempted control of respiration through separate or combined actions of ribs and diaphragm will be noted as specific techniques in subsequent chapters.

MUSCLES OF THE ABDOMEN. Activity which takes

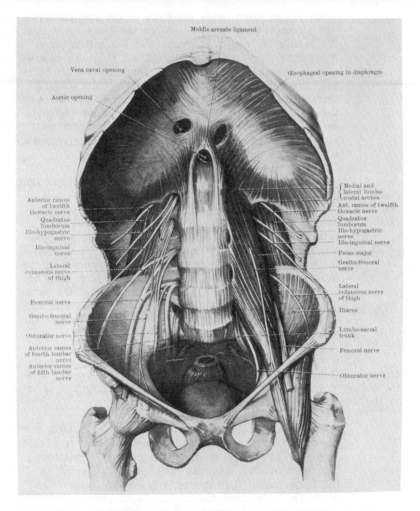

Plate 7. The diaphragm, with muscles and nerves of the posterior wall.

place in the abdominal muscles during respiration is of much significance in some vocal methods among the national schools and of little in others. These muscle pairs include the external oblique, the internal oblique, the transversus abdominis, and the rectus abdominis. (See Plate 8.) They compress the abdomen and support the viscera. These powerful muscles are both postural and expiratory; they can be

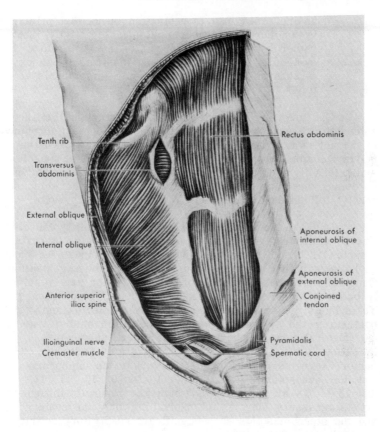

Plate 8.   Deep muscles of the abdominal wall.

expected to figure in an important way in some technical
systems of singing.   The degree to which they are considered contributive as breath-support muscles often determines
emphases within specific vocal pedagogies.   Scientific investigation, however, does not verify the importance attached
to them in certain breath management systems.   Indeed,
Campbell concludes in a chapter devoted to the function of
the abdominal muscles that

> the great power of the abdominal muscles is not
> used for respiratory functions except in coughing
> where it increases the kinetic energy of the air
> stream.   Moreover, during spontaneous breathing

an increased load to expiration is not met primarily by an increase in abdominal muscle activity, but rather by utilizing the recoil of the respiratory system by an increase in end-inspiratory volume through an increase of the inspiratory muscle activity. [8]

One must not conclude from this statement that the anterolateral group of abdominal muscles is of no importance in the act of expiration. By actively contracting when the pelvis and the thorax are in a fixed position, those muscles maintain a firm elasticity against the abdominal viscera; in so doing, they play a role in the muscular balance which so heavily influences the frequency of the respiratory cycle.

DORSAL AND OTHER Accessory Respiratory Muscles. The prominence given by some teachers of singing to certain muscles as breath management muscles is curious, inasmuch as little scientific evidence lends support to those contentions. Campbell examines a number of muscles which are commonly believed to serve as accessory muscles of inspiration. [9] He includes the scaleni (scalenus anterior, medius and posterior), the sternomastoids (sternocleidomastoids) trapezius, pectoralis major and pectoralis minor, subclavius, latissimus dorsi, serratus anterior, serratus posterior superior, serratus posterior inferior, quadratus lumborum, and the sacrospinalis group. (See Plates 9, 10, 11, 12, and 13.) "Of all the muscles which are generally thought to act as accessory muscles of inspiration, only the scaleni and the sternomastoids show significant respiratory activity in man" (Campbell, 1954). [10]

The same source finds it difficult to accept a major function in the act of inspiration for that favorite of several schools of singing, latissimus dorsi. (See Plates 9, 10, 11, and 12.) "The latissimus dorsi contains fibres which arise from the lower three or four ribs and which might be able to elevate these ribs, thus facilitating inspiration. Contraction of the muscle as a whole, however, compresses the lower thorax and therefore assists expiration."[11] Although vigorous contraction was observed during coughing, no evidence of activity was found during quiet or moderately increased breathing. Campbell's associates report some inspiratory activity in the latissimus dorsi during deep breathing and in some erect normal subjects during forced breathing.

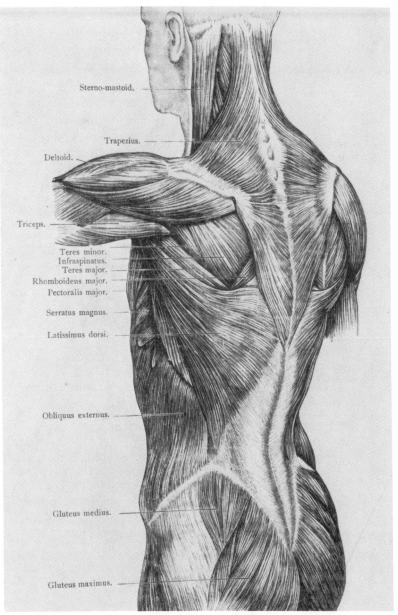

Plate 9.   First layer of the muscles of the back.

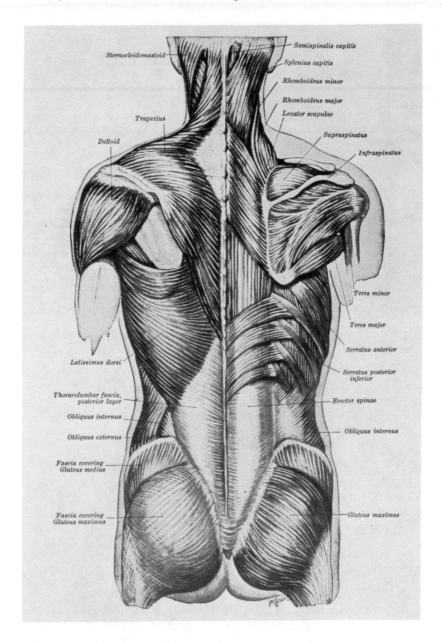

Plate 10.   Superficial muscles of the back.

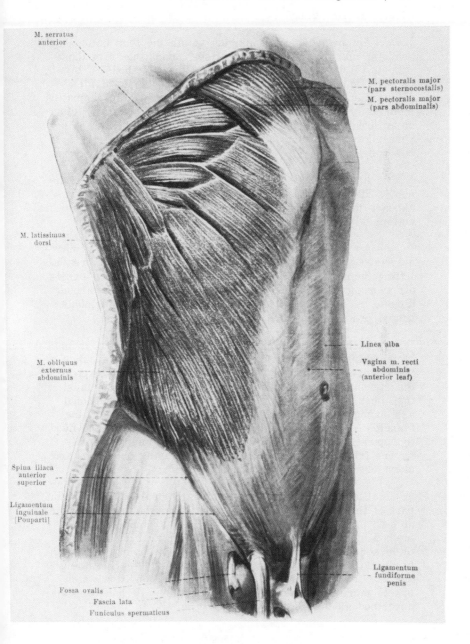

Plate 11.   Muscles of the trunk.

Clavicular Breathing

Among teachers of singing within the four national schools, and in most vocal treatises emanating from those schools, it is customary to mention three methods of breath support into which all vocal pedagogy supposedly divides. Many teachers identify clavicular, costal and diaphragmatic methods of breathing. Most of these sources dismiss clavicular breathing disparagingly, leaving only costal and diaphragmatic breathing (with abdominal involvement) for serious consideration.

Although clavicular breathing as an isolated phenomenon is discouraged in most pedagogies, it occasionally reappears thinly disguised to assist in specific kinds of support actions within some national schools.

As it occurs in singing, clavicular breathing is characterized by raising the clavicles with the intake of breath, letting them fall in expiration. Although such action expels air thoroughly from the lungs and therefore expels carbon dioxide as well, it poses problems upon subsequent inhalation if practiced cumulatively.

Such inspiration can be identified by a noisy, incomplete taking of the breath, the result of glottal resistance to the inspired air, and by noisy exhalation. During expiration, the sternum and ribs fall, as do the clavicles. All must then be repositioned upon inspiration, requiring additional assistance from the shoulder muscles. Increasingly, the muscles of the neck become involved as well. As the need to reposition the sternum and the ribs becomes markedly severe following expiratory collapse, heaving shoulders and chest are prominently to be seen.

Clavicular breathing precludes normal activity on the part of those components of the breath mechanism which are able to produce stabilized function. As a compensatory method of breathing, exaggerated clavicular breathing is often seen in violent activity, such as takes place during the final effort in sprinting. It is the kind of noisy breathing one also observes in hysterical crying, a condition which upsets more regulated breath coordination. It has been aptly described as "the breath of exhaustion."[12]

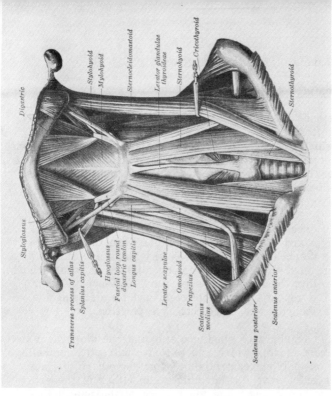

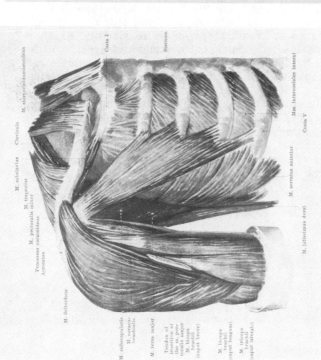

Left: Plate 12.   Muscles of the chest.   Right: Plate 13.   Muscles of the front of the neck.

Diaphragmatic Control

Methods of supporting the voice (breath management) generally attempt more or less conscious control of those muscles which act directly upon the diaphragm. Assumptions about the kinds of muscular action which are thought to occur during the breath cycle have produced pedagogical formulas within the four major schools far in excess of the three traditional methods cited above, although related to them.

The descent of the diaphragm, the concerted action of diaphragm and abdominal musculature, and the partnership of the diaphragm with the ribs and lungs are standard concepts in most vocal circles among all four national schools. There is within the schools a superfluity of techniques for retarding the ascent of the diaphragm and for delaying the collapse of the ribs and lungs during expiration.

Some teachers of singing claim that the diaphragm is an involuntary muscle which can be only indirectly controlled by the action of other controllable muscles; others attempt localized control over its movement. In either of these orientations, theories regarding the control of the musculature which regulates or influences the diaphragm produce identifiable techniques of breath management in singing, all of them recognizable as pedagogical doctrines of specific national schools. National schools of singing clearly indicate a lack of agreement as to how to approach breath management.

In this study, the degree of emphasis upon the dominant action of one or more parts of the muscular system determines the name of the specific method as it pertains to breath management. The reader should be aware, however, that teachers of singing often devise empirical language to describe these physical events.

Chapter III

BREATH MANAGEMENT TECHNIQUES
IN THE GERMAN SCHOOL

The typically German-schooled teacher of singing is
closely identified with clearly-defined principles of breath
management which characteristically point to low-breath techniques.

Inasmuch as the greatest expansion of the ribs upon
inhalation occurs below the sternum, teachers in this school
believe that even a moderately high chest may militate
against complete lung expansion. The Germanic teacher generally advocates a relatively low chest posture in singing.

Atemstütze (breath support), or more commonly
Stütze, is to be achieved by retarding the inward movement
of the epigastrium (abdominal wall) and the upward motion
of the diaphragm by exerting outward pressure upon the abdominal muscles, an action termed Bauchaussenstütze (distended belly support). Since it is difficult to maintain any
degree of sternal elevation while applying outward pressure
on the abdomen, the German-schooled teacher often prefers
a "relaxed," lowered thoracic posture. In order to acquire
increased support, the pelvic area is firmed, the buttocks
tightened, and an attempt is made to bring the low back muscles into play.

As a result of these convictions, several systems of
breath management have found wide acceptance within this
school. While each of these systems concentrates more fully
on one given function than another, there is an obvious relationship among them in that all embrace tensions in the
lower trunk. Teachers in the German School often imagina-
tively combine these various approaches to breath management.
In some instances, attention is drawn to specific muscles
which are to be activated; in others, more general admonitions of a somewhat subjective nature are the rule.

Lower dorsal expansion, gluteal-pelvic contraction, low diaphragmatic fixation, epigastric distention, lower abdominal (or hypogastric) distention, Stauprinzip (breath damming), delayed inhalation (or induced exhalation), and minimal breath approaches are among techniques which flourish within the German School of singing.

Low Dorsal Breathing

Lower back breathing is a technique based upon the assumption that during the inspiration-exhalation cycle the lower back muscles perform certain specific functions which are of special importance in singing.

A representative statement of the importance of dorsal sensation in singing was made at the International Congress for the Training of Musicians, held in Salzburg in 1953, by a major exponent of the German School:

> The best way to free the upper half of the chest from 'rising air' is to transfer a 'holding action' of the lower air masses to the back at the level of the lower ribs. The inhaled mass of air, which the student neither overpresses nor overloads in the lowerlying back regions of the lungs, and which must remain sucked in there and held firm, is the guarantee for a finer and finer spinning out of air into tone during the learning years.

> ... [T]he low-lying back lung areas are able to accept a larger quantity of air, and the resulting resonances in the bone structure of the spinal cord set up vibrations which react, like a connecting pillar into the skull.

> In the beginning this 'holding action' is the most important element in breath control. Once one can hold the opened air-spread position of the back ribs area, one can develop the correct muscular additions: one attempts to 'set' on the contracted inner abdominal muscle group. The reflexive action of the most important single abdominal muscle, the diagonal muscle, then comes into play. These muscles help to fixate the lowest position in the column of air. [1]

Numerous additional sources could be cited as evidence of the stress given by the German School of singing to the importance of the back muscles. One further source must suffice:

> The strongest muscles that attach the diaphragm to the thoracic cage are situated at the inner side of the back ('origins of the diaphragm'); that is the reason why the main impulse in proper singing occurs from the lower part of the back (what great singers have called 'singing with the back'). [2]

Later:

> The large movement responsible for erecting the mechanism of singing is directed mainly from the back; from the powerful origins of the diaphragm and the body-stretching muscles. [3]

Some Germanic teachers recommend techniques for spreading the back which are in direct opposition to action involving the intercostals and the diaphragm; by so doing, they actually induce a quicker rate of exhalation than would normally occur in the inspiration-exhalation cycle during singing. Exaggerated sensation which may be experienced in the lumbo-dorsal area during the breath cycle is for the most part the result of induced muscular antagonism unrelated to normal breath events.

As was documented previously, back-spreading as a breath management technique is difficult to support with scientific evidence. Consciously trying to spread the muscles of the lower back upon inhalation and during singing probably cannot significantly increase breath capacity nor directly influence the span of the respiratory cycle.

It should not be concluded that sensation is never discernible in the lower dorsal region during singing except as practiced in the German School. Singers who do not adhere to consciously-induced low-dorsal breathing do indeed experience some expansion laterally in the back during inspiration, especially near the sides, between the bottom ribs and the crest of the ilium (the top of the pelvic bone), but seldom as far into the center of the back as the spine. (Any spinal-caudal control of the breath must occur below the level of conscious manipulation and is not the result of induced back-

spreading sensations.) Singers often have a continuing awareness of lateral expansion during singing.

This particular phenomenon is caused by the descent
of the diaphragm and by the lateral extension of the lower
ribs through the participation of the intercostal muscles as
they act upon the surrounding supportive musculature.

Among many singers not trained in the German School,
considerable expansion at the sides and somewhat into the
back can frequently be observed upon inhalation. However,
such action can take place only when elements of correct
posture permit natural functioning of the inhalation-expiration
cycle.

The resultant sensation of this properly functional
breath should not be confused with that unique muscular
sensation in the lower dorsal area which results from the
slightly slumped torso that characterizes the low dorsal
breath of the German School.

Gluteal-Pelvic Contraction (Low Trunk Support)

Gluteal-pelvic muscular function as a means of achieving breath support is best known by such terms as pelvic
support, buttocks support, and (among English-speaking advocates of this typically Germanic technique) "the tilt and
tuck method. "

Although most practitioners of this approach to breath
control recognize that the lungs, the intercostals and the
diaphragm are the chief members of the breath mechanism,
they maintain that the muscular source of control for breath
emission lies very low in the trunk. They recommend that
the pelvis be tilted slightly forward (often with one foot somewhat forward as well), and that the buttocks be tucked under.
This posture is intended to provide essential gluteal-pelvic
support for the sung tone. Gluteus maximus, the largest
observable muscle in the gluteal area (see Plates 9 and 10),
is thought to be brought into tension by this posture.

Gluteal tension and sphincteral closure are often advocated as one coordinated physical action. Indeed, gluteal
tension is somewhat difficult to attain without accompanying
sphincteral activity. Such sphincteral activity is frequently
reserved for phrases requiring a high degree of energization,

at which time the singer may bring increased tension to the
buttocks, while squeezing the anal orifice.

Sometimes the singer is urged to "squeeze the dime"
(or such other appropriate currency as dictated by geographical location), to "sit on the breath," or to experience muscular and sphincteral sensations similar to those encountered
in childbirth or during the act of defecation. The technical
concept behind this somewhat bizarre practice is that the
lower abdominal area must experience muscular tension in
order to put into play those muscles which retard the upward
surge of the diaphragm, and to supply strength and firmness
to the entire vocal instrument.

Critical examination of gluteal-pelvic techniques certainly must recognize that muscular connection does pertain
between the pelvis and the thorax. This can readily be verified with an examination of rectus abdominis, the long flat
muscle which runs along the front of the abdomen, and which
has its origin in the crest of the pubis, attaching to the fifth,
sixth, and seventh ribs; in conjunction with several other
muscle pairs, this muscle is capable of compressing and supporting the abdominal viscera. (See Plates 8 and 11.) Controversy among the national schools of singing arises about
the extent to which muscles of the pelvis and the buttocks can
offer assistance in coordinating the action of the lungs, ribs
and diaphragm, and whether those muscles can perform the
task assigned to them by the advocates of gluteal-pelvic support.

Of gluteus maximus, it might conceivably be asserted
that a postural muscle which helps keep the trunk erect must
serve the total singing instrument. However, it is difficult
to sustain the claim that it is a muscle which functions importantly in controlling the breath cycle.

In similar fashion, it could be claimed that muscular
activity in the anal region, including that stemming from the
levator ani and the coccygeus, relates in some remote way
to singing. Elevating the lowly sphincter ani and the coccygeus to a place of pedagogical prominence is not uncommon
in the German School. Teachers in this segment of the German School insist that by consciously exercising control over
muscles in the buttocks and pelvis, a foundation is provided
for epigastric-thoracic muscular action upon which the activity
of the breath mechanism is dependent. However, the increase
of tension in the lower trunk is difficult to equate with the

ease and efficiency in breath emission such techniques are intended to bring about.

Scientific appraisal of the activity of these muscles does not offer convincing argument for their conscious role in breath management:

> The levatores ani constrict the lower end of the rectum and vagina and probably fix the perineal body. Together with the coccygei they form a muscular diaphragm which supports the pelvic viscera and opposes itself to the downward thrust produced by any increase in the intra-abdominal pressure. [4]

> The external sphincter can be voluntarily contracted and thus more firmly occlude the anus.... The tone of both internal and external anal sphincters keeps the anal canal and anus closed. [5]

From a functional point of view it is apparent that these muscles have to do with constriction in the lower trunk, especially in response to downward abdominal pressures. While such pressures seem momentarily to hold the muscles of the abdomen and might therefore be thought to assist breath management, the thoracic region is unable to resist the cumulative downward muscular pull, so that the sternum lowers, the ribs collapse, the diaphragm rises and the capacity of the lung is more quickly reduced. Nevertheless, gluteal-pelvic contraction continues to be urged by many teachers of singing associated with techniques of the German School.

Low Diaphragmatic Fixation

Theories of low diaphragmatic fixation assert that the upward movement of the diaphragm can be halted voluntarily by holding the diaphragm down during most of the expiratory act, although there exists fluoroscopic evidence to the contrary. Current advocates of the fixated low diaphragm often point to evidence of success in achieving localized diaphragmatic control in Eastern religious disciplines. Practitioners of low diaphragmatic fixation participate in a complicated system of visceral pressures which have only an indirect influence upon the emission of breath. The concept is best expressed by the admonition, "Hold the diaphragm low."

Such attempted control serves to impede function as normally encountered in the breath cycle. The system is fairly prominent within the German School.

Epigastric Distention (Distended Abdominal Breathing)

Distended abdominal breathing is characterized by outward pressure on the upper abdominal wall. Pressure is continued outward until the completion of the sung phrase and until the new breath commences.

Some German-trained singers who follow this method wear a kummerbund, corset or belt against which they push outward as a means of breath retention, and to increase muscular support. This in effect is to push out against the abdominal viscera and bears little relationship to the cycle of inhalation-exhalation as medically observed. However, a certain type of support may result, in that tension will also occur in the muscles immediately in contact with the diaphragm and in the epigastrium, somewhat retarding the ascent of the diaphragm. During these outward visceral movements, ribs and sternum tend to collapse at a rather rapid rate during exhalation, probably nullifying any advantages of diaphragmatic control.

A surprising number of proponents of this method are misinformed as to the exact location of the diaphragm, frequently placing it at the navel. As a result of this anatomical misconception, they confuse pouting out the abdominal wall and viscera with diaphragmatic-epigastric expansion. The method is a major one wherever the German School may be found, claiming the allegiance of a great number of singers. The technique is often referred to in English as "belly-breathing." It claims many North American adherents.

Hypogastric Distention (Low Abdominal Breathing)

Low abdominal breathing is an important variant of distended abdominal breathing, having its own distinctive features. While adherents of epigastric distention chiefly concern themselves with the relationship between the diaphragm and the upper abdominal wall during distention, those advocating hypogastric distention cite activity in the lower abdomen as the source of diaphragmatic control. Whereas the one attempts an outward thrust of the abdomen proper, the other strives for distention in both abdomen and lesser pelvis during inhalation and exhalation.

Not infrequently, this technique finds itself congenially coupled with gluteal-pelvic approaches. To facilitate this method of breath control, singers are requested to drop the torso as far as possible, to allow the shoulders to come forward, assuming the so-called "gorilla posture." Because of this calculated thoracic collapse during expiration, compensatory muscular action takes place in the lower trunk upon inspiration. In singing by this method, as the scale ascends, pressures of the lower trunk are increased as the singer continually presses down and out. Subjective notions of a trampoline action (down for high notes, up for low ones) are directed toward the lower trunk. Although somewhat less frequently endorsed than epigastric distention, advocates of hypogastric distention abound among teachers of the German School.

Stauprinzip (Breath Damming)

Breath damming is a technique of breath retention through marked sub-glottal muscular pressures. The flow of breath is stemmed by the glottis as a result of muscular tension similar to that experienced in a painful groan or grunt. The Stöhnlaut (groaning utterance) is to be developed into musical tone by the application of the Staufunktion principles which can be mastered through a series of exercises devoted to that purpose. The primitive power of the vocal instrument is thought to be present in this Stöhnlaut.

Although this method of elevating the primitive cry to a position of pedagogical centrality had previously existed, it was systematized and named Stauprinzip (damming principle) by George Armin, a notable figure in German vocal pedagogy. [6]

The system relies upon an initially high degree of muscular antagonism which has a direct influence on the flow of breath from lungs to larynx. The technique centers on the activity of muscles in the lower trunk, precipitating muscular tension throughout the trunk and neck. The laryngeal valve is under increasing pressure as it is called upon to assist in the damming process.

Attempting to call upon the Urkraft der Stimme (the original force, or moving principle, of the voice), the method

appears to activate all of the muscles utilized in normal inhalation-exhalation cycles plus muscles of the trunk and
thorax which have little to do with breathing but which do
become active in lifting and grunting. Such muscular antagonism causes congestion which is evidenced in the superficial
veins of the neck, in heightened facial color and in exaggerated postures of the trunk and head. Not inappropriately,
the term Stauprinzip has been disapprovingly translated by
one noted German vocal pedagogue as the "congesting method."[7]

This method may not claim as many followers among
German singers in the present decade as in the past, yet
a long list of successful German singers in this century have
given allegiance to it. A number of today's Heldentenöre
are numbered among its practitioners.

Induced Exhalation (Delayed Inhalation)

Delayed inspiration or inhalation is a technique meant
to bring about relaxed, muscle-free singing. In this system,
breath is taken in as rapidly as possible at first, with an
early breath emission immediately following. Much of the
inspired air is purposely emitted prior to phonation so that
one sings on little breath. The pedagogical direction is
"breathe deeply, commence emptying the lungs at once (or
begin expelling the breath), then begin to sing."

The purpose of taking a full breath in this pedagogy
is not to make use of it in phonation but to change the air in
the lung as completely as possible and to relax the musculature. Breath pressure must be considerably reduced before
phonation commences. Pressure below the larynx is caused,
it is thought, by accumulated breath, a condition detrimental
to relaxed vocal sound.

Teachers who present this system of breath control
generally are aware that the lungs are not literally emptied
out by induced exhalation techniques. However, they purposely advocate lowering the chest following the intake of breath,
trying forcibly to move the ribs inward during the sung
phrase. The act of singing then takes place during a conscious delaying of the impulse for a new breath, whence the
alternate name, delayed inhalation.

Sometimes teachers admit that until one has mastered

this technique there is a sensation of being somewhat out of breath during long phrases. It is claimed that this feeling decreases as one loses the fear of delaying the inspiratory act.

Following the considerable delay of the desire for a new breath, inspiration is often audible and somewhat forced in character. When phrases are of great duration, even some residual breath is called upon. There is a tendency for the singer to lean backward slightly from the hips as the phrase concludes, in part because of the inward pressure exerted on the ribs and the downward movement of the torso.

It is the intent of induced exhalation proponents that attention be directed away from muscular events which produce cumulative pressure beneath the larynx. This can best be accomplished, it is argued, by directing attention to inward and downward pressures in the abdominal and pelvic regions, following the release of large quantities of the inspired air. The method stands in total opposition to those techniques concerned with sterno-costal-thoracic action.

Minimal Breath System

Minimal breath techniques may take several directions, but are commonly characterized by the recommendation that a small quantity of air be initially inhaled in order to avoid over-crowding the lungs and to avoid inducing tensions during inspiration. In addition to advising the singer to take something less than a complete breath, it is recommended that one avoid trying to establish any direct control over its emission. It is believed that a minimal amount of breath, or perhaps even none, is necessary to set the vocal cords vibrating. Research which attempts to establish that the vocal bands can vibrate independently of the application of breath current is seen by some teachers as supportive of this technique. Thus the French researcher, Raoul Husson, has given an assist to this group of German-schooled teachers who minimize the importance of air-flow upon cordal action.

Husson has concluded on the basis of electromyographic studies that it is possible for the vocal cords to vibrate in the absence of air currents. Recurrent nerve impulses determine the frequency of phonic movements of the vocal lips and act independently of exhalation. Expiration affects

vocal intensity but not actual cordal vibration during phonation.   These theories, which are frequently disputed, appear
in a number of publications; brief reviews of several of these
articles are to be found in An Interdisciplinary Index of
Studies in Physics, Medicine and Music Related to the Human
Voice, edited by Wallace Heaton and C. W. Hargens (Bryn
Mawr: Theodore Presser Co. , 1968).

While at first blush it might seem that induced exhalation and minimal breath techniques of the German School
stand somewhat out of the mainstream of German breath
management techniques, it quickly becomes apparent that
they too favor an essential ingredient of techniques found in
that school: low thoracic posture which transfers emphasis
in breathing to the lower trunk.   Yet both of these techniques
have evolved as reactions to methods which exaggerate dorsal
and epigastric distention.

"Over-approximation" is not an exact scientific expression, but it well serves to describe the excessive tension
in the vocal valve which pertains in low-abdominal techniques
typical of the German School.   Among many teachers the
need to modify this tendency toward "over-approximation"
leads to complicated attempts to reduce tension at the glottis.

Chapter IV.

BREATH MANAGEMENT TECHNIQUES
IN THE ENGLISH SCHOOL

Typical breath management techniques of the English School fall into systems which deal with upper back activity, costal function, and diaphragmatic positioning. These techniques include upper dorsal breathing, fixed diaphragmatic breathing, elevated chest and contracted abdomen, and costal arrest (costal fixation).

Upper Dorsal Breathing

Although some teachers in the English School attempt to spread both the upper and lower areas of the back, upper dorsal breathers are more commonly encountered, whereas the German back-spreader concentrates more narrowly on the lower back.

"Raise the ribs with the back muscles" is a frequent request from the back-breathing English teacher. Often one sees an English-trained singer, especially in oratorio performances, with shoulders slightly raised and rounded over a score, trunk bent forward from the waist, neck somewhat extended, attempting to expand laterally certain muscles in the upper back.

Those who espouse upper back breathing generally position the shoulders in this "forward and up" posture because they mistake the spreading postural sensations in the trapezius and related shoulder muscles for inspiratory action. William Shakespeare remains an influential force on the pedagogy of the English School. His outstanding book, The Art of Singing (1921), contains the following passage:

How high should we breathe? As high as possible

32

without giving up the freedom and elasticity of the
points of the shoulders. Within these limits we
should feel an ample expansion at the back, especially under the shoulder-blades, but the chest
should be raised very little. [1]

Shakespeare has devised an exercise for acquiring this breath
action:

> Balance the body on one foot and touch the ground
> behind with the other.... Now extend both arms
> forwards and outwards, keeping the elbows in, the
> palms of the hands upwards, as though in the act
> of imploring. This position slightly twists the mus-
> cles under the shoulder-blades, and shows us, while
> drawing in the breath, whether we are using the
> important back rib-raising muscles. We now raise
> the chest but very slightly, and the points of the
> shoulders not at all; nor can we breathe too deeply,
> for we have already raised the ribs with the back
> muscles and contracted the diaphragm. (It is gen-
> erally recognized that the artist on the stage can
> sing better when acting or on the concert platform
> when holding the book well forward.) So much for
> position. [2]

Shakespeare goes on in the subsequent paragraph to suggest
that one should take a full breath as low down in front as is
consistent with its being felt high up at the back and with
the sense of interlocking of the muscles under the shoulder-
blades.

In a brief critique of Shakespeare's famous exercise,
William Vennard in his excellent work, Singing: The Mechanism and the Technic (3d ed. 1964), comments: "Our only
conclusion can be that at this point Shakespeare deceived
himself. He used shoulder muscles for inhalation and considered this all right as long as the shoulders were only
pulled forward and not raised. "[3]

While inducing these sensations of spreading in the
upper back, the clavicles tend to rise; during exhalation the
sternum and chest begin to sink. This occurs because it is
not physically possible to raise and expand the trapezius muscles without upsetting the muscular antagonism in the pectorals
and the thoracic area so essential to normal upright posture.

According to Campbell, it appears that the trapezius

may at times be made to function as an accessory muscle
of inspiration because the upper fibres may extend the neck,
and in so doing assist the sternomastoidal action, the remainder of the muscle affecting the action of the pectorals. [4]

However, even a slight extension of the neck induces
undesirable positions for the laryngeal muscles in singing.
There is little reason to doubt that the spreader of the upper
back is reintroducing clavicular breathing without realizing
it, and that there must result heavy reliance upon assistance
from the scaleni and sternomastoids.

John Newburn Levien deals, perhaps unwittingly, with
the trapezius and latissimus dorsi in his advice to singers:

> Draw the air into the lungs down to the waistline
> and, mind, amply yet easily, into the sides and
> back, allowing the stomach to remain flat and even
> to retract a little. Before drawing in the breath
> raise the shoulders very slightly, unobservably,
> with a suggestion of moving the elbows outwards,
> away from the sides. This will allow the upper
> part of the lungs to be well filled with air, without
> any movement of the shoulders being seen when
> breath is taken. [5]

It was mentioned in a preceding chapter that latissimus dorsi figures prominently in theories of back involvement
in singing. This muscle numbers a host of admirers among
back-spreading pedagogues. Such attraction to latissimus
dorsi is understandable; together with trapezius, it covers
large areas of the back, superficially observable. For those
committed to the belief that the back muscles participate importantly in breathing, no other muscles so readily present
themselves for consideration. Lying prominently as they do,
it could easily be assumed that together they must perform
back-spreading functions; for the most part, appearances in
this case are deceptive. (See Plates 9 and 10.) In spite
of its auxiliary relationship to certain breathing muscles,
latissimus dorsi serves chiefly as a shoulder muscle, concerned with movements of the humerus. Its most active participation in breathing occurs, be it noted, during clavicular
breathing.

While anatomically serratus posterior superior could
elevate the ribs, we have seen there is no laboratory evidence
to give positive support to such an assumption. [6] Rhomboideus

major and rhomboideus minor, located in the upper back, are muscles which assist in maintaining the poise of the shoulder, as do the levator scapulae. These act in association with the trapezius. (See Plates 10 and 13.) Little importance can be given them as actors during the course of the breath cycle.

In summary, singers who believe they are spreading the upper back as a method of breathing and of supporting the voice are chiefly bringing into play the shoulder muscles and the clavicles. Under such a guise does clavicular breathing effect an entrance into pedagogical legitimacy in the English School. These upper dorsal breath techniques are frequently combined with costal and fixated diaphragmatic systems.

Fixed Diaphragmatic Breathing

Fixed diaphragmatic breathing aims at stabilizing the actual position of the diaphragm. This hoped-for condition is to be achieved by expanding the epigastrium just below the sternum, to be followed at once by an inward pulling of the upper abdomen, at the same time raising the rib cage upward and expanding the ribs laterally. The theory which motivates this approach to breath control in singing is that the organs of the abdomen are pressed up into a supporting position for the diaphragm, thereby effecting an even emission of the breath.

It should be noted that the system is distinguished from related methods as regards costal action, in that the epigastrium first expands, followed by a second action which consists of an inward abdominal press and rib expansion, independent of inspiration.

David D. Slater's Vocal Physiology and the Teaching of Singing is an official volume which has served as preparatory source for the candidate and faculty examiners at the Royal College of Music and the Royal Academy of Music, historically two of the most influential institutions in vocal pedagogy in Great Britain. Anyone teaching voice in England who has achieved either of the desirable marks of certification (A. R. C. M., L. R. A. M.) has supposedly been examined on knowledge of the statement entitled "Correct Breathing" which succinctly and lucidly presents this view on breath application:

> The best method of breathing is a combination of intercostal and diaphragmatic.

If the breath be taken too deeply, thus causing distention of the abdomen, it will be impossible to obtain a free action of the ribs and a proper expansion of the chest.

Take breath down, until there is a slight expansion of the upper part of the abdomen (viz., the soft part just below the breastbone), and follow this immediately by pulling in the abdomen, and raising and expanding the ribs.

By means of this pulling in of the abdomen, the organs contained therein are pressed up into position, thus supporting, or as it is sometimes called, 'fixing' the diaphragm.

Do not raise the shoulders.

Do not expand the lower part of the abdomen.

Do not hold the breath at the throat, but do so by means of the diaphragm and intercostal muscles. [7]

A variant of this approach is found in a system of breath support based upon the notion that the diaphragm, unless strongly engaged by the abdomen, pulls the ribs upward (an assumption which cannot be supported factually). The abdomen is to be drawn in tightly so as to maintain the position of the diaphragm. It is claimed that the tense epigastrium engages the diaphragm and holds it firmly in a more or less stable location.

Elevated Chest and Contracted Abdomen

Sterno-thoracic elevation with contracted epigastrium is a breath application method which although sharing some aspects with other systems is based on a combination of factors which gives it a character of its own. "Sternum and chest high, diaphragm in" well summarizes the advice of its practitioners.

The diaphragm (in actual practice the epigastrium and the viscera) are pulled in at the outset of the breath intake. At the moment of inhalation, the midsection is already somewhat contracted inward toward the spine. The ribs are expanded as much as possible, with sternum fully elevated. This posture, achieved at the moment of inspiration, somewhat resembles that assumed by contestants displaying the musculature of the torso in body-building competitions.

This exaggerated posture of the trunk is said to bring the inspired breath into a greater state of compression and closer proximity to the larynx. The strong muscles of the thorax are brought more completely into play, supposedly increasing support for the musculature of the neck and larynx. This is known as "the position of strength."

It is sometimes remarked that such an excessive posture of the torso is also arrived at when heavy objects are lifted to chest level. Chairs or weighty objects are held out at arm's length during the act of singing, as breath-training exercises. Additional physical exercises for developing the pectoral and upper abdominal muscles are often devised. Attention is directed to the high rate of occlusion of the vocal bands and to corresponding sensations of support in the upper abdominal and thoracic muscles. At the same time, those who counsel singers to assume this posture try to avoid as much as possible any outward abdominal movement, believing it all must be inward. It is favorably pointed out that breath retention is prolonged during the course of such physical action.

Such support practices place the muscles of the trunk and neck into a high state of antagonism; they induce such a high rate of muscular impingement that flexible muscular activity in the region of the epigastrium must be precluded. Rigidity is induced both above and below the ribs. Although diaphragmatic ascent may be momentarily retarded, the breath mechanism cannot function freely because of excess muscular tension. Muscular relationships chosen for commencing inspiration in this technique are similar to those generally found at the completion of an action requiring considerable muscular impingement. Such a concept of breath application has a distinct result on the quality of sound which emerges from the larynx.

This technique can be encountered among some singers of the English School who are oriented toward the operatic literature. Coupled with upper dorsal activity, it produces in the singer an appearance of elevated chest and raised shoulders, with drawn-in stomach.

Costal Arrest

Advocates of prolonged costal distention promulgate the stationary rib cage as an ideal in singing. Those who teach prolonged costal distention believe that the collapse of the ribs, occurring with the ascent of the diaphragm and the accompanying diminution of lung capacity, can be obviated by a continued distention of the ribs through the direct action of the intercostal muscles. One attempts to fix the ribs at that same point of expansion which the ribs had attained upon inhalation; this posture is to be retained throughout the entire sung phrase.

Unlike the auxiliary muscles of breathing, the intercostal muscles relate directly to the process of breathing. That the ribs expand and that the intercostales externi and the intercostales interni are involved in the breath cycle is indisputable. However, as was earlier pointed out, the exact contribution of each of these groups of muscles continues to be questioned.

We recall that it is generally held that the external intercostal muscles are inspiratory, elevating the ribs during inhalation, and that the internal intercostals lower the ribs in expiration. Therefore, those who stress costal arrest try to maintain the firm, expanded condition of the intercostales externi and as much as possible to prevent the intercostales interni from pulling the ribs down again. In costal fixation techniques there is a conscious attempt to hold the ribs out during the entire inhalation-exhalation cycle.

That the ribs stay distended for a longer period of time during the slow breath emission in singing as opposed to the quicker emission in speech is quite clear. On the other hand, the inadequacies of this technique (localized control over the intercostal muscles as the answer to delayed breath emission) can be demonstrated by holding out the ribs while the sternum collapses, accompanied by rapid contraction of epigastrium and diaphragm. Advocates of stationary rib action generally heighten one aspect of the breath process to the detriment of the total concerted action.

In summary it can be said that breath application in the English School is largely directed toward the epigastric-thoracic region of the torso, with concern for upper abdominal action in conjunction with intercostal activity, and there is nearly total avoidance of the low-breath techniques practiced in the German School.

Chapter V

BREATH MANAGEMENT TECHNIQUES
IN THE FRENCH AND ITALIAN SCHOOLS

The French School

Less attention is directed toward conscious breath
management in the French School than in any other. Students are urged to keep good posture and to relax, but are
seldom directed to more specific procedures. Some discussion of diaphragmatic and costal action is occasionally encountered, but no systematic scheme of conscious breath control is typical. The French School for the most part is committed to that breath management approach best described as
natural breathing.

NATURAL BREATH. Natural breathing is a term
given general usage by a group of teachers philosophically in
line with the French School; they believe there is no essential
difference between the actions of the breath mechanism in
speech and those which take place in singing. With teachers
who believe that the heightened activity which takes place
during singing must demand increased muscular action on the
part of the breath mechanism, teachers of natural breathing
strongly disagree. They make suggestions such as, "You
don't have to think about breath in speaking, so don't think
about it when you sing. " Attention is directed toward musical
factors, in the belief that the phrase itself will dictate the
control of the breath.

The viewpoint of the French School has remained per-
sistent throughout the century, advice from an earlier decade
sounding much like contemporary studio admonitions:

> Breathing should remain instinctive--The pupil
> since birth has breathed to breathe and he hasn't
> managed badly; he learned instinctively to breathe
> for speaking; it remains up to him to learn every

bit as instinctively to breathe for singing.

> Breathing should remain instinctive. Nothing is
> more dangerous than to hand over too completely
> to cerebral intervention acts as automatic as that
> of respiration, and to try distinctly to become
> conscious of the mechanism of so complex an ac-
> tion.
>
> ... We think of the phrase and we breathe appro-
> priately. [1]

Natural breathing is a method of breath control only
in that it offers an option to those methods which directly
emphasize conscious controls. It avoids directing attention
to any local area. Awareness of costal, diaphragmatic or
abdominal action is engendered largely through imagery and
subjective suggestion.

Pedagogical perils abound in ignoring the breath
process, unless the singer has managed to achieve a coordinated breath technique through individual discovery, which is
exceedingly rare. Since what appears to be natural to one
singer will not be the same breath approach which comes
naturally to another, a number of techniques (or great deficiencies in the application of the breath) often exist, side
by side, within the vocal studio where so-called natural
breathing is taught. Whatever the student habitually has
done with the breath then generally continues to be done.

Singers trained in the French School often demonstrate
a shallow breath which brings the clavicles and shoulder muscles into play. Teachers check on the degree of "relaxation"
in breathing by asking the pupil to move the head loosely,
swing the arms, bend the waist, and make the torso limp.
The energization of the sound is at a lower level in the
French School than in any other. The typical French singer
is basically a high-breather because of the prevailing notion
within the school that attention toward increased breath activity is undesirable in singing, and because shallow breathing
is what most people make use of in daily activities.

The Italian School

There is an astonishing degree of uniformity throughout the Italian School with regard to breath management.

The inventiveness of German and English teachers toward
support methods is totally lacking.

The Italian School stands in direct opposition to
systems which advocate lowered sternum and collapsed
thoracic cage, and equally so to those techniques which aim
at fixing the costals or the diaphragm. Even more decisively, the Italian School considers the low-breathing techniques
and outward abdominal pressures of the German School to
be functional violations, contrary to natural processes.

APPOGGIO. Appoggio is the term used to sum up
the kind of muscular coordination on which the Italian system
of breath management is based. Although the word appoggiare
means to lean against, or to support, the term appoggio
can properly be described as encompassing sterno-costal-
diaphragmatic-epigastric breathing. Appoggio embraces a
total system in singing which includes not only support factors
but resonance factors as well (witness such terms as appoggiarsi in testa and appoggiarsi in petto). With reference to
breath management for the singing instrument, appoggio encompasses the interrelationship of the muscles and organs
of the trunk and neck, combining and balancing them in such
an efficient way that the function of any one of them is not
violated through the exaggerated action of another.

Appoggio begins as a postural attitude: the sternum
must remain at a moderately high, poised position throughout
the breath cycle. The sternum finds this position when the
arms are raised over the head and then brought down to the
sides of the body; at the same time the shoulders are relaxed,
making certain the sternum does not lower. In this position
the sternum could be raised still higher, which would be
too high; it could also be lowered from this posture by "relaxing" it, which would be too low. This noble posture is
perhaps the most visible trademark of the Italian-schooled
singer. It is the key to the Italian's breath coordination in
singing.

The position of the diaphragm itself is partially determined by posture. For example, the abdominal muscles
which engage the diaphragm are in a state of contraction in
the standing position but less so during sitting. Further, if
the sternum lowers, the diaphragm is unable to maintain the
proper degree of distention during the breath cycle, especially as required during the singing act; the rib cage, attached
to the sternum by the seven upper ribs, will tend to collapse

if the sternum is dropped. The ribs remain in a well-expanded position if the sternum and the costal muscles are poised. Because the muscles of the epigastrium (so often confused with the diaphragm itself) engage the diaphragm, a sensation of internal-external muscular balance takes place during the course of the sung phrase. This feeling of stabilized muscular balance increases with the demands of pitch and power.

Francesco Lamperti in A Treatise on the Art of Singing describes this sensation:

> To sustain a given note the air should be expelled
> slowly; to attain this end, the respiratory muscles,
> by continuing their action, strive to retain the air
> in the lungs, and oppose their action to that of the
> expiratory muscles, which, is called the lutte
> vocale, or vocal struggle. On the retention of this
> equilibrium depends the just emission of the voice
> and by means of it alone, can true expression be
> given to the sound produced. [2]

Upon inhalation, there is some outward motion in that area which lies between the end of the sternum and the navel. This action is not similar to the pouting-out of the lower abdominal wall which is thought to result from diaphragmatic expansion as practiced in the German School. Upon exhalation, in the Italian School, an almost imperceptible inward motion slowly commences. This motion is resisted internally by a sensation of balancing pressures, experienced chiefly nearest the navel.

The Italian-trained teacher requests that during the entire act of singing the sternum should remain relatively stationary, neither rising nor falling. This insures that the rib cage will remain fairly well positioned, the ribs moving inward only slightly (often imperceptibly) at the completion of exhalation on long phrases. If the hands are placed at the waist, bridging the anterior and posterior sides of the body, fingers on the epigastrium, thumbs posteriorly at the lowest ribs, considerable lower dorsal movement will be evident. A sensation of transverse expansion across the entire body is experienced upon inhalation and is present throughout the sung phrase.

The upper abdominal wall moves slowly inward, but the sensation of support is achieved by maintaining a feeling

of steady internal-external muscular balance as mentioned
above. This feeling of balancing muscular action is experienced in the entire posterior lumbo-dorsal area as well as
in the anterior thoraco-epigastric area. However, this action encompasses neither the action nor the sensation which
results from techniques of low-back spreading as they are
consciously sought after in certain Germanic techniques.
The latter inevitably upset the muscular balance of the entire
torso.

Because the lower abdominal area (hypogastric) is
muscularly connected with the upper abdomen (epigastric),
the singer experiences a sense of engagement throughout
the length of the abdomen, especially on phrases requiring
extensive energization. This sensation does not resemble
the outward muscular tensing in the lower abdomen which
most northern schools promulgate. The latter sensation can
take place only in conjunction with a different set of postural
considerations in the pelvis and thorax, as was previously
pointed out in some detail.

In the Italian School, muscular stabilization results
from postural alignment of the head, neck, shoulders, torso
and pelvis.

In the concept of appoggio there is no pressing outward
against the viscera upon inhalation, no pushing downward with
the abdomen proper, no pushing downward upon the viscera
during the singing of a sustained phrase. During singing,
muscles of the buttocks do not rigidly contract, the pelvis
is not tilted, and no muscular tension is placed in the legs.

Further, there is no sense of great expansion in the
pectoral area, although the pectorals and the neck muscles
form part of the supporting framework which results from
the relatively high sternal position. Muscular balance throughout the body is the aim.

Breathing is silent and can occur within a split second
or can be paced quietly over a number of seconds. Whether
taken quickly or slowly, through nose or through mouth, the
breath process functions in the same noiseless manner.
Naturally, following numerous cumulative phrases where
pauses for the breath are extremely brief, some limited
audible inspiratory sounds may occasionally be discerned.
However, the quiet breath is a mark of identification for
the singer who uses the appoggio technique of the Italian
School.

The singer is urged to feel that no changes of sensation occur in going from breathing to singing. Giovanni Battista Lamperti supports this position:

> 'How fast must I take in breath?'
>
> 'If you do not dissipate the sensation in your head of the last one, you can inhale as rapidly as you wish.'
>
> 'Breathe through your tone,' Lamperti said.
>
> 'Why?'
>
> 'Because that is the position of singing. Why should you get out of position, while adding more energy to your breath power?'[3]

Muscular resistance when inhaling is strenuously guarded against in the Italian School. Some singers in non-Italian schools mistake holding the breath for controlling the breath, during the singing act. Like little children who grab a "deep breath" and "hold" it before submerging their heads in water, those singers experience muscular resistance at the intake of the breath, which feels as though it were the result of lung expansion. The stretching feeling in the chest is not evidence of increased lung capacity, but of muscular resistance. In contrast, the Italianate singer is exhorted not to crowd the lungs upon inhalation, but to satisfy them.

The muscular balance of the appoggio posture permits the singer to utilize the amount of breath necessary to the demands of the phrase, while retaining a sense of continuing breath resources. Breathing in and singing out seem not to be opposing actions.

When viewed within the findings of scientific investigation, it can logically be affirmed that in breath application techniques singers trained in the tradition of the Italian School do less violation to natural physical function than do singers trained in several other schools. Appoggio demonstrates that unimpeded physical function produces the most efficient breath management in singing.

Chapter VI

TECHNIQUES OF VOWEL FORMATION IN SINGING

It is somewhat artificial to consider vowel formation apart from concepts of vocal resonance because the action of the combined resonators which plays a role in vowel differentiation also helps determine the kind of "focus" or "resonance" the vocalized tone will have. In spite of this obvious interrelationship, the two subjects can be most clearly understood if separately treated.

Before proceeding to a consideration of vowel formation techniques as they develop within the national schools, some brief attention must be given to several acoustical matters concerning the voice.

Acoustic Properties of the Vocal Tract

Although the following statements were written with an eye to speech, similar articulatory conditions prevail in the vocal tract during singing:

> The character of the vocal cord buzz is modified by the vocal tract's acoustic properties. These acoustic properties depend on the shape of the vocal tract. During speech we continually alter this shape by moving the tongue and the lips, etc. These movements, by altering the acoustic properties of the vocal tract, enable us to produce the different sounds of speech. [1]

With regard to actual vowel formation, Dr. John S. Kenyon lucidly presents the interrelationship of the resonators to the fundamental tone:

> These cavities (mouth, pharynx and nose) definitely shaped for each vowel, are believed to reinforce

45

those partial tones of the complex voice-tone whose
pitches correspond to the natural resonance of the
cavities so shaped, independently of the pitch tone.
Thus in pronouncing any vowel, however the voice
as a whole be raised or lowered in pitch, these
partial tones will automatically become prominent
which fit the forms assumed by the mouth and
pharynx for that particular vowel. Hence the characteristic pitch or pitches for each vowel remain
fairly constant, and so identify the vowel to the
ear. The same vowel may therefore be heard,
though the voice as a whole may vary in pitch. [2]

If these generally acknowledged viewpoints are accepted,
it follows that the vowels themselves must be permitted to
provoke specific postures within the resonance chambers,
thereby reinforcing the laryngeal sounds. That these assumptions are not accepted equally by all national schools of singing, both this and the following chapter will illustrate.

THE GERMAN SCHOOL

Fixed Buccopharyngeal Principle

It is a frequent maxim of the German School that
in order for all the vowels to remain equalized throughout
the vowel spectrum (that is from [i] through [u]), the basic
postures of the pharynx and the mouth should remain as constant as possible.

In order to accomplish this, a fairly open buccal
posture is required. Of course, the demands of articulation
modify this spatial arrangement, but the goal is for a minimal amount of movement. These limitations placed upon
shaping and combining the pharyngeal and buccal cavities
do not permit the detailing of postures found in the same
spoken vowels.

This unique buccopharyngeal posture which is kept
during singing can only mean that the reinforcement of "those
partial tones of the complex voice-tone whose pitches correspond to the natural resonance of the cavities, " definitely
shaped for each vowel, must be achieved by physical events
in singing which differ from those which occur in speech.
These actual events are more fully explored in the following
chapter.

To ears which do not embrace the fixed buccopharyngeal principle, to hear the vowel (i) as in Liebe formed by a
mouth posture not far from the vowel (a) as in Labe, is to
perceive a distorted version of the vowel (i) or a newly designated vowel. To listeners who do not share in this characteristic Germanic aesthetic regarding sung vocal quality,
the maintaining of one basic throat and mouth posture during
the articulation of several vowels produces a common quality
of distortion throughout them all.

Buccal Rounding

Another technique which influences vowel formation in
the German School is the process of buccal rounding (rund-
lippige Vokale) produced by a slight pouting of the lips.
(Occasionally this shape is suggested by the term, Schnutchen
machen, a somewhat dialectical expression.) This buccal
posture is well in line with an attempt to diminish the horizontal "smile position" which the German-trained teacher sees
as an excess in the Italian and French schools. A pleasant
expression, the German teacher believes, can just as easily
be maintained with the mouth well-opened and rounded. Actually, the "rounded lip" position does relieve the starkness
of the set mouth posture which results from the fixed bucco-
pharnygeal principle. It contributes to a more pleasant facial
expression than would otherwise be possible.

Preferred Vowels for Vocalization

It is not merely coincidental that this unique posture
which has been described is best achieved through the use of
the umlaut (ö). More than any other vowel, (ö) is the basic
vocalizing sound in the typical German School. In singing
this vowel, the mouth is usually opened somewhat farther
than it would be for the same vowel in speech. Frequently,
the umlaut (ö) serves as the postural center for vowel pro-
gression in such a vocalise as (ö - e - i - ü - o - a). (ö)
is considered a good vowel for determining basic mouth posture, and the singer is asked to keep the position of the
initial umlaut, as far as possible, throughout the vowel series.

Further, it is maintained that this vowel combines in
itself the advantages of the high formant vowels (i) and (e)
and the lower formant vowels, such as (ɔ), (o) and (u),

provoking the ideal posture for singing. (It is phonetically
questionable that this sound can achieve such a functional
wedding.) This Doppelgriff principle (literally, double grip)
is often encountered as the basis for vowel formation in the
German School. A typical exposition may be found in Josef
Kemper's Stimmpflege (1951). [3]

Other vowels favored by the German vowel technician
are (ü) and (Ü), as in fühlen and füllen, which vowels also
assist in producing the "rounding" posture.

In addition to the Umlaute, many German-schooled
teachers make much use of (u), as in Mut, and of (U), as
in Mutter, for vocalizing, tending to avoid the high vowels
almost entirely. Many times these vowels are used as single
syllables throughout the vocal range in melismatic vocalises.
They are also given prominence in sustained vocalises devoted to the accomplishing of an even scale. When utilized
in this way, they are not intended, as is the case in some
other schools, as a means for accomplishing vowel modification in the upper range of the voice; rather they are used to
induce a basic buccal posture throughout the sung scale.

Equalization of Vowel Sounds

The use of specific vowels which stress the rounding
aspects in singing, tends to bring about a reduction in the
brilliance of the sound. Further, when vowels at the brilliant end of the vowel spectrum, (i) and (e), are encountered,
they frequently are modified toward lower vowel formations,
regardless of pitch or accompanying register factors. Without such modification, these vowels are too bright for the
Germanic ear in any part of the voice; only the modification
detailed above will fit them into an equalized vowel spectrum.
The search is for the ausgeglichene Vokale (equalized vowels),
in which no individual vowel sound will stick out from its
neighbor because of excessive individual color. The technique for achieving these equalized vowels, it is thought, lies
in the fixed buccopharyngeal posture.

THE FRENCH SCHOOL

The teacher trained in the French School wishes above
all to preserve the sound of the language in singing, and
proper vowel formation is considered a means to that end.

Buccal Posture

French teachers believe that the mouth should be well opened, especially in its forward area near the lips, but in such fashion as to permit the retention of the "smile" posture. The jaw is not dropped at the rami (hinges). Whereas among some non-French singers the jaw hangs and the mouth is rounded or pouted, the typical French singer seems to raise the upper maxillary area, including the cheeks, nearly as one does in laughter.

The Vocalizing Vowel

The smiling facial posture evolves out of an exaggeration of the position assumed in singing the vowel (a), as in parle; this vowel is almost universally the primary vocalizing sound in the French School.

Especially when executed with well-opened mouth, this vowel requires a slightly higher tongue posture than does the vowel (a) as in the Italian cara or in the German Vater. Serving the function of basic vocalizing vowel, it may well explain the tendency toward "openness" which prevails in much of French-schooled singing. Although in careful speech the vowel (a) is not given a nasal modification, the high tongue position and the low-hanging velum which generally are present in the French School tend to direct much of the sound into the nose and to narrow the pharynx. The combination of high tongue, low velum, narrow pharynx and the open-though-smiling mouth, tends to produce a rather bright, reedy, thin quality throughout the vowel spectrum.

Labial Mobility

As a counteraction to the somewhat widely-opened mouth, great mobility of the lips is demanded, while still keeping the smile position. Whereas in the German School relatively little mouth and jaw motion occurs in singing, except as necessitated by consonantal demands, the mouth and lips of the gallicized singer seem in almost constant motion, albeit within the smile, as they form vowel positions. To an observer, the French-schooled performer appears to sing "on the lips" and in the forward portion of the well-opened mouth, regardless of which language is being sung.

THE ENGLISH SCHOOL

Despite a native language of diphthongs, triphthongs and numerous transition sounds, the typical Anglicized singer seeks to find a balanced relationship between the shapes of the resonance cavities and the laryngeal sound, which will permit reinforcing partials to be present within the constantly changing vowel patterns. Many teachers in the English School advocate the quick, flexible adjustments of the resonators above the larynx which, it will be shown, form a major premise of the Italianate school with regard to vowel formation.

Jaw Function

The admirable tenet described above, regarding the acoustical influences of the vocal tract upon the sound which emerges from the larynx, is much impeded by the English preoccupation with the dominant function of the jaw in singing. Repeatedly one hears English teachers opine that English singers do not open their mouths sufficiently in singing, when a comparative study decisively reveals that they have their jaws distended far in excess of any other school of singing, including the German. (The German School is not concerned with the jaw posture as such, and does not achieve the enlarged pharyngeal position through forcing the jaw downward. The buccal posture of the Germanic school does not resemble the English "long-faced," "relaxed" or "dropped" jaw posture.)

There is a jaw controversy within the English School, which is not a new condition. Harry Plunkett Greene in his remarkable article on "The Straight Line in Singing" (1912) deplored the "chief bottle-washer" duties assigned to the jaw in the English School. [4] A significant number (though a minority) of writers and teachers in the English School campaign against it. Both the written attention directed to the jaw and present-day concert experiences attest to its continuing central position in the English performance world. The "jaw" flourishes among solo singers in all areas of repertory, and is a hallmark of technique which seems basic to English choral sound. Indeed, it is difficult to find a major choral organization in England (their number is legion) whose members do not seem to have been caught in a "freeze" while gaping. (Of course, any device which removes upper partials from the sound will serve to prevent blatant voices in an ensemble from "sticking out. ")

Much technical study in this very sizable segment
of the English School is directed toward learning to drop the
jaw as far as possible in order to "relax" it, with the hope
of finding freedom in singing. It is often recommended that
the mandible drop so as to require the ramus on either side
to glide forward, leaving a depression just below the lobe
of the ear.

> A sufficient opening of the jaw will give a little
> concavity which can be felt by the finger--between
> the jaw socket and ear. This is due, mainly to the
> separation of the back teeth which should always
> have attention. [5]

Later, from the same source, "Remember that the mouth
should be felt to open at the socket of the jaw, rather than
in front (at the lips). "

Sometimes it is recommended that the jaw be dropped
far enough to accommodate the width of two fingers placed
between the front teeth. (Such a posture produces for most
mouths an aperture not far from the fullest distention of the
jaw, actually.) This "relaxed jaw" position is to be retained
while enunciating all the vowels.

W. A. Aikin, by all accounts a major figure in English vocal pedagogy, in a section dealing with the resonant
pitch of the vowels, presents a somewhat more restrained
yet a typically British attitude toward jaw action and vowel
formation:

> In order to prevent any impairment of the resona-
> tion of the mouth we must adopt the open jaw for
> all vowel positions--that is to say, the changes by
> the lips and the changes by the tongue are to take
> place without any movement of the jaw, which re-
> mains definitely open to the extent of an inch be-
> tween the front teeth. This demand may at first
> sight appear to be excessive, but it is designed
> with a view to obtaining the maximum of phono-
> logical effect without destroying the character of
> the vowels, in order to show more clearly their
> true nature as well as to indicate a phonological
> method of their improvement. [6]

Later, he continues:

> Most people, when they first attempt to make good
> vowel-sounds, discover that they have not been in
> the habit of opening the jaw sufficiently, especially
> in the positions ee and oo, at the two extremes of
> the Resonator Scale. Attention, therefore, should
> first be given to the position of ah, which has al-
> ready been defined, and the same opening of the
> jaw maintained for all the other vowels [emphasis
> added]. 7

Following the above quotation Aiken presents a complicated system of adjusting for the problems which may occur by forming (i) (ee) with such a low jaw, as well as the
suggestion to maintain an open jaw on (i) even "if necessary
with a prop of wood an inch long between the teeth. " It
should be noted that this extended jaw posture is recommended as standard procedure in singing and is not reserved
simply for range extremes or for specific practices related
to vowel modification. It can also be easily verified by a
moment's trial that to open the mouth the extent of one inch
is to have it in a position seldom encountered during speech.
W. A. Aikin, author of the above suggestions, is the distinguished contributor of the article on "Singing" in the 1928
edition of Grove's Dictionary of Music and Musicians.

The Preferred Vowel

As a result of the attention tendered to the lowered
jaw, (ɔ) is the favored vowel for purposes of vocalization in
much of the English School, and it serves as the basic singing position for the formation of all vowel sounds.

An even more radical expression, but by no means
rare in the English School, exhorts the singer to place the
jaw in a completely relaxed position (meaning one in which
the mandible falls out of the rami) and then to form the
vowels using the tongue alone without altering the shape of
the mouth.

> First, drop the jaw in a completely relaxed posi-
> tion and then form the vowels using the tongue
> alone, and without altering the shape of the mouth.
> Control over the pharynx will be experienced and
> the student will have the feeling that the vowels are
> being formed in a low position; if the vowels are
> not produced in this same low position during singing
> one may be sure that the throat is not open.

> ... [P]ractice trying to produce the vowel sounds
> with the pharynx alone and without the use of the
> mouth, as does the ventriloquist ... abandon the
> normal positions for vowel formation used in speech
> and substitute for these the low position described
> above in which the mouth is of secondary importance
> and the pharynx becomes the main resonator of the
> tone. Any deviation from this low position or a
> return to the normal use of the mouth as in speech
> will result in closing the throat no matter how hard
> the singer tries to make it 'feel' open or how hard
> he tries to pull the base of the tongue forward. [8]

Plainly the aim here is to <u>refrain</u> from adjusting the shape of the vocal tract to accommodate changing vowel sounds in singing. This pedagogical tenet stands in direct opposition to most scientific findings, which admonish that the tongue, lips, palate, cheeks and jaw alter the acoustical shape of the vocal tract. (Yet science is called upon to support these pedagogical viewpoints.) To maintain that no such alteration of the component parts of the vocal tract occurs in sung vowels, while admitting their occurrence in spoken vowels, is surely to present a double acoustic standard for singing and speaking which does not accord with principles advocated by a number of non-British teachers of singing.

Within Anglified vocal methodologies, the activity of the jaw in mastication is cited in support of the hung jaw. However, in chewing, the action of the jaw tends to be both horizontal and vertical. Were one to place the jaw in the hung position required by many English teachers of singing, food would fall out of the mouth during mastication. Chewing even the thickest portion of steak, or even the child's immense wad of bubble-gum, simply does not include such vertical jaw distention as hung-jaw practitioners advise. Relevance to vowel formation seems even more remote.

It should be noted that the jaw normally can be found in this distended posture only in some forms of yawning, regurgitation, drunkenness, snoring, idiocy and death.

When the jaw has arrived at that location brought about by "dropping it as far as possible," the pharynx actually has decreased in size, and the larynx, unless consciously depressed, is pressed upon and restricted.

In spite of the claim that the vowels can all be clearly articulated with the jaw hanging at its lowest point, the best that can be said is that by Gestalt the ear cultivated to such auditory experiences can supply the missing characteristics of indicated vowels, nothing more. Degrees of success in delivering understandable diction are frequently startling in performances where "hung-jaw" adherents are juxtaposed to other approaches to vowel formation. Much of the poor diction which is proverbially associated with the Anglicized singer can be traced directly to this physical source.

That the English have learned to accept distorted diction as part of a national vocal aesthetic is generally conceded. Perhaps it is indicative of such a viewpoint when distinguished critical evaluation, in the report of a recital by "one of the most versatile and talented of our young singers," states that the artist sang fluently in four languages, but "Because she understands and cares for words, she can convey the meaning without using conventionally precise diction"[9] [emphasis added]. It is self-evident that among typically English-trained singers, diction in any language is sadly victimized by hanging that sturdy English jaw.

As was previously indicated, not all English singing teachers share this viewpoint on jaw activity. A somewhat radical statement in opposition to the majority view comes from a noted English teacher:

> The mere fact of opening the mouth to sing is often enough to induce rigidity of muscles. The student must be encouraged to allow the jaw to drop loosely instead of pushing it down forcibly. Most singers tend to lower the jaw too much; there is nothing whatever to be gained by this, and a great deal to be lost; it cannot be done without muscular contraction, involving tightness of production; it leads furthermore to much superfluous movement of the jaw in the articulation of consonants. The result is not only unmusical to hear but distressing to watch. Such singers deserve to be reminded that singing and mastication are not to be indulged in simultaneously without inelegance. It is difficult for most of us to look attractive while singing so the least we can do is to try not to appear aggressively repulsive. For quite ninety per cent of the singer's work his jaws need not be further than one finger's width apart. If he can arrive at that with easy production he can be trusted with the remaining ten per cent. [10]

THE ITALIAN SCHOOL

The Italian language may well enjoy a favorable position in the mechanics of singing with regard to the limited
number of vowels it possesses. (See Chapter XVII, The
Role of Language in National Pedagogies.) Nevertheless, in
all languages, regardless of the incidence of vowels and consonants, an almost constantly changing acoustical motion takes
place in speech. In singing, the adjustment of tongue, lips,
jaw, velum, cheeks and resonators occurs more distinctly
than in speech because of the prolonged duration factor; there
is in singing a better opportunity for the resonators to arrive
at and to maintain the proper posture for reinforcement of
the partial tones of the various vowels. "In-between" positions are minimized, and acoustical changes occur more
cleanly, avoiding the gradations of sound occasioned by the
continual movement of the speech organs which prevails in
spoken language.

However, a stationary acoustical posture in singing
is possible only until the new vowel or consonant comes
along, at which time the complicated laryngo-buccopharyn-
geal resonatory mechanism may move cleanly from one
vowel posture to a neighboring one, or may leap from one
end of the vowel spectrum to another (or arrive at an intermediate position), or adjust to produce a consonantal phoneme.

Relationship of Speech and Song

In the Italianate school it is believed that the sung
vowels evoke the same mechanical patterns in the jaw, tongue
and lips as in speech, except that they occur more deliber-
ately. (Sometimes, however, texts in the Italian vocal literature can be very rapid indeed!) These activities tend to
become more pronounced with pitch and power (as they also
do in speech), but the vowels always keep their spatial relationship to each other.

"Mi aiuti," as a mild request for assistance, involves
a buccal aperture far less extreme than would "Mi aiuti!"
as a frantic cry for help in a loud, high voice. (Imagine,
for example, the difference in buccal apertures between saying "Help me with this matter" and calling "Help!" if trapped
in a burning building.) For increased power and for rising
pitch, the mouth opens wider, yet each vowel retains its own

posture in relation to its companion vowels. Vowel differentiation remains at any pitch or dynamic level.

To arduously practice forming vowels and consonants without moving the organs of speech other than the tongue is for the Italianate singer a patent absurdity. In this attitude the Italian stands in direct opposition to many practices found in other schools. Articulation in the Italian School is not accompanied by a dropped mandible (as in much of the English School), by an exaggerated buccal aperture (as is common in the French School), nor by a preset, constant buccopharyngeal posture (as is often true in the German School).

The Italian maestro di canto (or maestra) attempts to avoid most of the physical events by which some other schools strive to induce proper vowel formation. The Italianate teacher believes that distortion of tone in unskilful singing is often caused by the very inability of the resonators to flexibly match the laryngeal position demanded by a specific vowel sound. The Italian-trained pedagogue does not find it possible to position the mouth in one "ideal" posture through which all the vowels are then sung. "Chi sa ben respirare e sillabare, saprà ben cantare" (he who knows how to breathe and syllabify well, will know how to sing well). [11]

Unless previously-induced rigidity is present, the teacher trained in the Italian tradition never directs attention to the jaw. If the jaw is tense in singing, one simply seeks to re-establish normal speech positions. The "loose jaw," the "relaxed jaw," the "idiot jaw," the "drunken jaw," the "snout," the "rounded mouth," the "frontally extended mouth" are not admonitions to be heard in the Italian School, nor are they postures to be found in normal speech in any language. It can be said, without qualification, that the "long face" which results from the hanging mandible (moving independently of the rest of the face as it drops out of the rami) is not to be seen in Italian voice studios the entire length and breadth of the peninsula.

"Come si parla" (as one speaks) is the sum total of the wisdom of the Italian School with regard to buccopharyngeal adjustment in the formation of vowels in singing.

Vocalizing Vowels in the Italian School

Mention was previously made that (ɔ) is the favorite

vocalizing vowel among typically English-trained singers,
(a) among French, and that the German-schooled singer tends
to vocalize chiefly with the Umlaute, especially (ö), relating
the higher vowels to them posturally. By contrast, the Italian teacher generally uses (i) (ɛ) and (ɑ) as centralized vocalization postures.

Many Italian vocalises, especially those of a more
sustained nature, follow the vowel spectrum from its highest
to its lowest vowel (i - e - ɛ - ɑ - ɔ - o - u), with
the high vowels initiating the series. Frequently vocalises
not only begin with the high formant vowels but return to
them, as for example, (i - e - ɑ - e - i), (i - e - ɔ - e -
i), (i - e - o - e - i). Generally in singing, (i), (e) and
(ɛ) are regarded as brighter vowels, (U) and (u) as darker
sounds, with (ɑ) and (ɔ) as balancing vowels in the middle.
It is obvious that whereas the typically German-schooled singer strives to bring the high, close vowels nearer to the
acoustical condition of the low vowels, the Italian works from
an exactly opposite premise.

The vowel (ɑ) is frequently used in vocalization in
the Italian School, both in sustaining and in agility, but generally only after the singer has learned to keep the vowel
well balanced with regard to fundamental and upper partials.

Chapter VII

TECHNIQUES OF RESONANCE IN SINGING

Vocal pedagogy often expresses itself in placement imagery which is intended to describe or to elicit sensations in the resonating cavities of the vocal tract. The term voice placement (also tone placement) is used by many singing teachers to denote those identifiable vibratory sensations experienced during singing.

Among most singers, the term resonance is seldom given a scientific usage, but loosely refers to vocal timbre. Sensations of resonance indicate the manner in which sound originating at the vocal bands is modified by the resonators.

Inasmuch as neither sound nor voice can literally be placed, some few teachers avoid such imagery altogether. In all four major schools, those teachers who make use of placement imagery seldom believe they literally are placing the sound. They find that the kind of timbre they consider desirable can be induced by mentally placing or directing the flow of tone. The physical events which correspond to these sensations thus become, to a certain extent, controllable through imagery.

Resonator Combining

That the manner in which resonators are combined determines the resultant tone has long been established. Indeed, Sir Richard Paget demonstrated that when two resonance cavities are joined they do not necessarily have the same pitches they would separately have. [1] Moreover, the resonant quality of the voice (actually the timbre), although initially dependent upon laryngeal function, is further determined by the interrelationship of the combined resonators, responding to the laryngeally-produced sound.

These resonating cavities include those in the chest (trachea and bronchi), the larynx itself (especially the ventricles of Morgagni, it is sometimes thought), the pharynx (which for purposes of further clarity in identifying resonance activity can be subdivided into the laryngopharynx, the oropharynx and the nasopharynx), the mouth, the nose and the sinuses (which are probably mostly agitated by sympathetic resonance). By variously combining these resonators, vocal timbre can be considerably altered.

> Sounds of the pitch desired, with admixture of overtones, are produced in the larynx; in man they are of pleasing quality because of the character of the vocal folds, neither too sharp edged nor with too wide a surface of approximation. The sounds produced in the larynx are amplified and selected in the pharynx, mouth and nose, and in these cavities some of the overtones can be strengthened while others are subdued or suppressed. The relative size and shape of these cavities are subject to considerable voluntary variation. Other sounds can be produced by the action of the nasopharyngeal and labial stops, and hissing sounds produced at the teeth. [2]

Whereas in speech little attention is directed to this process, the ability to consciously alter and control the shape of the vocal tract in singing receives much technical attention in some methods. Such interest would appear to be justified by the findings of investigative work connected with telephony:

> ... the pitch of notes is determined by the vibration of the vocal cords; the vowel sounds are conditioned by the cavities of the pharynx and mouth; the richness and quality of the voice is determined in the main by the head resonances arising from the various cavities, nasal and sinus. [3]

This is the material of voice placement.

Anyone associated with teachers of singing, or familiar with literature on vocal technique, will be aware of the many advocates of forward placement and the formidable number of teachers who adamantly reject the concept. Regardless of which viewpoint they hold, almost all singers believe some part of the distinguishing characteristics of timbre and quality are determined by the changing shapes of those resonators which lie above the larynx, specifically the cavities of the mouth and pharynx, and by the extent of nasal conjunction with them.

Others would include the sinuses, the chest and the larynx itself. It should be briefly noted that the possibility of chest resonance does actually exist in terms of the more or less unalterable sources of resonance stemming from the trachea and portions of the bronchi. Although at times it may feel like a source of resonance, the remainder of the chest cannot be included among the actual sources of resonance. Within the larynx itself are several possibilities which indicate that it may be a greater contributor to actual resonance than its size might lead us to suppose. An excellent treatment of "The Larynx as a Resonator," and of resonance in singing in general, is to be found in William Vennard's Singing: The Mechanism and the Technic (3d ed. 1964). [4]

It was suggested in the preceding chapter that a singer can consciously influence the size and shape of the mouth and pharynx. This can be proved by any observant person. That the singer can at will exclude or introduce nasality into the tone is equally demonstrable by simple experimentation. Direct control over the sinuses, the larynx and the trachea as resonators may be considerably more difficult to document.

It is exactly at the point of determining how the size and shape of any of these several resonators can be determined and with what favorable results, that vocal teachers find themselves in confrontation. It will be shown that pedagogical positions on placement theories can be delineated to a large extent on the basis of their allegiance to national tonal aesthetics.

Some familiarity with the muscular system which controls the several resonators is essential if techniques of the national schools are to be understood and compared.

The Buccopharyngeal Muscular System

The relationship of mouth to oropharynx is an obvious one; the oropharyngeal isthmus communicates between mouth and pharynx, being visible as one looks into the throat. One sees the isthmus of the fauces, the region between the palatoglossal and the palatopharyngeal arches. (See Plate 14.)

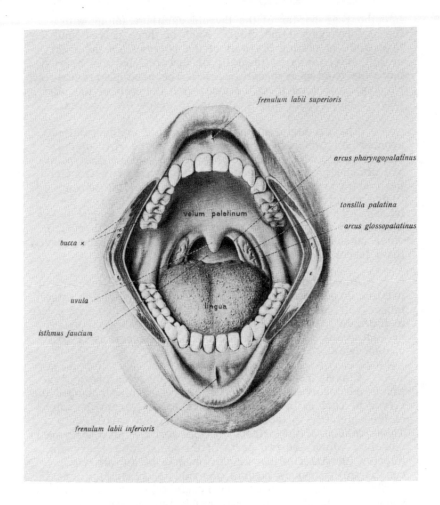

Plate 14.   The Cavity of the Mouth.

These two pairs of arches consist of muscular fibres which
extend downwards and laterally from the uvula.   They can
be easily identified as lying on either side of the tonsil, the
palatoglossal arch being more frontally located.   The oral
part of the pharynx extends from the soft palate down to the
top of the epiglottis.

The palatopharyngeal muscles themselves are inserted

into the rear border of the thyroid cartilage (along with
the stylopharyngeal muscles). Each of these paired muscles
is capable of pulling the wall of the pharynx (on the right
or left side) forward, medially or upward, and can approximate the palatopharyngeal arches. The palatopharyngeal arch,
running as it does from the uvula into the wall of the pharynx,
plays a major role in any attempt to shape the pharynx.

The palatoglossal muscles originate in the palatine
aponeurosis (which in turn is attached to the rear of the
hard palate, and to which all the muscles of the soft palate
are attached), from where they pass downward in front of
the tonsils and are inserted into the sides of the tongue.
These muscles, working as a pair, serve to narrow the
fauces. They can also pull up the root of the tongue (being
attached to the tongue), and by acting together with certain
other muscles they can assist in closing off the buccal cavity
from the oropharynx.

Among other muscles of the pharynx, the levator veli
palatini (see Plates 15, 16, and 17) elevates the soft palate;
tensor veli palatini acting separately, can pull the soft palate
to the side, or acting as a pair can tighten the soft palate
or flatten out its arch; the musculus uvulae serves to pull
up the uvula.

Closely related to this group of muscles are others
which are involved in swallowing and which also act upon the
laryngeal part of the pharynx (which extends from the top
of the epiglottis to the bottom of the cricoid cartilage).
These consist of the cricopharyngeus and the thyropharyngeus
muscles, which are two parts of the constrictor pharyngis
inferior (the inferior constrictor muscle of the pharynx),
constrictor pharyngis medius (the middle constrictor muscle
of the pharynx), constrictor pharyngis superior (the superior
constrictor muscle of the pharynx) which in turn consists
of four major parts: pterygopharyngeal, buccopharyngeal,
mylopharyngeal and glossopharyngeal. These three major
sets of constrictor muscles form the actual walls of the
pharynx. (See Plates 17 and 18.)

It should be noted that the cricopharyngeus attaches
to the cricoid, and the thyropharyngeus to the side of the
thyroid cartilage (and by a small strip, to the inferior horn
of the thyroid cartilage). The buccopharyngeus joins the
buccinator, the mylopharyngeus attaches to the lower jaw,
and the glossopharyngeus attaches to the floor of the mouth.

(For more complete explanations of the functions of this complex muscular system, the reader is advised to consult a recognized source on anatomy. Unless the singer has some solid information relating to function, it is difficult and hazardous to make judgments regarding the merits of opposing techniques in singing.)

This intricate muscular system of the buccopharyngeal area (see Plates 16, 17, and 18) comprises a complex structure, the parts of which are so interrelated that the difficulty in adjusting some part of the system locally without influencing action of the entire laryngopharyngeal mechanism must be at once apparent.

Attitudes toward the possibility of localized control over this exceedingly interdependent mechanism clearly set apart the national schools of singing in their approaches to vocal resonance.

THE GERMAN SCHOOL

Role of the Pharynx

The clue to resonator adjustment in the German School lies in recognizing the specific quality of sound desired by that school, a sound which can only be produced by altering the pharynx from normal speech postures. Application of techniques which will produce this specific quality largely separates typical German pedogogy from that of other schools, with regard to voice placement.

Within the Germanic school it is commonly believed that the pharynx is readily adaptable to spatial enlargement, as in the yawn. It is thought that the increased "room in the throat" which results, produces a fuller, richer sound. Because the glottis is to some extent capable of functioning independently of the parts of the vocal tract which lie above the larynx, it is claimed that laryngeal action will not be impaired by more or less mechanical adjustments in the pharynx.

Because the palatopharyngeal muscles which help in positioning the palatopharyngeal arch are inserted into the back ends of the thyroid cartilage, it is impossible to spread the fauces without also somewhat influencing the posture of the thyroid cartilage. The palatoglossal muscles which are

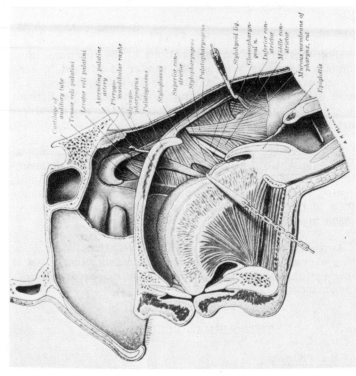

Right: Plate 16.   Interior of the pharynx.

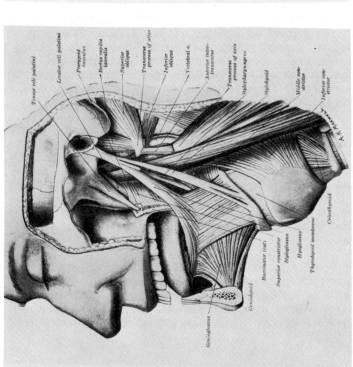

Left: Plate 15.   Muscles of the tongue and pharynx.

inserted into the sides of the tongue cannot function without involving the tongue to some extent. In enlarging the throat wall by "relaxing" it, most of the muscles of the buccopharyngeal area are placed into new relationships with each other.

The sound which results from these practices is produced by a change in pharyngeal size; shaping the pharynx so as to increase its size places the laryngeal muscles in such tension that registration events of the vocal instrument are affected. Whatever the accompanying results, it is claimed that the greater the space in the pharynx, the better the emerging sound. Accommodatingly, the pharynx lends itself to conscious sensations and controls.

This approach to pharyngeal positioning stems from a wider pedagogical view which affirms that singing and speaking represent different functions. Indeed, it is held, the organs of speech were not originally intended for speech but for more basic animal functions. Further, all of art consists of an altering of, or an improvement on, nature. Singing is not a "natural" art but a "learned" art. Criticism that natural function has been violated is therefore not accepted as pertinent by adherents. (Perhaps such a viewpoint with regard to singing begs the question as to whether it is appropriate to disturb the physical processes by which nature has improved herself.)

The system which develops from this vocal philosophy is a total one in which new relationships are sought between laryngeal posture, resonator adjustments and breath management, all of which create an improved vocal instrument thought to be better able to produce sounds which match a particular cultivated aesthetic ideal.

Stimmbildung

Stimmbildung (formation of the voice) is a favorite expression among German teachers. While to some the term simply signifies concern with coordinated skills in singing, to a majority of German-trained teachers, both that term and the term Stimmaufbau (voice building) have nothing to do with singing as an art but rather only with the mechanistic functioning of the voice as an Apparat (machine). In any case, certainly no other school devotes so much time to the theory and Technik of voice production as does the German School.

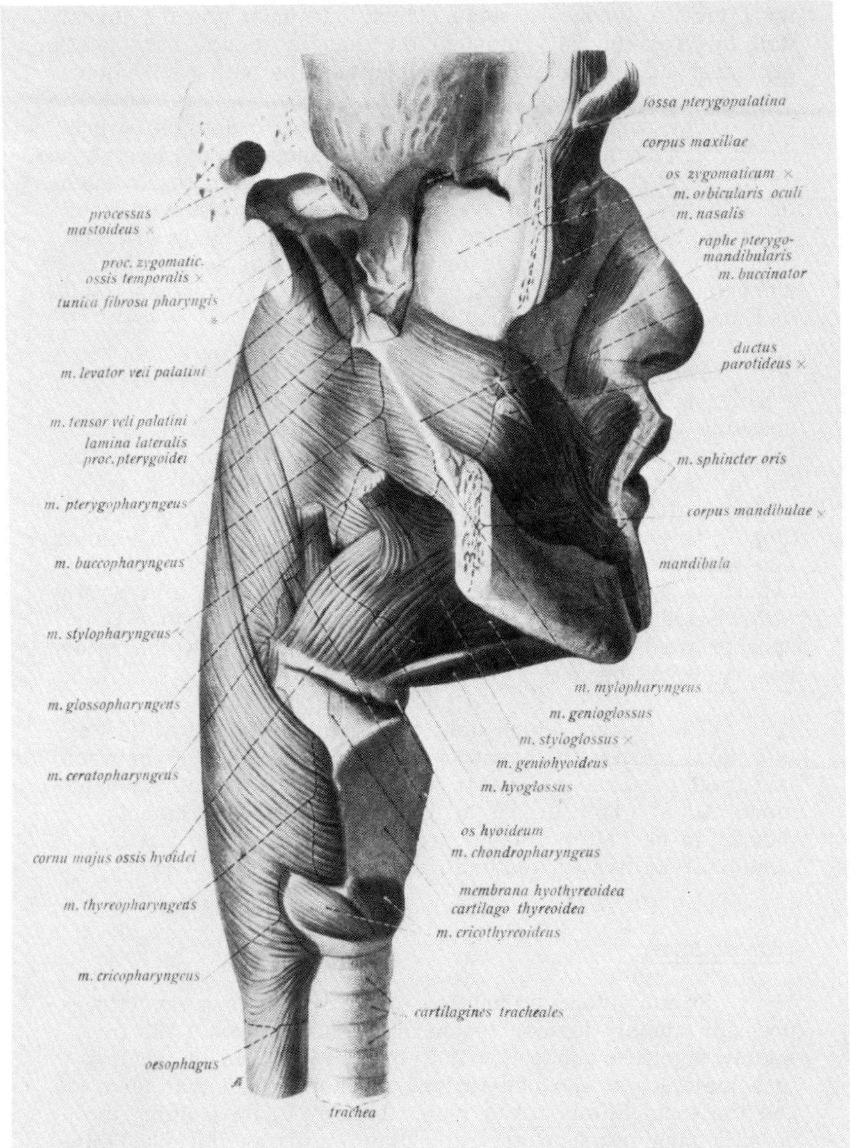

Plate 17. The muscular wall of the pharynx viewed from the right side.

Frequently it is maintained that the voice must first be taken apart, the component parts developed and then reassembled into a mechanism which will function in accordance with new kinds of coordination. The voice must be neugebaut (rebuilt).

Out of such philosophies a number of pedagogies within the German School have emerged which claim to have rediscovered primitive coordinations lost by modern man. These methods often claim to be able to make singers of everybody, to double the size of any voice, or to produce vocal ranges extending far beyond those normally thought to exist in given vocal categories.

Even though such highly complex methods often stress some one particular mechanistic aspect in singing, they all share concern for buccopharyngeal positioning, and for determining the direction the tone takes when it leaves the larynx.

Posterior Sensation

Some teachers in the German School describe specific muscular action which should engage the singer's attention. However, most of them rely upon sensation as the guiding indicator of technical proficiency. Both types typically adhere to the Prinzip des Nach-hinten-Singens (principle of singing toward the rear), which recommends that in "opening the throat" the tone be "placed" at the back of the throat wall. "Hinten ganz breit machen" (widen in the back) is often to be heard among German teachers, referring to the throat wall.

Imagery in this school includes such expressions as "fill the throat with sound," "imagine that the throat is a cave," "feel a potato, apple, orange, grapefruit, (the list is as extensive as the imagination) in the throat," "imagine the throat is a cone with the large end at the nape of the neck through which the tone flows out," etc. Or, closely related to the same kind of sensation-producing suggestions, "sing from the throat down into the body" or "send the tone down the spine." "In den Körper hinein singen" is a frequent request from the German teacher.

All of these expressions, and innumerable others similar to them, induce posterial sensations which are meant to enlarge the pharynx, improving it acoustically for singing.

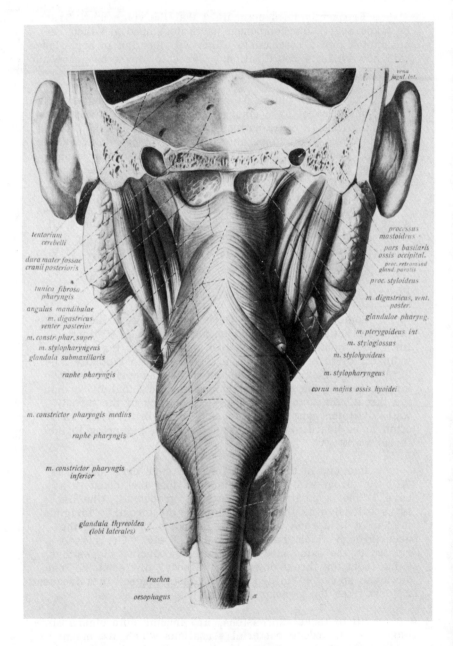

Plate 18. The pharynx with the constrictor muscles behind.

Distending the pharyngeal wall and the fauces is equated with "relaxing" and "opening" the throat. In the typical German School, placement sensations originate "nach hinten."

It can be acoustically demonstrated that pharyngeal enlargement increases the influence of the lower partials at the expense of the upper. As a result, singing with an enlarged pharynx tends to give the character of Rundung (roundness) so beloved by a great number of German singers. Because there is a loss of upper partials through this rearrangement of resonator interaction, the tone often partakes of a somewhat muffled, hollow quality. A kind of bigness is achieved, yet the tone may seem to many non-German listeners to be lacking in that illusion of "focus" which characterizes certain other kinds of productions.

A counterbalance to this loss of tonal brilliance, however, is to be found in a certain hardness of tone which results from the spread fauces. This "pharyngeal ring" coupled to the "round" quality often produces a kind of timbre which to ears trained in the Germanic vocal aesthetic indicates an enriched sound. Other listeners often perceive it as manufactured or falsely colored.

Such a sound often seems to emerge not directly from the mouth of the singer but rather from the pharynx. There is good evidence that this kind of tone sounds louder to the person producing it than it may to someone listening to it.

A vast compendium of current quotations from voice studios, from singers and from pedagogical literature in the German language could be assembled to illustrate this preoccupation with pharyngeal enlargement. The following is typical:

> When yawning we feel very wide and free in the
> throat. If we look in the mirror we can see the
> throat wall. The palate is like a curtain with the
> uvula raised high; we see the back part of the
> tongue lying low and wide. We feel so free in the
> throat because the pharynx is open. After yawning
> we continue to hold the mouth open in the yawn
> position. We feel how the lower jaw hangs and
> how the tongue feels the lower front teeth. The
> pharynx has its widest and most favorable position
> for the formation of tone: the wide pharynx. [5]

The concept of the widened pharynx, it will later be seen, also figures importantly in low laryngeal positioning as well.

The viewpoints summarized above stand in opposition to much of what has been determined by physicists and acousticians. There is no evidence that increasing the size of a resonator acoustically improves it.

> The combining of the various cavities to create the proper resonance is not a matter of absolute dimension but a matter of relative dimensions.

> ... [I]t is the conductivity factor between the cavities that creates the wide range of possibilities in the human voice ... [and] to a certain degree, cavities of the mouth and throat opened or closed beyond a certain optimum or normal usage is useless effort.

> ... [L]arger than optimum diameters show almost no increase in frequency. Therefore, beyond comfortably open constrictions or conductivity passages between the resonating cavities, there is no point in making the connecting channels larger. [6]

The interrelationships of the resonating cavities must be properly maintained in order to supply the correct resonance factors for a given sound. To aver, as does the German School, that one basic, enlarged pharyngeal posture should constantly prevail, is to preclude the quick, resonatory adjustments necessitated by pitch and general articulation.

Kopfstimme

A second major characteristic of the German School in the area of vocal resonance is the preoccupation with that quality of sound known as Kopfstimme. It would not be unexpected to assume that this term could be equated with voce di testa, voix de tête and head voice. The term does parallel these expressions among some teachers in the German School, but Kopfstimme as typically used cannot be taken as identical to them.

Kopfstimme is a vocal timbre peculiar to placement practices of the German School. It is true that a related sound can be found in some specialized areas of the English

School, but nothing comparable is to be encountered in either the French or Italian Schools. Because it is frequently used at piano dynamic, the French disparagingly refer to the sound as piano allemand and the Italians disapprovingly call it piano tedesco, considering it to be but a breathier counterpart of the voce finta.

Although the terms voce di testa, voix de tête and head voice are used, at least in part, as register designations, the term Kopfstimme is frequently used among German teachers as a descriptive quality designation without absolute registration connotations. (Brustton [chest tone] tends to be connotive of registration designation, however.) A schwebender Ton (hovering tone) is asked for in the Kopfstimme, which must be sanft (soft) and flötenähnlich (flute-like).

The Kopfstimme quality is almost universally approached in the German School through vocalizing the vowel (u) at pianissimo level. It is marked by the presence of Duftigkeit, which term as a tonal description signifies the presence of a large admixture of breath. (This added breath mixture induces muscular laxness which contributes to registration practices peculiar to the German School.) Much of the vibrancy of the tone is eliminated as a quality component of the sound. Although nach hinten singen still prevails as a concept in the Kopfstimme quality, placement is often achieved through directing the tone "up the back of the throat wall and over into the forehead," or by "directing it along the base of the skull, then over into the forehead." At times the hand is placed on the forehead and the tone is to "strike" against the hand. In fact, Stirnresonanz (forehead resonance) is a familiar term in German pedagogy.

A variant of this placement concept is to send the tone "up the throat wall into the dome of the skull." In this case, the hand is often placed on the top of the head, the calvaria (skull cap), and the tone is to be "placed" against it.

This "up and over" approach, with interesting variations, can be found with great frequency both in vocal studios where the German School flourishes and in German publications devoted to the technique of singing. It stands in opposition to the Vornesingen (forward singing), which for most of the Germans is a pejorative term, denoting shallow, nasal singing. When Vornesingen is not used as a deprecatory term among Germanic teachers, it usually means to "move the sound forward" after sensations have already been established in the back of the throat or in the dome of the head.

A by no means extreme example of this tendency can be found clearly presented in a volume which opposes those methods which recommend that one should <u>nach vorn singen</u>, considering them to produce nasality and to lose <u>Schädelgefühl</u> (sensation in the skull). It is suggested that the student should be told to hum initially into the back of the head ("<u>er sollte in den Kopf, möglichst den Hinterkopf, hineinsummen</u>"). However, the tone is finally to arrive at the front of the head:

> ... to the sensation in the skull comes the increasingly strong tendency with open throat and low-positioned larynx, to bring the voice along the base of the skull into the frontal resonance chambers of the head and there to let it sound. [7]

This sensation, it is stated, is what the Italians call <u>voce aperta in testa</u>. (It is doubtful that any Italian teacher would recognize that definition as corresponding to the sound described.) The same source also speaks of <u>Schädelstütze</u> (skull support), a term frequently met with in German pedagogy. "Open throat," "low laryngeal position," "forehead resonance" and "skull support" thus combine to produce <u>Kopfresonanz</u>.

Inasmuch as it is patently clear that anatomically one <u>cannot</u> direct the tone or the breath up the back of the throat wall or along the base of the skull, or into the back of the head and from thence into the forehead, what do such admonitions actually achieve? (Clearly, this kind of imagery must produce a sound which satisfies the aural aesthetic of a particular group of listeners.)

The physical result of such imagery could probably be determined in great detail, but cannot be undertaken within the limitations of this work, other than in some general observations: concentrating on spreading the pharynx or the pillars of the fauces, and on directing the tone up the back of the throat wall into the dome or forehead, eliminates the impact of the high partials which normally reinforce unimpeded vocal sound; this is because the positioning of the pharynx in one distended posture makes difficult the intricate combining and adjusting which the resonators above the larynx make when freely functioning without such controls.

It is a matter of scientific record that each vowel sound has at least two particular frequencies of fixed pitch. In the vowel (i) there are both 375 c/s and 2400 c/s, while in the vowel (u) are found 400 c/s and 800 c/s. The higher frequencies in the vowel (i) help to give it its characteristic color. If one radically changes its form, either at its laryngeal inception or in the mode by which it is modified by the resonators, one is no longer truly producing the sound (i). By a subtle process of adjustments, the vowel timbres can be much altered, although some conditioned ears may still perceive approximately the same vowel. This conditioning follows cultural habits as found in specific national schools of singing.

Brilliance can be reduced by modifying the vowel at its inception at the larynx, through altering the size and shape of the resonators, and by increasing the degree of unvocalized breath introduced into the sound. (By-noises of other sorts involved in speech may also be present.)

"Aiming the breath at the forehead" or "feeling the warm breath in the throat and head before the tone commences" or "whispering the attack" are all means of meeting the demand for breath mixture in the tone. Such a mixture of breath in the tone is perceived in the German School as part of the tonal quality, producing Sanftheit (gentleness, softness); cordal approximation is less complete than it might normally be for those particular pitches and articulated sounds.

This induced loosening of the vocal valve, resulting in a higher rate of breath mixture in the tone, counteracts the resistance to accumulating breath pressure below the vocal bands and produces a less intense tone, achieving a kind of breathy, shimmering lyricism. Even apart from the Kopfstimme quality, many Germanic teachers search for the "soft" attack which induces a slight breath mixture at the commencement of phonation. (See Chapter I, the Attack.)

The resultant sound of Kopfigkeit (heady quality) has a rather muted character with little brilliance in its make-up. Ears unconditioned to the tonal aesthetic out of which the sound emerges find the sound lacking in vitality and incapable of dramatic impact. Indeed, some teachers find it more adaptable to the gentler emotions of the Lied or the oratorio than to dramatic, operatic literature.

To those who dislike the quality of Kopfigkeit, the

tone seems markedly "hooty," "breathy" and "diffused," whereas to its admirers it is "soft" and "flute-like." Typically Germanic teachers often request <u>Flötentöne</u> (flute tones) in this "heady" production. Sometimes the sound is humorously referred to by its German detractors as <u>Blockflötentöne</u> (recorder tones).

To those who practice it, the <u>kopfig</u> quality is more lyrical than are the sounds produced in other schools. German teachers of singing quite often believe that they alone continue a tradition of <u>voce di testa</u> which they assume has somehow been lost by the Italians (inasmuch as the Italians do not make use of this timbre). To the German-schooled ear, the firmly centered, vibrant Italianate sound is often considered unlyrical, even at pianissimo level. Conversely, what to the German is a sound denoting hovering lyricism is to the Italian singer <u>un suono incartato</u> (a boxed-up sound), or a form of <u>piano tedesco</u>.

There can be little doubt that in searching for the <u>schwebender Ton</u>, exemplified by <u>Kopfigkeit</u>, the German-schooled singer often indulges in technical devices which vitiate the center, the core, the "focus" of the tone.

Frau Franziska Martienssen-Lohmann, in her influential and interesting volume <u>Der Opernsänger</u> (1943), with reference to training the lyric soprano voice, writes:

> Not the bright, shining vocal character but the softness, roundness and sweetness of the head tone and the tender line are characteristic. In training this natural lyric it is of great importance through intensive cultivation to bring to flower high onset and head-tone leading over the entire vocal compass. [8]

However, Frau Martienssen-Lohmann felt the need to guard against too much <u>Kopfigkeit</u>, for by exaggerating this softness in the tone, intensity, kernel and compactness of the sound can be lost. Such caution is often not exercised and the kernel of the sound is very frequently destroyed in the search for <u>Weichheit</u> (mellowness, softness).

Given the kinds of abdominal tensions in the German School that are a result of low-breath techniques, subglottal pressures on the vocal bands are often excessive. The sudden loosening of the vocal valve through the introduction of breath mixture permits stark contrasts in sound, producing decisively different tonal quality. Thus lyrical, piano singing in the more dramatic voices often has little relationship to vocal quality produced in forte passages. The kopfig character of sound, especially in the upper voice when suddenly introduced, recalls the general problems of breath support techniques in the German School.

That this heady sound has a place in the tonal palette of an accomplished singer cannot be denied. It is one of the many colors a singer may wish to call upon. To use it as the primary vocal quality in lyrical singing is to invite problems of tonal imbalance of a serious nature, in addition to being vocally debilitating. To recommend it as the standard sound for much of the literature is to prescribe a system of inefficient breath management coupled with violation of resonator function. Such methods consist of an amalgamation of compensatory actions which preclude clean cordal approximation. It should be remarked that within this commonly-encountered approach to lyricism, some readjustment is made at times in the balance of tonal factors, by the introduction of degrees of nasality. However, when maladjustment is initially the basis of vocal production, it is difficult to salvage the sound by such localized resonance corrections.

Some intimate, communicative and artistically satisfying sounds can result within a limited repertory, through the use of these techniques. It is highly doubtful that they serve with the greatest degree of efficiency throughout the repertory.

Once again, it is essential to indicate that some of the most devastating criticisms of posterial placement and Kopfigkeit come from German teachers who do not embrace the more typical national aesthetic which produces these techniques. Some teachers, a minority in the German School, speak disparagingly of Tutentöne (tooting tones) where their colleagues find a desirable Kopfresonanz. Within this atypical group of German teachers, the same tonal intensity found in the Italian voce di testa is the ideal; they dislike the shimmer of breath which is so often found in the more general notion of Kopfstimme. This group of German pedagogues also finds the enlarged pharyngeal techniques to produce a Knödel (literally, a dumpling) in the throat. Although this term is used to describe several kinds of throat sound, it always has to do with tone which seems to be produced by the stretched pharynx. The atypical German teacher, critical of the cavernous sound which often results from such techniques, also speaks of the sound as Höhlenton (hollow, or cavelike).

THE FRENCH SCHOOL

Contrary to those German colleagues who concentrate on the spaciousness of the pharynx, the typical teacher of the French School looks for ways to increase buccal and nasal resonance. While it is true that the best French singing clearly differentiates between nasals and non-nasals, there tends to be rather consistently a veil of nasality in French vocal tone which is the product of the slightly-lowered velum. Tenor Nicolai Gedda, in an interview given John Higgins in The Times (London) in 1972, may have had this tendency in mind when he said:

> I've always enjoyed singing in French enormously and have never had any difficulty with the language. Indeed, some of the French have told me that foreigners sing the language better than they do: we don't have the nasal sounds that they tend to overemphasize with bad effects on the vocal line. [9]

Role of the Mask

It is well known to what extent concepts of chanter dans le masque have dominated vocal pedagogy in France in this century. De Reszke is credited with bringing the system to prominence and acceptance in France, but it would seem more logically to be the result of national linguistic tendencies and tonal ideals. (Although de Reszke considered "the nose" to be highly important in singing, it is doubtful that he recommended the degree of nasality, as opposed to nasal resonance, which is characteristic of much current French vocal production.)

Uniformity of ideals with regard to timbre is characteristic of the French School. Instructional admonitions repeatedly center on such expressions as plus en avant, sur les lèvres, dans le masque, sur le masque, ouvrez la bouche, participez avec la bouche, and comme on parle.

One almost never encounters any advice to place the tone at the back of the throat, in the dome of the skull, or in the forehead. Tone is all directed toward the middle

front, or to the lower portions of the face and to the lips.
(All of these locations are frequently rolled together into one
physical gesture of forward placement.)

It can be stated emphatically that there is little correspondence between the German and French Schools in the
matter of voice placement. In the French School, the rapidly changing postures of the mouth tend to produce large buccal
movements, because the singer is expected both to articulate
with the lips and to achieve an open mouth position.

A frequent French pedagogical device is to place the
fingers lightly on the face of the singer, third finger above
the upper lip, thumb on the chin, forefinger just below the
bottom lip, scissors-like. This is to insure that the student
extend the aperture of the mouth fully, keep the lips mobile,
and feel the tone in the front of the face. The student tries
to remain flexible with lips, tongue and jaw while returning
as quickly as possible to the general position of the open
mouth.

Elevated Tongue

In the case of ascending pitch, the tongue often is
rounded upward, concavely, the tip still remaining in contact
with the lower front teeth, in an exaggerated (i) position,
further increasing brilliance, often to the point of harshness.
On the most upper notes of the range, the singer's tongue
often seems to loll out and over the lower teeth, the tip of
the tongue being in contact with the anterior side of the
teeth, near their tops. This is meant to "get the tongue
out of the throat"; the action obviously raises both the hyoid
and the larynx.

If the term forward placement is admissible as a
description of resonance concepts in singing, it surely more
appropriately matches the resonance goals of the French
School than any other.

THE ENGLISH SCHOOL

Cathedral Tone

There is a recognizable part of the English School
which is devoted to the cathedral tone in boys and in adults,

whether male or female. A straight, vibrato-less quality is much admired by the English in some of the solo song literature, in church music, and in early music. The absence of vibrato is thought to produce a tonal purity and bears a resemblance, to a certain extent, to the Kopfstimme of the German School, although avoiding most of the pharyngeal aspects of that production. This distinctive English quality is produced by concepts of "up into the back of the head and over into the forehead," which of course reduce the upper partials and the vibrancy of the tone.

However, a considerable number of teachers affiliated with the English School adhere to a good balance of pharyngeal-buccal-nasal resonances which is very much in line with those attitudes shortly to be described as an Italianate approach to placement. It must be stated that this theoretical adherence to resonantal balance is as often as not distorted by the demands of the hung jaw.

THE ITALIAN SCHOOL

The Italian School adheres to concepts of forward placement in singing. It could more accurately be stated that the placement goal of the Italian singer includes forward sensation but without the narrow concentration on forward placement as found in the French School. The Italian-schooled singer is taught to feel the tone pass through the face, to place it out in front, without emulating the French tendency to retain the tone in the masque.

Sensations recommended by the Italian teacher are indeed forward when compared with the posterial sensations associated with the German School. Posterial, up and over sensations, to be followed thereafter by skull-cap or forehead sensations, are seldom encountered among typically Italian-trained singers (although Caruso is often brought forth by German teachers as having claimed to experience both; there is a tendency among German pedagogues to conjure up the ghost of Enrico Caruso in support of any and every vocal technique.) In contrast, sensations immediately perceived frontally, in all areas of the face, even at times the forehead (particularly in the very upper voice) are definitely encouraged in the Italian School.

To the Italianate ear, the properly balanced sound is both bright and dark, the combined chiaroscuro tone. The

Italian teacher abhors the frontal blatancy of the French School as well as the dull posterior production of the German. The chiaroscuro (bright-dark) sound is obtainable through the natural function of the balanced resonators.

Gola Aperta (The Open Throat)

The Italian School avoids sensations in either the laryngopharynx or the oropharynx. Any reference to open throat has to do with sensations of openness in the nasopharynx. Such openness is arrived at by "inhaling through the nose as though filling the lungs with the fragrance of a rose," a suggestion to be heard in nearly every studio in Italy. When breathing is accomplished through the mouth, the same "inhalation of the fragrance of the rose" is attempted, without any spreading in the oropharynx or the laryngopharynx. The slightly-suggested smile is almost constantly present. There is no conscious basic buccopharyngeal posture to be arrived at in the Italian School; physiologically and phonetically the Italian premise is totally in accordance with natural function.

Voice Placement

L'impostazione della voce is the Italian expression for placement of the voice. (This term should not be confused with l'impostazione dell'organo fonatore, a term used to describe the position of the vocal bands at the point of vocal emission.) L'impostazione della voce is inextricably bound up both with vowel formation and the appoggio. (Although the term appoggio includes concepts of breath management, it unquestionably also relates to resonance sensations as well, which are in petto, in testa, or in both simultaneously. Imposto, however, means "placement.")

It is not true that appoggiarsi in testa and appoggiarsi in petto are terms which denote opposing kinds of breath management, nor is it true that the two terms refer to separate registration actions. One does not appoggiarsi in testa for head voice, then appoggiarsi in petto for chest voice. The Italian maestro or maestra will use either term as the student's needs require, to remind the singer of the two facets of the singing sensation; these two aspects are often presented simultaneously, depending upon range and desired timbre.

Impostazione and Appoggio

The technique of appoggio is made possible by the well-maintained chest posture that is associated with sterno-costal-diaphragmatic-epigastric breathing. The appoggio accomplishes sensations of impostazione which originate in the frontal area of the face, projecting from that point forward. The singer commences the sound simultaneously at two points, the region of the epigastrium and the facial area. These two areas of activity comprise the appoggio. (Voce di testa and voce di petto are largely registration terms, whereas appoggiarsi in testa and appoggiarsi in petto are chiefly placement and support terms.)

The Italian has never been able to erect a separate science of breath application in singing, an ability which flowers within both the German and English schools. (Nor has the French School exhibited an interest in that area.) As a result, in the Italian School the focus of the tone (the placement) and the control of the breath are considered to be one action. Further, in the Italian School, these two aspects are bound together with diction as well, inasmuch as the phonetic event dictates the shape of the vocal tract and demands a corresponding breath assistance. What happens above the larynx must match what happens within the larynx, which must be matched by the proper application of breath. In the Italian School, articulation is thought to control resonance factors automatically and to regulate diaphragmatic action through the occurrence of vowel and consonantal happenings within the sung phrase. This notion is recurrent in much of the pedagogical literature of the Italian School.

"The desire to feel the 'touch' of the 'point' of tone, becomes the objective guide to the breath," advises Giovanni Battista Lamperti.[10] The same source indicates that diction combines and directs the activity of support and of resonance.

In the Italian School the vitality of tone, the "focus," is never at the mercy of dynamic level. This constant quality is expected to.remain even in pianissimo singing, in both male and female voices. Francesco Lamperti formulates this Italianate rubric in very clear language:

> Piano should, in all respects, with the exception of intensity, resemble the forte, it should possess with it in equal degree, depth, character, and feeling; it should be supported by an equal quantity of breath,

and should have the quality of tone, so that even
when reduced to pianissimo it may be heard at as
great a distance as the forte. [11]

Timbre Terminology within the Italian School

For purposes of analysis of the sort attempted in this
work, it is necessary to treat separately matters of vowel
formation, resonance, laryngeal position and registration.   It
is one of the conclusions of this study that less conscious
separation of these technical matters occurs in the Italian
School than in the German and English schools, or even in
the French School.   This overlap of technical concerns causes
confusion with regard to terminology in the Italian School;
some further clarification of terms which occur in this study
may be in order at this point.

Although voce di testa is congruous with head voice
and voix de tête, the latter sound as currently practiced in
much of the French School is typically an open sound, whereas voce di testa is always closed.   (We have previously seen
that Kopfstimme represents a different tonal aesthetic.)   In
the Italian School, the open sound of the French School is
termed voce aperta.   The well-trained Italianate singer entirely avoids the open sound which is considered to be characteristic of the French singer; this is accomplished in the
Italian School by a fuller participation of the pharynx in general and of the nasopharynx in particular, in a naturally-
balanced relationship.   Furthermore, it is achieved by a
total involvement of the laryngeal mechanism, as well as by
appropriate registration techniques typically associated with
the Italian School.

Voce chiara (bright voice) in no way corresponds to
voce aperta.   The former is to be cultivated while the latter
is to be avoided.   The open voice (voce aperta) is lacking in
that balance of fundamental and appropriate overtones which
comprises the fully resonant sound throughout the voice.   In
the voce di petto (or more commonly, just petto), una voce
aperta lacks the body and depth of sound which issues from
the right combination of breath energy and adequate tracheo-
pharyngeal resonance.   In the voce di testa register, (or,
more popularly, just testa), una voce aperta is caused by
disregarding vowel modification which should take place in
register transition, and by improperly-assumed postures of
the pharynx.   The latter occur when no consideration is

given the needs of the mouth, which should open for ascending pitch.

La voce chiusa, the closed voice, is a desirable condition in the Italian School, standing in opposition to la voce aperta. It does not correspond to la voce oscura (dark voice) which is never a pedagogical aim in the Italian School. An Italian teacher may work toward la voce chiara, but except in voices of excessive brightness, will not strive for la voce oscura unless as an emotive coloration. Voce oscura is reserved to designate a cupo (dark, gloomy) quality which is sometimes required in sinister moments in dramatic literature. This coloration may occur in any range of the voice; as an indication or description of registration events, the term cupo is used sparingly. Cupo should not be equated with the German Deckung (cover); coperta in some respects is accordable with Deckung, but exists only with regard to graduated registration events. Those happenings are necessitated by vowel modification, being far less drastic in nature than Deckung. (See Chapter X, Vocal Registration and National Attitudes.)

The favorable conditions then, of voce chiusa, and voce chiara, produced by applying the appoggio, result in the fully resonant chiaroscuro timbre of the Italian School. This vibrant resonance is an essential quality of the Italian School; the complete sonority of the voice, at whatever dynamic level, is characteristic of the best in Italian singing. Vitality of tone remains constant, even in pianissimo singing, in both male and female voices.

> Especially in singing, it is necessary that the voice
> have the maximum sonority, for which all the parts
> of the resonance cavities must participate, particu-
> larly the nasal cavity, and any impediment to which
> constricts the throat, causing it to become exces-
> sively dark, as can often be verified among singers
> of Northern origin. [12]

An alignment of physical functions obtains in the Italian School which consists of flexible resonator adjustments, poised laryngeal position, mobility of tongue, lips, cheeks, jaw and soft palate, and sterno-costal-diaphragmatic-epigastric breathing. These functions coalesce into a specific method of singing, expressed in the appoggio concept of the Italian School.

Quite logically, one may assume that low abdominal breath techniques, laryngeal depression (see the following chapter), pharyngeal enlargement, static posture of mouth and mandible, and practices of posterial tone placement combine to present an alternate technical avenue, in direct opposition to the practices of the Italian School.

Chapter VIII

LARYNGEAL POSITIONING

What is the most efficient position for the larynx to assume during inspiration and during the act of singing? Not all teachers of singing are in agreement; answers to this question vary from school to school.

In theory, there are only two possibilities for positioning the larynx: the larynx remains in a relatively static position during the breath cycle; the larynx descends somewhat drastically with proper inspiration and is retained in a low position during the act of singing. In actual practice, a third position exists: the slightly elevated larynx. (The bobbing larynx, frequently to be seen among untrained singers, is not a method.)

The Elevated Larynx

The elevated larynx is so frequently visible during singing, especially within the French School, that the conclusion must be made that either it is considered to be a desirable laryngeal position or that it involuntarily occurs as an undesirable compensatory action.

That it is entirely a compensatory act unrelated to technique is disproved by the fact that a high laryngeal position must of necessity follow when the head is elevated in singing. Raising the head somewhat, in order "to free the larynx," is a pedagogical device frequently encountered in the French School. To determine that the throat is relaxed and free, the French-trained teacher often has the student raise and rotate the head, arriving at a final posture where the head sits lightly on the neck, however in an elevated posture, chin tilted slightly upward.

84

Although it may not be completely accurate to assert that teachers in the typical French School specifically request a high laryngeal position, such postural admonitions invariably produce it. The extrinsic muscles of the larynx and of the neck are placed in a less active role, and the support of the external muscles of the larynx is lessened. This posture is sometimes achieved through suggesting that the chin should be up and out of the way in order to free the jaw and the larynx. It often accompanies clavicular-sternocleidomastoidal activity during inhalation.

Furthermore, the laryngeal position is a high one in the French School because of a habitual tendency (as was earlier pointed out) toward the slightly elevated tongue as found in singing the vowel (a) as in parle. When tongue elevation is somewhat exaggerated for all vowel sounds, the hyoid bone and the laryngeal cartilages are also placed in comparatively higher positions. The practice of using (a) as the basic vocalizing vowel in the French School has an effect upon laryngeal position throughout the entire vowel spectrum.

A tight-necked quality of sound manifests itself more frequently among French-trained singers than elsewhere in the four major schools. In its most extreme example, a high degree of nasality is present. The sound which results is produced by a narrowed pharynx, raised tongue, and hyoidal and laryngeal elevation.

In the Italian School an elevated larynx is occasionally to be seen in the production associated with some leggiero tenors who on occasion make use of voce finta quality in the upper register of the voice. Some coloraturas of the Italian and the French schools often resort to the elevated larynx, producing a sound which is characteristically white, shrill and blatant. A high laryngeal position in the upper voice is also to be found with frequency in many tenors of the English School, where an edgy sound is mistaken for brilliance. It should be noted that the high laryngeal position is almost never to be found in voices trained in the German School.

The Depressed Larynx

The history of the low-positioned larynx is a long and depressing one. It is not the discovery of twentieth-century German or American voice science, as is often assumed.

The low larynx was known to Garcia, and he appears to have endorsed it for certain kinds of vocal quality in an 1841 paper read to the Academy of Science, published as a "Report on the Memoir of the Human Voice."[1] However, it cannot definitively be determined to what extent he recommended its general usage in all voices at all times. He is reported to have taught the low laryngeal position as early as 1832, but to have repudiated it later on in life. Garcia is universally cited as an exponent of the "old Italian School," having been trained by his father, Manuel del Popolo Vicente Garcia, as were his sisters, Maria Malibran and Pauline Viardot-Garcia. However, Manuel Garcia's singing career terminated at age twenty-four, which does not provide us with an encouraging endorsement of his understanding of his own voice. His early endeavors indicate a search for new directions in the field of pedagogy if not in the art of singing itself. With the invention of the laryngoscope, he made a major contribution to the study of vocal function.

However, there is some evidence that his general viewpoint on the value of mechanistic thinking on the part of the singer may have considerably modified with passing years. At age ninety, in 1894, he presents a well-balanced perspective on the value of anatomical information for singers and teachers:

> The study of the anatomy and physiology of the vocal organs is not indispensable to the pupil, but might be most useful to the teacher. It will enable him, when a defect is to be amended, to detect the organ which is at fault, and to suggest the proper correction. For the pupil it is enough that, localising his sensations through his master's explanations, he should learn to distinguish the various parts of his instrument and the manner of using them.[2]

The Maestro died in 1906 at the age of 101.

Depressed laryngeal technique was given considerable currency in the late nineteenth century by Julius Stockhausen, a pupil of Manuel Garcia and personal friend of Johannes Brahms, in his two-volume work, Gesangsmethode, published in 1886 and 1887. Another publication, Gesangstechnik und Stimmbildung, added to his stature as vocal pedagogue, particularly in the German-speaking world.

Additional respectability in Germany was given to this

"tiefe Stellung der Kehle" (low-positioning of the larynx) by
such "scientific" endorsements as the following:

> The low position of the larynx which is favorable
> for the full quality of the voice, and which should
> be anticipated in singing, can be achieved in the
> same way as by yawning. Even the non-singer can
> easily convince himself that in the yawn-position,
> the production of the full tone is made more favor-
> able. [3]

It is curious with what frequency subjective judgments
on the quality of sound make their appearances in nominally
scientific reports. This passage stems from a scientifically
reputable source (Wilhelm Nagel), but from a lay source with
regard to the art of singing. The passage implies that the
sensations of the spread pharynx in singing have been given
scientific sanction; possible adverse physiological ramifications
of this "voller Ton" appear not to have been given any real
consideration by Nagel.

Some advocates of the depressed larynx indicate the
specific vertebral alignment the larynx should assume (generally, fifth, sixth, or seventh, depending somewhat upon
accuracy of anatomical detail). Others recommend the larynx
should visibly drop some specific distance (one-quarter inch,
one-half inch, even three-quarters of an inch if possible),
and the physical movement is to be practiced independently
of singing.

Following the initial lowering of the larynx upon inspiration, the singer strives to anchor the larynx low in the
throat. Whatever the specific or suggestive advice may be,
singers of the depressed laryngeal school all have the tucked-
in-chin appearance which is an accompanying feature of this
production. Chin and mandible exert pressure upon the
larynx, inhibiting its ascent. The larynx itself is drawn
down as a result of contracting the infrahyoid muscles and
"relaxing" the suprahyoids.

Gertrud Nicolaus, in her essay, Die Gesetzmässigkeit
der richtigen Vokalbildung jeder Tonhöhe als Vorbedingung
für Schönheit und Dauer der Stimme (Berlin: Selbstverlag
Gertrud Nicholaus, 1973), presents an interesting survey
of pedagogical viewpoints on the topic of the low-positioned
larynx, to which the reader is referred.

Raoul Husson devotes some attention to idiosyncratic approaches to the lowered-larynx phenomenon,[4] mentioning Garcia, Frau Fernau-Horn's Weitung und Federung Principien, and Guilliaume Ibos' principle (more fully explained in Georges Loiseau's Notes sur le chant[5]). Husson includes a short critique of George Armin's Stauprinzip, which he classifies as a low-laryngeal technique.

Low-laryngeal positioning is the logical consequence of techniques which induce sensations of pharyngeal enlargement. As Nagel pointed out, the low position of the larynx follows from the yawn posture. It remains the favored laryngeal position in the German School because it contributes to the production of sound demanded by the aesthetic ideal of that particular national school. Further, it induces the kind of placement sensations associated with that ideal.

As a means of accomplishing the concept of enlarged pharynx and breath mixture (Duftigkeit) in one concerted action, the yawn is combined with a sighing sound. A frequently encountered vocalise in the German School begins with a high pitch in either Kopfstimme or falsetto, concluding via a portamento which combines the "sigh" and the "yawn" on a low note. Such an exercise is held to be beneficial in that it both "relaxes" the vocal instrument and puts it in a favorable posture for commencing phonation; tension is supposedly released. In defense of this technique, it might be postulated that were the larynx unnaturally elevated and the constrictor muscles contracted, such a vocalise might indeed relax the throat. More probably, such an excercise stretches the pharyngeal wall; the only benefit for the "relaxed" throat could be the return to the unstretched pharyngeal posture which normally obtains in the throat. In short, the efficacy of this exercise as an important technical device is doubtful.

Although the low-positioned larynx is less frequently found today than in recent decades, it continues to command the loyalties of a number of adherents. Its heyday was convergent with the upsurge of high hopes that mechanistic techniques ("voice science") would transform vocal pedagogy. These views still predominate in the German School. The low-laryngeal position appeals to the assumed need to do something in the throat, to give vocal technique a visible and controllable handle; it offers a localized control which produces results that can be quickly seen, taught and heard. Unless a singer is versed in acoustical principles and has some prior knowledge of laryngeal function, the system appears logical and "scientific."

Some attention has already been devoted to acoustical aspects and to resonance factors in singing which indicate some of the physical problems connected with pharyngeal enlargement. At this point, a brief analysis of some of the physical events which involve the total musculature of the neck in laryngeal action might be appropriate.

The extrinsic muscles of the larynx have points of attachment which lie outside the larynx, by means of which they exercise various pulls upon the larynx from the mandible, skull and sternum. Because of the heightened energization which occurs in singing, these muscles are of much greater importance in singing than they are in speech.

Between the mandible, and the clavicle and sternum, lie muscles which serve a number of functions, but which to some extent provide "support" for the vocal mechanism. (See Plates 13, 17, and 18.) Of importance during singing is the considerable supportive value given to the laryngeal mechanism by the sternocleidomastoids. They have their origins at the sternoclavicular joint, passing over the sternohyoid, sternothyroid and omohyoid muscles. They also play a role in elevating the thorax in certain circumstances. The digastric muscle lowers the jaw and can raise the hyoid bone. Inserted into the hyoid bone, the stylohyoid can raise the hyoid bone and can draw it backwards.

A ligamentous band, the stylohyoid ligament, is attached to the styloid process of the temporal bone and to the hyoid bone itself by the lesser cornu. From it originate the highest fibres of the constrictor pharyngis medius (middle constrictor of the pharynx) which is closely related to the sides of the oropharyngeal wall. This fibrous cord, it can be seen, relates both to the hyoid bone and to the pharyngeal wall and illustrates well the kind of interdependency which pertains among the parts of the vocal mechanism.

When the hyoid bone is fixed by its depressors, the suprahyoid muscles are capable of depressing the mandible. The platysma, in its thick anterior portion, may assist in depressing the mandible; the very weight of the mandible may contribute to a lowering action. The hyoglossus arises from the body of the hyoid bone (and from the greater horn) and is attached to the side of the tongue. It is in relation with the digastric (the anterior body of which serves as a mandibular depressor), the stylohyoid, styloglossus, and mylohyoid. Chondroglossus emerges from the hyoid bone and from the side and base of the lesser horn, blending with muscle fibres

of the tongue. In addition, it should be recalled that trapezius, covering as it does the back of the neck and the shoulder (see Plates 9 and 10), is a postural muscle which helps
to position the head backward and laterally.

To some extent then, all of the muscles of the neck
provide a support for the larynx. A vocal technique which
attempts to readjust this natural support and to locally control the relationships of the muscles of the neck to the torso
and to the larynx itself, risks presumptuousness.

In holding the larynx in either a raised or a depressed
position, the muscles of the face, neck and pharynx, including
those which involve the larynx both directly and indirectly,
must assume a sustained relationship of postures which, anatomically, is normally intended for briefer periods of time.
Distention of the pharynx is a specialized action which is
naturally encountered for periods of relatively brief duration,
which can be beneficial, as in the yawn. When this condition
is prolonged, as in singing with a low-positioned larynx, the
cooperating parts of the vocal mechanism are called upon to
sustain that position. It is sometimes argued that inasmuch
as such action has been mechanically accommodated in the
act of yawning, it can be extended at length for the purpose
of singing. This is somewhat like suggesting that the muscular stretch in the arms and torso which often accompanies
yawning should be developed into a normal posture for action.

Leaving aside for a moment any unfavorable physiological considerations, one discovers that it is not possible to
place the throat in the yawn position, or a near variant of it,
without having some of the same distorted quality in the singing voice which the yawn produces in the speaking voice.
The size of the voice has not been increased, only the quality
has been changed.

Believing that muscular relationships are in constant
change and motion, and that no particular relationship is
more natural than another, admirers of the depressed larynx
argue that function is not violated, but that what has been
customary is now simply readjusted. The answer to such a
pedagogical viewpoint is that freedom of movement cannot
take place within the mechanism if a set position is forced
upon the musculature. To locally rearrange and control a
mechanism as complicated as the hypopharyngeal-respiratory
one for considerable periods of time is probably not an
achievable goal. It is fairly certain that many singers who

believe themselves to be exercising such local control are
in fact managing to do so less completely than they wish.

A pedagogy which attempts direct controls over the
pharynx must resort to a number of recognizable sensations
to which the attention of the singer is urged.   Whereas most
other pedagogies direct the singer's attention away from the
throat, low-laryngeal teachers direct attention to it.

It is highly questionable that such technique produces
a bigger sound which will better compete with the modern
orchestra, supposedly one of its advantages.   Concentration
on the increased role of the pharyngeal resonator through lowering the larynx diminishes the participation of those resonators above the larynx which bring brilliance to the tone.   An
illusion of spaciousness in the tone is achieved at the expense
of upper partials which are needed to provide vocal projection
and focus.   Thus the carrying power of the voice often appears blunted in the low-laryngeal school, with dullness and
weightiness of tone prevailing rather than fullness.

Indisputably, the low-positioned (depressed) larynx is
typically a major pedagogical rubric in the German School.

In the Italian School, the depressed larynx is almost
universally avoided.   (German teachers who advocate laryngeal depression frequently believe that Caruso used the technique.)   If it be true that Garcia at one point in his life
began recommending the lowered larynx as a means of achieving the voce oscura, his lesson falls upon stony ground in
Italian teaching circles of this century.   In fact, it would
appear to be nearly a physical impossibility to maintain low-
laryngeal posture and pharyngeal enlargement together with
the thoracic posture of the classic Italian-trained singer.
The vocal mechanism would be squeezed between the two
pressures.

Neither does the English-trained singer make much
use of laryngeal depression, unless adopting an obviously
imported pedagogy.   When it makes its appearance in the
English School, laryngeal depression is generally restricted
to oratorio basses, and to the few remaining members of
that disappearing breed of English oratorio contraltos who
formerly flourished ubiquitously on the island.

Laryngeal depression is not a characteristic device
among French-trained singers, even though Ibos recommended
it to his countrymen.

Laryngeal depression, pharyngeal enlargement and lower abdominal breath techniques have a natural affinity for each other. They seem to internalize rather than to externalize the sound. Although practitioners of these techniques are scattered widely throughout the Western world, these methods most nearly match the tonal aesthetics of the German School.

The Stabilized Larynx

Many teachers of singing recommend a laryngeal position which remains stable, neither rising nor sinking excessively low with the intake of breath. They believe the larynx remains poised throughout the singing act, with no more motion than occurs in the small laryngeal movements which accompany the various sounds of speech.

Breath can be taken so as to entail varying degrees of laryngeal descent. Most persons experience some slight laryngeal descent in increased breath activity; the larynx may indeed lower slightly with inspiration, but it never reaches the low position urged in depressed laryngeal technique. Beyond a slight downward movement in inhalation, the larynx lies relatively quiescent throughout the breath cycle. In singing, breathing should remain inaudible, there being no grabbing or forcing of the breath. In the normal breath cycle, the larynx is not retained in one depressed location by the application of muscular pressure. Although stabilized, some flexibility of movement must be allowed in the formation of vowel sounds. "Anchoring" the larynx to one immutable low position interferes with its normal function. Nor must the larynx be allowed to rise and fall with pitch changes or with register transitions.

Medical sources which are unfamiliar with the techniques of the professional singing voice sometimes add confusion to this latter point. For example, Dr. John Simpson et al. in A Synopsis on Otorhinolaryngology (1957), has this to say: "The larynx moves upward on deglutition and on singing high notes."[6] One wishes that scientists who frequently make comments on events in singing knew a greater number of professionally trained singers.

The quiet, poised larynx is almost universally advocated in the Italian School, with the occasional exception of laryngeal elevation in the vocal categories previously mentioned.

Chapter IX

VIBRATO AND NATIONAL TENDENCIES

Stylistic Uses

The phenomenon termed vibrato is a basic ingredient
of most Western cultivated vocal sound (occurring in some
non-Western cultures as well). Its absence is usually by de-
sign, out of consideration for interpretative or musical style.
It is sometimes claimed that early Baroque vocal music
(seventeenth-century) was devoid of vibrato, although an examination of the vocal requirements found in the literature
of the period may prove otherwise. Inconsistently, some
musicological stylists find it appropriate to use the nearly
straight, vibrato-less tone to execute eighteenth-century vocal
works, including Bach and his contemporaries, while providing accompaniment to such music with vibrant strings. This
practice seems to indicate an unawareness that string vibrato
is quite clearly in imitation of the human voice. Other vi-
bratoed instruments such as the flute also fall within the
same temporally acceptable vibrato rate as does the human
voice.

The straight, vibrato-less tone also makes its appearance as an occasional expressive device among many
singers of Lieder, in some recitative styles, and in a number
of contemporary vocal idioms. It is, in addition, basic to
the folk-singer and to the amateur singer in general. Aside
from stylistic considerations, there are schools of choral
singing which concentrate on eliminating vibrato from voices
in order to "blend" them.

Physical Factors

A number of thoughtful studies on the vibrato have
been made, notably those of Carl E. Seashore and associates,

from which it can be determined that "a good vibrato is a pulsation of pitch, usually accompanied with synchronous pulsations of loudness and timbre of such extent and rate as to give a pleasing flexibility, tenderness and richness to the tone."[1] Further, it can be shown that a frequency rate of six to seven times per second is accepted by most ears as an enhancement of vocal quality without disturbing the perception of pitch. A vocal vibrato as slow as five times per second is found to be desirable in some pedagogies, while being quite unsatisfactory in others. We shall see that these differences in acceptability relate to national tonal aesthetics.

The terms tremolo and oscillation are both used at times to describe an unsatisfactory vibrato rate without discriminating as to their exact meanings. Among most singers, tremolo is used to refer to a vibrato rate which displeases because of its excessive rapidity; oscillation defines a vibrato rate which is slower than the acceptable level, producing a tone of wobbly character.

The physical sources of vibrato in the human voice have not been definitively determined. One of the most complete surveys of vibrato theories is contained in Michael Smith's article, "The Effect of Straight-tone Feedback on the Vibrato" (1972):

> Although experiments have shown definite relation-
> ships between the activities of certain muscles and
> vocal vibrato, no cause and effect has yet been
> established.... Metfessel (1932) contended that the
> seat of the vibrato lay in the muscle synergism
> within the supralaryngeal area, which accounted for
> frequency fluctuations in the vocal folds. Schoen
> (1922) believed that tremors in the laryngeal sus-
> pensory system caused pitch fluctuations, and that
> intensity variations had their origin in the base of
> the tongue. Stetson (1931) correlated oscillations
> in the rib cage musculature with vibrato rate, and
> Westerman (1941) assumed that the basic rate of
> repetition of nerve impulses affected the rate of
> pitch and intensity variations. Mason and Zemlin
> (1966) detected an out-of-phase relationship between
> the cricothyroid and the mylohyoid muscles in sing-
> ing, and suggested that this could be intimately in-
> volved in the pitch and intensity regulatory process.
> Most recently Vennard, Hirano, and Ohala (1970)

detected by means of EMG (Electromyography) some correlations between the phases of pitch vibrato and the energy peaks in the intrinsic and extrinsic muscles of the larynx. Deutsch and Clarkson (1959) proposed a 'control loop' theory.... The 'control loop' theory somewhat removes the vibrato from the realm of pure physiology in that the factors which determine frequency modulation and extent here originate as products of acoustic-kinetic forces, that is, due to the acoustical situation, a body or mass (vocal cords) is continually energized as a result of its own motion (pitch fluctuations as a corrective mechanism). A singer produces this kind of energy during phonation while he is hearing his own voice (auditory feedback). If this auditory event is a principal determinant of vibrato, then the physical actions of the muscles or muscle groups, which actually cause pitch fluctuations, are of secondary importance. The 'control loop' theory may provide substantial clues to both a solution to the problem of the origin of vibrato and also the pedagogical approaches to vibrato training in the voice studio. [2]

Perhaps the only empirically verifiable contention is that the kinds of relationships which exist between the respiratory muscles and those directly involved in phonation produce the phenomenon known as vibrato. Differing vibrato rates which result from the several approaches to breath management (possibly explained by the 'control loop' theory) give support to this assumption. What we perceive as vocal quality in a singer is inextricably bound up with the vibrato speed of his or her voice.

It is worth noting that those voices which possess an excess of upper partials, resulting in shrill quality, most suffer from excessively quick vibrato rates; conversely those voices which are weighty and dull in timbre tend toward vocal oscillation. It might seem tempting to conclude that higher voices, therefore, which tend toward greater brilliance, show faster vibrato rates than do lower voices. This conclusion is not supportable; one finds many sonorous bass and mezzo-soprano voices characterized by a quick vibrato rate, while many soprani and tenori suffer from oscillation. Not the vocal type, but the vocal production is chiefly the cause of vibrato rate.

Not infrequently a slower vibrato rate, with wider

pitch variant, is also the mark of declining powers in a singer. In such cases, it would appear that the slower rate is
the direct result of general muscle tonus and to conditions of
aging within the larynx, such as pronounced ossification.
These considerations do not figure in the present study.

Differences in the speed of the vibrato can be clearly
heard as a result of pedagogical concepts. The typical vibrato rate of a singer trained in one of the four major
schools provides an important clue for identifying his or her
allegiance.

The Italian School

There is a direct relationship between the concept
of chiaroscuro (a proper balance of fundamental and upper
partials in the tone) and vibrato speed. When the deeper
oscuro elements of the sound are emphasized, the vibrato
rate becomes slower and wider; when the chiaro aspects
predominate, the frequency of the vibrato is faster, as can
be verified by some extremely brilliant Italian coloraturas.
The well-trained Italian singer keeps both oscuro and chiaro
factors in balance. The tone has both "bottom" and "top."
When this is the case, the vibrato rate falls within the six-
to seven-per-second cycle. In the appoggio, the Italian
School combines resonator adjustment (which determines the
relationship of chiaro and oscuro acoustical elements) and
efficient breath management. The muscular events which
prevail in sterno-costal-diaphragmatic-epigastric breathing,
produce a result in pitch, intensity and timbre which includes
the characteristic vibrato rate of the Italian School. No
doubt the kind of auditory feedback the ear of the Italian
singer is attuned to is determined by the vocal aesthetics
of the school.

The German School

A slower vibrato rate than that found in the Italian
School forms part of the weightier, round quality of sound
which pleases the typical Germanic ear. It is the result of
that total voice production which includes emphasis on pharyngeal enlargement, low abdominal support, and posterial placement sensations. The tendency toward a vibrato rate of approximately five per second is too frequently heard among
singers trained in the German School to be passed over as
the result of individual vocal idiosyncracies.

Sometimes it is postulated that vibrato rate may be dependent upon the kind of vocal line required by the literature performed. For example, one is much more aware of the tendency toward slower vibrato rates among some singers in a performance, say, of Der fliegende Holländer than in a performance of Aïda. Both operas involve voices of dramatic scope and power, and both present sustained phrases and orchestral competition for the voice; the kinds of vocal demands between the works cannot entirely explain matters. Rather, the technical approaches employed by the kinds of singers who are likely to appear in the German dramatic literature as opposed to the Italian dramatic literature are at variance with each other. This comparison becomes even more marked in a day and age when artists trained in one school cross over into the repertory of the other and we find a singer to be much less satisfying in Verdi than in Strauss, although his or her vocal category should embrace both.

In the Kopfstimme itself, when the admixture of breath in the tone is increased, the tone straightens out; when some vibrancy is added, the percentage of breath not turned into tone which passes over the vocal bands still remains high. When the fuller aspects of the voice are called upon, requiring a cleaner cordal approximation, the straight-tone disappears in favor of a more consistent vibrato, however at a rate still often not much above five per second.

The extrinsic muscles of the larynx are in a unique relationship when one drops the sternum, distends the abdomen, and enlarges the pharynx; such techniques are associated with the typical vocal production of the German School. This relationship appears to affect the nerve impulses as well as the synergetic activity of the muscles which function within the hypopharyngeal system; one result is manifested in the slower frequency of the vibrato rate.

The French School

The typical French vocal sound is characterized by a rapid vibrato rate, difficult to separate from the thin, nasal quality peculiar to much of the least desirable French singing. It can be deduced that this sound results from the narrowed pharynx, elevated tongue, raised larynx, and the emphasis upon placing the tone in the masque; the excessive brilliance of the French vocal production, accentuating as it does the upper partials and the harder surfaces of the resonators, seems to increase the frequency of the vibrato rate.

The accustomed ear formed by cultural milieu demands the unmistakable quality of the French vocal sound; muscular balances (muscular synergy) adjust within the vocal tract to produce those results. What strikes some non-gallicized ears as a tremulous throatiness (what the Italians call voce di capra, or goat voice and what others have termed "the goat in the throat") apparently is an aesthetically pleasing sound to many French ears. That this quick, tremulous character of sound is present in much of French singing is attested to by the attention devoted to its elimination in the teaching of an atypical minority group of French teachers.

The English School

With regard to vibrato rate, as in a number of other matters, the English School approaches attitudes held by the Italian School. Special coloristic considerations which prevail within the English School tend to modify this position, especially with reference to the stylistic uses of the straight tone. Moreover, the predisposition to make considerable use of exaggerated costal action in breathing, of spreading in the upper back, as well as the high incidence of the hung jaw, produce certain variants of vibrato frequency. When excessively practiced, the distended lower jaw alters vibrato rates because of the acoustical distortion of the mouth; this habit is most remarkable in the typical English contralto and bass oratorio singers.

However, aside from the two vocal categories just mentioned, a slow vibrato rate is not one of the chief characteristics of the English School, especially among operatic voices. Whatever the inadequacies of breath management techniques which stress costal action at the expense of other coordinations, the intensity of the breath emission remains relatively high. In fact, one of the most obvious concomitants of high costal-high dorsal breathing is the rapidity of the vibrato rate, a continuously high pressure of the breath being maintained directly below the larynx.

When the English singer resorts to some of the exaggerated high-breath techniques which grow out of costal excesses (as he and she are prone to do, particularly in the upper range), the resultant sound approaches a rapid shake. When such excesses do not prevail, the vibrato pattern typically falls into that acceptable mean frequency of six to seven per second, as it is experienced among well-schooled Italian singers.

Chapter X

VOCAL REGISTRATION
AND NATIONAL ATTITUDES

The number of registers which are said to comprise
the singing voice have been variously listed as none, one,
two, three, four, five, six, or seven, with some other
teachers of singing insisting that each note in the vocal compass should be called a register. Such confusion in register
designation serves to indicate that the physical events of registration can be induced or modified to some extent, and that
a singer can learn to emphasize or de-emphasize certain
kinds of muscular coordination within the laryngeal mechanism.

Empirically, the singer notes sensations which are
perceived as thoracic, pharyngeal, buccal, nasal or facial.
He or she may experience these sensations more or less
markedly as they sharply occur or as they overlap at noticeable points of demarcation. In the past these sensations
gave rise to notions that registers result from resonator
action, working independently in various parts of the voice.
Most teachers of singing in all four national schools currently believe that register phenomena (if accepted at all) result
from laryngeal function in conjunction with corresponding
resonator adjustment.

Register Transition and Muscular Function

Much of the scientific investigation into the physical
function of the singing voice is devoted to determining the
kinds of laryngeal action involved in register transition. Perhaps the most complete bibliography available on literature
relating to vocal registration is included in a 1972 article by
John Large, "Towards an Integrated Physiologic-Acoustic
Theory of Vocal Registers."[1] Dr. Large lists 149 sources,
representing a historical sweep from 1840 through 1970.

99

His suggestion with regard to future investigation in the area
of registration, were it to be adopted, would be of great
assist in clearing away much of the current confusion:

> it would ... be helpful in bringing some order into
> this confused area of research if (1) speech scien-
> tists would report their findings relative to vocal
> fry, modal register, etc. under the category of
> speaking registers, (2) the results of studies of
> men's registers were reported separately from
> those of studies of women's registers, and (3)
> greater attention were given to controls in design-
> ing experiments in which register is the variable
> of primary interest. [2]

No one is yet able to claim absolute knowledge of
the complex registration operations of the vocal mechanism
such as occur during the singing of a two-octave scale, or
which take place in leaping the interval of a twelfth.   Dr.
Victor A. Fields, after reviewing much of the pedagogical
and scientific literature on the subject in "Review of the
Literature on Vocal Registers" (1970), concludes:

> We draw the conclusion from a survey of vocal
> literature that the theory of registration is in con-
> troversy, as is nearly every aspect of vocal tech-
> nique; that definitions are vague and contradictory;
> that authors disagree as to the nature and existence
> of this phenomenon.   The action of registration is
> nowhere clearly explained and the exact causes
> remain undecided. [3]

But in spite of this confusion, there exist vocal pedagogies
which center around specific theories of vocal registration.
Laryngeal muscular action is so complicated that it can
occur only at a level below consciousness, in response to
nerve impulses.   Yet in both speech and song certain conscious activity must be initiated if pitch and syllable are to
take recognizable form.   Conscious mechanical control is
obviously impossible; consciousness of certain kinds of coordination which produce mechanical control are possible.   Such
awareness of coordination in singing is induced by psychological attitudes and by the imagery which awakens them.   These
attitudes effect the kinds of muscular coordination which determine the actual techniques of singing.

The extent of compensatory muscular action which

can be induced by imagery during singing is considerable.
It is therefore important that mental attitudes and verbal
imagery do not call into play physiological patterns contrary
to efficient physical function. Concepts of tone placement,
breath support and registration events largely determine the
kind of muscular coordination which identifies a specific technique and a national tendency. Functional adjustments tend
to differ from school to school depending upon the language
of imagery within those schools. Some consideration must
be given to the probable physical events in registration.

The transition from one extreme of the vocal range
to another, or from one neighboring note to the next, entails
delicate instantaneous adjustments of the laryngeal mechanism
which have no counterpart in any other musical instrument.
In untrained voices, vocal quality will seldom be unified
throughout the entire vocal compass, tending to display characteristic timbres in certain segments of the voice. To some
extent, several distinct qualities of tone can be produced on
identical pitches, resulting from different kinds of muscular
action within the larynx. These several qualities often are
perceived by the singer as varying resonance sensations.
The adjustments in muscular balances within the larynx which
produce these sensations directly correspond to what singers
term factors of registration.

W. J. Henderson, in Early History of Singing (1921),
remarks that the handling of vocal registers has long interested writers on the art of singing:

> The study of the voice itself undoubtedly began early,
> for about 1300 the division of the scale into regis-
> ters was known. At what time attention was first
> directed to this much discussed matter cannot be
> determined. But from various hints we may rea-
> sonably conclude that the teachers, while recogniz-
> ing the registers, made no attempts at equalizing
> the scale, except such as would occur naturally in
> the search after smoothness and beauty. Marchetto,
> a writer of about 1300, tells us that one of the or-
> naments of singing in his day was to pass from
> the chest to the falsetto--after the manner of a
> jodel. The student of the subject may find some-
> thing to ponder in the words of Jerome of Moravia
> (13th century): 'Different kinds of voices ought not
> to be mingled in the chant, whether it be chest
> with head or throat with head.... Generally low

voices and basses are of the chest, light and high
voices of the head, and those of the throat intermediate. They should not be mixed in chant, but
chest voice should remain such just as the voice
of the throat or the head.' ... Falsetto voices were
common at least as far back as this period and
were condemned by severe disciplinarians.[4]

Even though the stylistic uses of registers may have undergone great change since Jerome's commentary, the awareness of vocal sound experienced as register sensation would
appear to have a lengthy history.

Although the following account of movements of the
vocal folds during phonation does not specifically relate to
registration in singing, it may help provide some clues to
the sensation of registers to which singers have attested over
the centuries (see Plates 2 and 3):

Preparatory to phonation the intermembranous and
intercartilaginous parts of the glottis are reduced
to a linear chink by adduction of the vocal folds,
the degree of tension determining the pitch of the
sound. As the pitch rises, the tension of the folds
increases and they may lengthen by as much as
50 per cent in the highest notes. The photographs
suggest that the lengthening affects both extremities
of the folds, indicating that the Cricothyroids act
not only on the cricoid cartilage as described above
but also tilt the thyroid cartilage downwards and
forwards.[5]

The tilting process, downward and forward, of the
thyroid cartilage is of probable significance in the events of
registration. In order for the thyroid cartilage to move forward as well as downward, while maintaining the same degree of longitudinal tension, the cricoid would also have to
move. Alternately, if the cricoid cartilage stays in a more
stationary posture than does the thyroid cartilage, then the
forward action of the thyroid cartilage is caused by movement involving the cornua inferiori (lower horns) of the thyroid cartilage at the points of articulation with the cricoid
cartilage, thus providing a change in longitudinal tension of
the bands. In either case, there are implications that such
actions may produce the kinds of changes in sensation and
quality associated with vocal registers. Such physical processes could well help clarify the tendency toward register

"breaks" in untrained voices and the ability in the trained
singer to coordinate muscular action, often through resonatory sensation, so as to replace sudden and undesirable postural changes within the laryngeal mechanism by more graduated ones. Such probable action of the thyroid and cricoid
muscles in registration events has been noted by Vennard. [6]

A more frequently encountered explanation of registration phenomena deals with the manner in which the vocal
folds vibrate either in almost all of their mass or in a more
limited part of it, especially with regard to chest voice (voce
di petto) and head voice (voce di testa). Much of registration
literature deals with this concern for cordal involvement.
Many standard works on anatomy offer excellent descriptions
of these actions and should be consulted by anyone in need of
greater specific information than this and the following discussion can offer.

Voce di Petto

In voce di petto (chest voice), the longitudinal tension
of the vocal bands is reduced because the cricothyroid muscles are relatively inactive, and the vocal folds are thickened
as the thyroarytenoid muscles contract. The glottis opens
rather wide, and the folds are at their thickest, closing firmly and opening decisively, beginning at the bottom. As pitch
ascends, the cricothyroids begin to change the shape of the
glottis, and with the increasing tension, the vocal folds become thinner, with vibration taking place in the anterior part
of the folds. Photography reveals that this action increases
as the cords reach their maximum length; the bottom of the
glottis no longer engages in closing and opening actions, the
entire glottis being more or less equally involved.

As the pitch ascends, the thyroarytenoids which play
an important role in the low voice only gradually alter their
activity. When they continue a high rate of opposition to the
cricothyroids, as pitch ascends, the heavier quality of sound
found in the low voice continues to be perceived by the ear,
although the pitch is rising. The vibrations from this
"heavy" production are transmitted to the trachea and the
bronchi in such a fashion that they are perceived by the
singer as chest voice. This is the heavy mechanism of the
two-register pedagogue. For a more detailed discussion of
muscular action in vocal registration, perhaps the best source
to consult is William Vennard. [7]

In speech, if a male places his hand on the center of his chest, he experiences a kind of vibratory rumble (as does the female if she speaks in chest). This sensation remains throughout the normal speaking range, although its intensity lessens as the voice is inflected to pitches near the upper range limit of the speaking voice. At a certain point, the speaking voice cannot be inflected any higher without an accompanying radical change of quality. By calling or yelling, additional pitches can be produced in an area encompassing roughly a fourth or fifth.

In young male singers untrained to take into account breath application adjustments for rising pitch, this first point in the scale is often indicated by a slight raising of the larynx and by a distinct lightening of the tonal quality. This event corresponds to what some teachers designate as the first register break (the primo passaggio of the Italian School).

However, it is physically possible, though technically undesirable, to carry this heavier sound still higher (perhaps by as much as a fourth, or by considerable effort even more), beyond the point at which initially the additional muscular antagonism and breath energy were applied, to a second point, at which either a sudden adjustment must be made or the sound will break off. This is the point at which even the calling voice terminates. Were a male to try to speak or call beyond this second point, he would have to scream in a fashion both painful and injurious. This event corresponds to the second register break of some pedagogies (the secondo passaggio of the Italian School).

In a young baritone, the end of the comfortable speaking voice may end around b, with the forced call extending through e^1 or f^1. In the terminology of the Italian School, b would mark the occurrence of the primo passaggio, e^1 the second passaggio, with the area in between being designated zona di passaggio, or zona intermedia. (Because the second terminal point indicates the most radical change in the mechanics of registration, the term passaggio, when not indicated as either first or second, generally refers to the second terminal point.)

If the heavier muscular action is continued up through the second terminal point, it is impossible to relax the muscular tension and to readjust without the voice "breaking," without going into falsetto, or without the laryngeal muscles

attempting in some way to compensate for the continued action
of the thyroarytenoid muscles. The antagonistic action of the
laryngeal muscles has reached a point where immense strain
is experienced; they can no longer function without a sudden
change of relationships. The pitches above the second terminal registration point (the secondo passaggio of the Italian
School) simply cannot be made, even by increasing muscular
antagonism and increasing breath pressure (forcing) within
this adjustment, because the muscles have reached a state
of rigidity and must give way.

Pitches beyond this point can be made by three kinds
of vocal production in the male voice. Two of these three
are discredited in some pedagogies, considered to be qualities unsuited for general use in serious vocalism except as
demanded by unusual coloristic demands; they are falsetto
and voce finta. (The third sound, the legitimate voce di
testa, will be considered later.)

In the female voice, two kinds of sound are possible
for about a fifth beyond the secondo passaggio (which in the
soprano typically occurs at $f\#^1$, fifth line, treble clef
to g^2), one being the legitimate upper register, the other
being the voce finta. Some teachers, especially those associated with the German School, postulate a female falsetto
that is identical with the voce finta; those who claim that
anything other than chest voice in the female denotes falsetto
give the latter term a specificity which removes it from the
common parlance of vocal terminology.

Falsetto

Some male singers can begin to produce falsetto with
a certain amount of ease beginning at the first register point;
it is even possible for male falsettists to develop the timbre
downward, nearly to the lower end of the normal chest
range. Further, most untrained singers can no longer resist resorting to falsetto when they reach the second register
point.

In a discussion of registers, it is tempting to join
the twentieth-century battle over the meaning of terminology
within the Italian schools of the seventeenth, eighteenth, and
nineteenth centuries. The question is by no means a purely
academic one, inasmuch as a number of current pedagogues,
to be found in Germany, France and England (and of course,

in America) stress the use of falsetto as a means of accomplishing the upper male voice, believing themselves to be practicing an old Italian method, supported by historical evidence. (For a reader who wishes to pursue early sources on voice registers, including falsetto, the most complete compilation of material probably is to be found in Philip Duey's 1951 Bel Canto in Its Golden Age. [8])

In the eighteenth century, Tosi spoke of chest voice (voce di petto), head voice (voce di testa) and falsetto, [9] while Mancini seemed to designate only two registers, chest and head, the latter also called falsetto. [10] The question is complicated by our knowledge that eighteenth-century pedagogical interest was still largely directed toward the castrati.

Pertinent questions are (1) did falsetto mean, in former centuries, the imitative female sound it indicates in Italy today; (2) was this imitative female sound an accepted stylistic practice prior to the late nineteenth century; (3) did falsetto designate what is currently called "middle voice" (voce intermedia); and (4) is voce di testa, as commonly practiced in the current Italian School, equivalent with what falsetto may have meant in previous centuries? The answers supplied to these questions determine the pedagogical assumptions upon which teachers build registration techniques.

The waters are muddied still further by Garcia's interesting use of the term registro di falsetto-testa, with charts designating the falsetto register as lying between petto and testa registers. Indeed, Garcia breaks down his falsetto-testa register to specifically indicate that falsetto corresponds to the medium male vocal register. [11] This is the area which the Italian School today treats as the zona intermedia, where register blending is important but where none of the sounds of falsetto (as understood in the current Italian School) would ever make an appearance. Further complicating matters, Garcia offers a chart showing that falsetto can commence at d (middle line, bass clef) in the male voice, and that the entire extent of falsetto in the female reaches about a fifth, from the pitch a (second ledger line below the treble clef) to $c\#^2$ (third space, treble clef), an area extending from the chest voice through the conclusion of lower-middle voice, for most sopranos. Clearly, Garcia cannot be brought forward in support of current falsetto practices.

Francesco Lamperti does not help us much more

with his designation of two registers in the male voice consisting of chest voice and mixed voice. 12 He offers a chart
with six overlapping notes; the reader could assume these
notes are to be sung either in chest, in mixed voice, or in
some further "mixture" of those two. It is surely more than
a coincidence that F. Lamperti's mixed register and Garcia's
falsetto register occur within the areas generally designated
today as the zona intermedia or zona di passaggio. It is
clear that these two terms used by Garcia and Lamperti bear
no correspondence to the practices of some contemporary
teachers (none of them associated with the current Italian
School) who devote much time to the development of falsetto.
In the face of an on-going singing tradition, can one really
believe that a little over one hundred years ago falsetto as
it is understood in the Italian School today was cultivated in
the middle of the male singing voice? Regardless of what
falsetto may have meant in the seventeenth and eighteenth
centuries, it appears highly improbable that in the nineteenth-
century Italian School (from which stem traditions which are
vital to operatic performance today) the term falsetto universally meant the imitative female sound practiced in the
last decade or two (often under the claim that bel canto has
been rediscovered).

     Searching for a physiological justification for falsetto
usage, some teachers in the non-Italian schools claim a relationship between the thinning of the vocal bands in the effeminate falsetto sound and a similar action in the light
mechanism of the voce di testa, and conclude that the laryngeal muscular events which serve falsetto and head are
similar. Indeed, there can be little doubt that the internal
thyroarytenoids are differently activated in head and falsetto
than they are in chest. However, researchers have often
grouped several kinds of register action under each of these
headings; as a result, serious conflict in terminology exists.
Therefore, when twentieth-century scientific evidence is called
upon to prove that nineteenth-century Italian falsetto was the
"false voice" of some twentieth-century vocal pedagogues,
we can only remonstrate that researchers do not understand
the term with any degree of commonality.

     Within the English, French and German Schools there
are groups of teachers who believe that the legitimate male
head voice can be developed through exercising the effeminate
falsetto sound, reinforcing the sound with an increase of
breath pressure, so that considerable intensity (volume) can
be produced. Because of incomplete cordal occlusion, a

great deal of breath energy is needed to accomplish this
timbre. The reinforced falsetto feels supported; the increased energy which it requires serves as proof to some
teachers in these schools that the tone has legitimacy.
Much attention is then directed toward bridging over this
sound into the middle voice in such a manner as to avoid
any noticeable break into the legitimate voice.

Other teachers within these schools approach falsetto
purely as a device for strengthening some of the musculature
believed to be involved in legitimate voce di testa. In this
latter viewpoint, the actual reinforced falsetto sound is not
incorporated into the sung scale but reserved only for developmental purposes. No attempt is made to bridge the
break between falsetto and legitimate voice, nor is the falsetto sound used during performance.

In the French School, the falsetto sometimes comprises the entire upper range of the tenor voice, and a considerable portion of the upper range of the light baritone, as
well.

Falsetto plays no part in either the pedagogy or the
performance of the Italian School. It is sometimes resorted
to for "marking" in rehearsal if a singer is unwell and does
not want to use the full energy of the instrument, but even
then its use is looked upon with disapproval. Falsetto as
a coloristic effect in the top voice is considered an indication of technical deficiency among teachers of the Italian
School. The Italian aesthetic would permit an inappropriate
forte on a high note in preference to falsetto, in the event
the singer does not yet possess the technical facility to com-
ply with an ideal legitimate piano.

One would be hard put to find an Italian teacher of
singing who could be convinced that "the old Italian bel canto
method" can be rediscovered through the development or use
of the effeminate falsetto in the male voice, a viewpoint
heavily endorsed by some groups of teachers in the English,
German and French Schools. Were such a technique to become accepted practice (and such acceptability has been
marked in the non-Italianate schools in the current decade),
it could revolutionize the sound of the cultivated singing
voice, much to the detriment of the vocal art.

Failing to understand the mechanical practices of traditional vocal registration (and therefore unable to direct

the student toward access to the legitimate upper voice), a number of pedagogues in the non-Italian schools seem increasingly to be persuaded that the "easy, effortless" falsetto upper voice is preferable to the time-consuming rigors of ironing out the techniques of passing into the fully resonated upper voice. In some instances, this trend is supported by already existing tonal aesthetics which are observable in certain segments of the national schools which have been noted elsewhere in this work.

To claim that formerly voce di testa was identical to falsetto (as do a number of proponents of falsetto usage) is to close the mind and the ear to a number of compelling considerations as well as to apparent historical discrepancies. In addition to probably misreading early pedagogical materials with regard to falsetto, it should be noted that advocates of falsetto ignore the logical assumption that the presence of the powerful though sweet voices of the castrati would have made falsettists unlikely in the truly professional vocal circles of the seventeenth and eighteenth centuries. Indeed, the male falsettist seems to have flourished only in certain liturgical literatures--especially in more limited circumstances where the castrati were unavailable, and where vocalism was still an unsophisticated art.

What purpose would the male solo falsettist have served at the courts of worldly cardinals and princes where the castrati were held in near veneration for their vocal prowess? To assume that the reinforced falsetto could equal the quality of the castrato is to assert that castration was unnecessarily undertaken. (The moral problems of castration were not ignored during the period in which the castrati flourished. Anthony Milner offers a brief, informative study of the church's attitude toward castration, with an excellent bibliography on the subject of the castrati, in "The Sacred Capons," The Musical Times, v. 114, no. 1561 [March 1973], 250-2.) Nor can the advocates of falsetto singing support a claim for lineage with the bel canto tradition by pointing out that castrati were less frequently admired in some northern areas, therefore necessitating the existence of male falsettists. Clearly, such falsetto singers lay outside the Italian vocal tradition.

The operatic composers of the late seventeenth, eighteenth, and nineteenth centuries make demands in intensity and breath management which the most skilful users of falsetto would be hard-pressed to meet, because of the physiological nature of falsetto production. An even scale obviously was required by the bel canto literature; the demands of cantilena and fioritura are only met when the complete tonal balance of the voice is present. Inasmuch as this would be possible with both the castrato voice and the legitimately registered male voice, why is it to be assumed that non-altered males worked on a different technique producing a less complete sound in the upper voice, except as an occasional vocal coloration?

Further, it would seem strange that such a tradition suddenly would have disappeared in the early years of the nineteenth century, had it really existed. In fact, at a period of time when the sweet, ringing castrato voice (sometimes described as the female sound and range with the added power of the male) was still in evidence, though with less frequency, the male falsettist would have seemed a totally inadequate substitute. Female voices increasingly replaced the castrato, and the vocal categories of the modern era became more clearly delineated. It is equally difficult to believe that the normal male vocal instrument has undergone some fundamental physiological mutation in the last 150 years, or that a unified scale in the male voice which avoids obvious shifts in registration timbres became an ideal only within the past century.

One strongly suspects that, beginning with the establishment of the vocal art associated with the Neapolitan Opera School, any extensive use of falsetto as a habitual mode of negotiating the upper voice was always a dodge for the individual singer with an incomplete technique. The vast literature of the Neapolitan Opera School tends to support this viewpoint. (Much of the literature written for high voices was intended for the castrati.) The falsetto was probably cultivated among some liturgical choristers and amateur solo singers of hearth and court.

Today, certainly, quite apart from historical speculation, no singer of international repute who can sing his top voice legitimately (be he bass, baritone or tenor) will resort to falsetto in public unless he is ill (with the exception of certain stylists who will be noted when individual categories of voice are examined); falsetto is reserved for the amateur, the so-called counter-tenor, the ensemble singer (particularly of pre-Renaissance music), and that segment of modern schools of singing wherein it is believed that falsetto techniques are the rediscovery of the old Italian voce di testa as it was executed among practitioners of bel canto.

Proof that the contemporary Italian School has forgotten, according to its detractors, the falsetto usages which are said to produce head voice, is the use of the <u>do di petto</u> (chest c, the tenor full high c), which is a near prerequisite for any career today in the Italian operatic repertory. This term, in much use among Italian-trained singers, is thought by some to provide solid evidence that the Italian singer approaches the top voice through the chest voice mechanism. From the foregoing discussion of laryngeal function in register transition, it can be seen that it would be physically impossible to produce the tenor high c in chest registration (most tenors can't even <u>yell</u> a sound above the second passaggio, g^1, let alone negotiate a pitch at the range extremity, a fourth above). The term <u>do di petto</u> refers to a legitimate sound with complete resonantal balance which is not disconnected from the rest of the voice and which is in direct opposition to the falsetto. <u>Do di petto</u> is ringing, vibrant with upper partials, and is the characteristic sound of the operatic tenor voice. (Can one imagine "Che gelida manina" being sung in an Italian opera house by means of a reinforced falsetto c?)

Emil Behnke, in The Mechanism of the Human Voice (1881), while lamenting that tenors do not use falsetto, makes the claim that in former years tenors had sung the upper voice solely in falsetto. In support of this contention he quotes an incident from "The Opera and the Art of Singing" by Gloggner-Castelli (here considerably truncated):

> In the field of singing a new man arose, who, in spite of great personal attributes, worked destructively for the future, and whose influence upon the later manner of singing is seldom truly recognized. I mean the singer Duprez. Hissed off at first in Paris, he turned to Italy, where he stayed several years, and then returned to the French capital. When he came to use his magnificent vocal resources, as he did in the Fourth Act of <u>Tell</u>, where he brought out the High C in the chest voice with all the might of his colossal organ, it was all over with the fame of all his predecessors. Nourrit, till then the favourite of the Parisians, a distinguished tenor singer, recognized the rival's power. His day was over, and in despair over his lost and irrecoverable glory, he flung himself from an upper window upon the pavement, and so made an end of his life. Duprez may justly be considered one of

the greatest dramatic singers of our time, and the main features of his method soon spread themselves all over Europe. After hearing of Duprez, and how the chest register could be cultivated even into the highest regions of the voice, the public were no longer contented with the use of falsetto.... How widespread is this mistaken notion, that the use of the falsetto is contrary to art, we hear frequently enough in the expressions of individuals when some unlucky tenor happens to get caught on one of these tabooed falsetto tones. Thus the school founded by Duprez, important in itself, has called into life a manner of singing, the ruinous consequences of which we can see daily. [13]

Emil Behnke was born in Stettin in 1836, began a promising career as an operatic singer, lost his singing voice, and turned to the study of vocal function, on which he lectured in England and Scotland. His volume cited above made him beginning in the 1880's an influential force in English pedagogy. A later collaboration with Lennox Browne resulted in the volume Voice, Song and Speech, which firmly established him as a major figure in British vocal pedagogy. Much of English conviction regarding the uses of falsetto may well be traced to this source.

Certainly Glogger-Castelli's historical interpretation of the triumph of do di petto over falsetto fits very nicely into Behnke's own theories regarding the decline of the art of singing. One must assume that Duprez's sound corresponded to the legitimate ringing high c of the Italian School. (He apparently went to Italy to learn precisely that.) The chronicler admits that Duprez's role in changing vocal style is "seldom recognized"; he relates the despair and the unhappy end of the falsetto-using Nourrit in the face of the public's response; he indicates that all over Europe the "High C in the chest voice" was the only acceptable sound, falsetto being tabooed so that any tenor caught using it was "unlucky." In short, his comments present a strong case for establishing the same disapproval of the falsetto sound in the mid-nineteenth century as one finds in the twentieth. (Nourrit left Paris in 1837 and went himself to Italy to study. He was to have debuted in Donizetti's Polyeucte, but the production fell into trouble with the censor. There were successes in Naples, but he sang mostly mediocre roles at La Scala. His suicide took place at Naples in 1839.)

Then as now, some skilful artists were able to please the public with the "agreeable effect" of the falsetto for top tones. The Duprez-Nourrit incident can hardly serve as firm historical evidence that one singer converted the world away from the general usage of falsetto overnight, in 1836. The incident might better illustrate the growing international standards of vocalism expected in opera houses where audiences were no longer content with male singers who could not properly registrate the upper voice because of technical limitations. Nor should it be overlooked that Duprez found his remarkable top voice after a long period of training in Italy.

A considerable body of operatic literature generally thought to exhibit qualities and techniques of the bel canto style has re-emerged as an important part of the current standard repertory. This in turn, has led to much speculation (as well as to some sound historical investigation) as to the probable nature of vocalism in the early decades of nineteenth century. Increasingly, it has become a favorite pastime of some bel canto buffs to collect examples of exceedingly high-lying cadenzas, especially for the tenor voice, and to cite the large number of current performing artists who would be unable to execute them; the thesis is that today's techniques of singing cannot accommodate the demands of the bel canto repertory. It then follows, they reason, that the use of falsetto must be postulated to explain the negotiation of such passages, and of the upper voice in general.

Such a simplistic explanation overlooks several probable factors. First, there are today indeed tenors who can produce pitches above high c, including occasionally even f above high c, in legitimate head voice, especially when those pitches occur in rapid, melismatic passages, but such singers seldom possess the size of instrument which pleases today's listener; in all probability, as a result of our Verdian and post-Verdian aural experiences in the opera house (often of large size and of small acoustical advantage) the contemporary listener would find these voices inappropriate to such an opera as say, Bellini's Adelson e Salvani (were it to be performed!). Second, the incidence of such astoundingly high-lying cadenzas in the bel canto literature as compared with less spectacular writing is smaller than some critics would lead us to believe. Third, these cadenzas in some instances may have been but a remnant of the sort of writing appropriate to the castrato voice of the preceding centuries; certainly, the incidence of such passages quickly diminishes

as the century progresses. And fourth, there is little historical evidence to support the viewpoint that every singer
who sang certain roles was expected to execute the exact
cadenzas indicated.

It is entirely possible that an occasional "effect"
with an interpolated high f in falsetto was by no means unusual, just as such an effect is not unusual today in performances of I Puritani. It does not therefore follow that
the tenor of the early nineteenth century was expected to
produce in falsetto all notes above g^1, a popular notion among
contemporary writers who wish to prove that such an approach
characterized bel canto vocalism.

Then as now, the tenor high a (and any pitch to be
negotiated above) probably was often delivered in a light head
voice. (Admittedly, for some special coloration it even at
times may have been executed in falsetto as well, exactly as
that term is understood among practitioners of the current
Italian School.) Such use of the light head voice was dictated
by the exacting dynamic requirement of much of the writing
for tenor voice in the early nineteenth century. Dramatic
intensity was not given high priority; sweetness and gracious-
ness were often the chief aims of the early nineteenth-century
composer when dealing with the tenor voice. These qualities
have always been part of the technique of the legitimate tenor
voice.

During this intriguing transitional period in the historical development of the art of vocalism, conventions with regard to the utilization of treble voices in roles designating
male characters were undergoing revision. Indeed, the tenor
voice as a vehicle of heroism in the lyric theater was only
beginning to emerge; increasingly, women and castrati cast
as male protagonists were no longer entirely acceptable to
the developing vocal and dramatic tastes of the era. (On
the other hand, it should be remembered that both Pasta and
Malibran, as well as other celebrated prima donnas of the
period, sang the role of the Rossini Otello even into the
fourth decade of the nineteenth century.)

Although one may wish to question the Gloggner-Castelli interpretation of the Duprez-Nourrit incident, it would
be musicological blindness to ignore its implications; it is
a parable of the new realization of the fuller potential of the
legitimate tenor voice, manifested through the stylistic enlargement of the potential of the voce di testa dynamic range.

This expanded dynamic capability was an unneeded dimension
in the treble castrato production, although the bomba is
historically documented as an exciting "effect." With the
great Rubini, a new aura, incorporating this added dimension,
was brought to the tenor vocal category. Giovanni Battista
Rubini, as immortal as any brief actor on the mortal stage
may become, stands midway between his predecessors (who
were indubitably dwarfed by the overpowering vocal stature
of the reigning eunuchs) and those future tenor vocal athletes
of the Italian School who would soon emerge in response to the
dramatic necessities of Verdi.

It is equally clear, in any consideration of the constantly evolving role of the tenor voice as a romantic-heroic
vehicle in the lyric theater (based upon contemporary accounts
of public performances), that the non-altered high male voice
did not normally attempt to actively compete in full measure
in the pyrotechnical feats so much expected of the castrati;
as a result the tenor was less admired, in general, than was
the phenomenally-equipped castrato. In discussing this professional hierarchy, Henry Pleasants in his highly informative
and engaging work, The Great Singers, remarks that

> If tenors fared better than basses it was because
> they learned, under the tutelage of the castrati, to
> use a light head voice and falsetto in such a way
> that the best of them could approximate the embel-
> lishments, cadences, portamenti, roulades, trills
> and turns established by the castrati as basic de-
> vices of good singing. [14]

However, Pleasants somewhat balances out this favorable
picture of the condition of the early nineteenth-century legitimate tenor voice by reminding that such tenors were
probably lower pitched than are our current operatic tenors;
their natural range may very well have been much closer
to that of the average church choir tenor. [15]

That a marked change in attitude toward the existing
expectations for tenorial sound came about in the early decades of the nineteenth century (an era which offers some of
the most exciting developments in the entire history of the
vocal art) is clearly indicated by the vocal writing itself, as
exemplified in the works of Rossini and his contemporaries,
including Bellini and Donizetti. Without doubt, a more robust
quality than had heretofore been demanded, was brought
about by a greater degree of breath energization and the

balanced activity of the intrinsic musculature of the larynx. The new style, increasingly emotive and dramatic, requested a correspondingly new relationship between those parts of the laryngeal mechanism which engage in a delicate dance, a balancing of tension and relaxation which characterize the fully-realized tenor instrument. (This sound, the legitimate upper register of the high male instrument, is more fully discussed when <u>voce di testa</u> is considered.)

Earlier in this discussion, it was mentioned that all schools recognize two kinds of sound as being possible in the female voice in its extension above the <u>secondo passaggio</u>, one being the legitimate upper register, the other being the sound which the Italian School identifies as <u>voce finta</u>. Significant segments of the French and English Schools postulate a female falsetto, but it falls to the German School to develop this assumption into a full-blown vocal dogma.

Among some German teachers, female <u>Kopfstimme</u> is thought to be but a further, desirable development of female falsetto; it is brought to fruition through vocalises which are executed at piano dynamic level, generally on those vowels which are low in upper partials. (See Chapter VI, Techniques of Vowel Formation.)

The existence of the female falsetto is an intriguing hypothesis. To some pedagogues it appears logical that the same phenomenon which exists in the male vocal instrument should exist in the female. Indeed, it is thought by some researchers who classify male registration into chest and falsetto (the latter held to be the same as head) that falsetto events nicely parallel each other in the male and female. (Male and female register parallelisms will be dealt with shortly.)

An opposing viewpoint seriously undermines the intellectual neatness of this hypothesis: it is questionable that the falsetto, as it pertains in the post-pubertal male voice, has an exact equivalent in the female vocal apparatus; the latter does not undergo anything like the developmental changes experienced during puberty in the male larynx. In any event, it is exceedingly clear that the female is incapable of making as disjunct a sound in her upper voice as can the male; it is exactly that imitative female timbre in the adult male voice which the Italian School describes as falsetto.

To speak of a female falsetto would never occur to a representative pedagogue of the Italian School, despite Garcia.

Whatever the merits of falsetto practices (easily confused among some writers and teachers with voce finta practices), they figure in varying degrees within some segments of the several national schools, excluding the Italian. A few additional comments on the use of falsetto practices will be made when specific vocal categories within the national schools are described.

Voce Finta

This clearly identifiable vocal quality can be described as light and somewhat disembodied in character, being but a shadow of the fully energized tone. Voce finta (feigned voice) results from lessening the muscular connection between the head and the torso. The larynx elevates slightly, with the observable assistance of the sternomastoids and the muscles of the back of the neck. As a result of neck distention, the normal supportive muscles of the torso are largely kept out of play. Moreover, there is a fairly high rate of breath mixture in the tone because of insufficient cordal occlusion which results from this lack of structural support. While avoiding the quality of female imitation which characterizes falsetto, the male voce finta has a marked character of its own and can readily be distinguished (among vocal cognoscenti) from the somewhat similar falsetto timbre.

This finta quality can commence at the first terminal registration point (primo passaggio) and can be extended several notes beyond the second terminal point (secondo passaggio) (more readily in light voices than in those of a more spinto character), but cannot usually be continued into the most upper region of the voice except in the case of the very light leggiero or the tenorino whose passaggi points occur much higher than is the rule in most male voices.

Voce finta is permitted in the male voice in the Italian School only as an occasional vocal coloration. At best it sounds sweetly ethereal, at worst somewhat emasculated. It can only be produced at a low dynamic level, a fact which reveals this specific timbre for the mild registration violation that it is.

In the Italian School (as distinct from the German, in particular), voce finta is almost never encouraged in the female voice; in the female, finta quality is so "feigned" as to be unacceptable in its artificiality. As was earlier mentioned, in some non-Italianate schools this female finta quality is termed falsetto.

Thus far in this discussion, falsetto and voce finta have been described as two of three possible approaches to the vocal sound which can be produced beyond the second registration point (secondo passaggio of the Italian School). Their legitimacy as standard vocal approaches has also been questioned in this study, with regard to efficiency of function and desirability of quality. Yet another timbre remains to be considered.

Voce di Testa

The legitimate sound of the upper register, the third and correct approach to that range of a fourth or fifth which lies above the pivotal point of the secondo passaggio as viewed by the Italian School, is clearly of one cloth with the rest of the voice, in both male and female. It is the product of increased action on the part of the cricothyroids as earlier described, in which the distance between the angle of the thyroid cartilage and the arytenoid cartilages is increased, the vocal folds become long and thinner, vibration occurs in the anterior part of the folds, and the action of the thyroarytenoids is appropriately altered with the ascent of pitch. (Yet who can claim exactitude in describing physical function as it actually occurs in the rapid register fluctuations encountered in the dramatic coloratura of the nineteenth-century Italian operatic literature?)

This sound is the head voice, the lighter mechanism of some pedagogies, the voce di testa of the Italian School. It should by now be clear that the sensations perceived by the singer in this area of the voice are in contradistinction to those sensations experienced during the use of the heavier mechanism, the chest voice.

However, head voice sensation in the Italian School is not reserved solely to those notes above the second register terminal point, but is already discernible in the intermediate zone between the first and second terminal points. Within this zona intermedia, sensations of the lighter mechanism are

noticeable and become so predominant at the secondo passaggio that distinct head sensations result. To the singer, the
upper register which lies beyond the secondo passaggio may
seem to resonate entirely in the head. It seems logical to
theorize that the "downwards and forwards" tilting of the
thyroid cartilage, an action earlier described, closely relates to that laryngeal position which together with cordal
elongation and thinning brings about the events of the secondo
passaggio area.

It is precisely at these two passaggi, and particularly
at the upper one, that special emphasis is directed in the
Italian School toward an increase in breath energy. It is
held that unless breath energy increases at these points in
the scale, the voice will tend to sound sectionalized and unskilfully registrated; support is essential to the accomplishment of successful register transition. This viewpoint would
appear to be substantiated by laryngeal photography; changes
in vocal quality which accompany laryngeal adjustments can
best be gradated by an increase in energized breath application
and appropriate muscular antagonism. By such means are
register transitions minimized and the equalized scale realized. Supportive of this theory is the phenomenon accompanying unenergized vocal sounds within some segments of
the non-Italian schools, where falsetto and voce finta make
appearances precisely at the point of the secondo passaggio,
thereby violating the principle of equalized registration transition into the upper voice.

By inducing the same kinds of head sensation which
occur above the second register point as early as the first
point, and by increasing breath energy, certain physiological
events are encouraged: probably the activity of the thyroarytenoid muscles is modified so that other muscular actions
(as previously described) may take place in a more gradual
fashion, permitting the upper register to be integrated with
the rest of the voice. Indeed, most teachers of the Italian
School recommend retaining some awareness of the frontally
located head sensation throughout the entire voice, in both
male and female (except for female open chest sounds).

Bell Register

A vocal register acknowledged and used by many
teachers in all four schools, but especially by the French
and Italian, is designated as beginning roughly a fifth above

the secondo passaggio in the female voice. (It is claimed by some teachers in the German School to be the female counterpart of the male falsetto.) This register often extends about a fourth or fifth above the voce di testa, and can be illustrated by those sounds in a light soprano voice from about d^3 upward to g^4 or beyond, or corresponding pitches for lower female voices. Frequently considered an extension of the head voice, this range can be phenomenally long, sometimes extending nearly an octave beyond the actual head timbre. Those physical events which produce the head voice now become extremely acute, to such a degree that a change of timbre and sensation are experienced.

A number of descriptive terms in several languages have been applied to this register, including the following: bell register, flageolet register, whistle register, flute register, piccolo range, echo voice, voce di campanello, petit registre, registre de flageolet, flute registre, Pfeifestimme, hohe Quinta and zweite Höhe. Some further comment regarding this register will be found in sections of this work dealing with the specific vocal categories.

Male and Female Register Parallelisms

Sometimes it is suggested that there are direct registration parallels between female and male voices, with events located at the removal of an octave. This is not the accepted opinion in the current Italian School, although there is evidence that it may have been, among some earlier noted Italian writers on vocal pedagogy.

There is much to be said for the assumption that the physical events which occur in the female chest voice correspond to those which occur in the male chest voice, and that because of the difference in cordal size and in mutational histories, the female singer has a shorter chest voice than does the male, and conversely, a long head voice.

This pedagogical position assumes that the thyroarytenoidal action is comparable in both male and female chest registers and that the stretching action in ascending pitch on the part of the cricoarytenoids begins sooner in the female than in the male in relation to the bottom of the vocal range, chiefly because of differences in general laryngeal location within the muscular structure, actual laryngeal dimensions, and overall pubertal development. The same functional

registrational explanations then are thought to apply to both
female and male voices.

As agreeable as this explanation may appear to be in
establishing correspondence between the sexes on vocal registration, there remain certain unanswered questions.   For
example, most sopranos experience an urgent need to come
out of chest into middle voice by at least e^b above middle
c, and generally do so much earlier.   At the point of emergence from chest, they experience another quite distinct register sensation.   Certainly the tenor voice does not experience, on a comparable note one octave lower, anything like
the shift from chest to lower head or lower middle.   (To
ignore the entire lower octave in the tenor voice and equate
his zona di passaggio with the soprano transition out of chest,
as has been done by some theorists, is to display an em-
barrassing confusion.)

The tenor of average vocal weight typically experiences
his first register event around $c^{\#}1$ or d^1 (written in the
octave above middle c), which might compare with the soprano sub-register of the middle voice, as defined in the Italian
School.   He also typically encounters a register sensation at
$f^{\#}1$ or g^1 (upper line and space immediately above treble
clef), which might correspond to the soprano registration
sensation of head voice an octave above.   This is also the
pivotal point at which he can readily go into falsetto if he
does not want to use the full compass of his legitimate head
voice, or if he does not know how to negotiate it.   However,
if we liken his chest voice to that of the soprano, he has
only fairly begun to sing the notes of his chest voice when
the soprano leaves her chest voice.   She then begins with
the long, mixed, middle voice, at least a sixth or an octave
prior to what is his practice.   She also stays in it for over
an octave, and he for considerably less.   Even if he is taught
to bring head sensations down throughout the range, the vibratory chest rumble is present throughout at least his bottom octave.   On the other hand, the chest voice of the
soprano ceases normally at least by $e^b 1$.

Further, if one equates the tenor's second pivotal
point (secondo passaggio) with the soprano's low $e^b 1$ chest-
head transition point (which can be done only by arbitrarily
lowering it a major second or a minor third to e^1 or $e^b 1$,
as some pedagogues do), we are left with the briefest of
chest voices in the tenor, in contrast to his extended speaking voice, which takes place largely in chest.

When this octave parallelism is advocated (keeping our tenor as a point of illustration), a long register is then proposed extending from low e♭ to f♯1 an octave above, likening that register to the soprano head voice. Then both soprano and tenor ranges above the f♯ are described as falsetto registers. This explanation can be encountered among some English, French and German teachers; it cannot be found among Italian-schooled teachers.

As mentioned above, this usage embraces a concept of falsetto which does not correspond to the term as encountered in the lingua franca of international operatic circles. When the so-called female falsetto is amplified, it becomes the legitimate female head tone; the male falsetto can be increased to great intensity and never lose its imitative female character. Thus, attempts to identify direct registration correlation between the two vocal categories appear to be more the result of codifying minds than of actual physiological events.

Still some other teachers in the English, French and German schools solve the registration discrepancies which emerge as a result of parallelism by maintaining that the tenor sings in chest through the first 12th or so of his range, until he strikes the f♯1 or g1, at which time he goes into falsetto voice. This explanation totally ignores the existence of the male middle voice, but more glaringly, must term the soprano range covering the comparable 12th, head voice, while terming everything above the f♯2 or g2, female falsetto. This leaves the female chest voice as a timbre without correlation in the male voice. (Some German teachers do indeed totally ignore the female chest voice, believing it to be undesirable under any circumstances, and falsely induced.)

The reputed vocal habits of the castrati would seem to indicate that--when pubertal voice changes have been avoided--the events of vocal registration in the male will closely parallel those of the female vocal organ. Such assumptions can safely be made on the basis of literature and contemporary reports as to the quality, range and technical proficiency of the castrati. It is noteworthy that it is inevitably easier, especially with regard to registration aspects, for a female soprano to sing literature written for altered male soprano voice than for the legitimate tenor voice to do so, and that it is more appropriate for the mezzo-soprano to sing literature written for male contralto than for either

baritones or tenors to do so. Interestingly, at times this
argument is presented as evidence that male vocal techniques
have deteriorated through the loss of falsetto practices, when
of course the castrato voice was quite distinctly not the male
instrument. (Who is so foolish as to attest that the counter-
tenor is comparable to the castrato virtuoso with regard
either to vocal function or technique, not to mention the timbre itself?)

Many who believe in parallelism of registration events
in male and female tend to believe that no register distinctions
exist with regard to vocal categories, particularly in the male
voices. The passaggi of both baritone and tenor are thought
to occur at the same medium point in the scale (generally
e♭1, second ledger line, bass clef), thereby confusing the
primo passaggio of some categories of light tenor voice with
the secondo passaggio of some lower-voiced males. A cor-
relative pedagogical tenet is that there are no differences in
the points of register demarcation among the soprano, mezzo
or contralto voices, the passaggi of the female voices being
e♭1 on the bottom and f♯2 on the top; register handling then
differs only in regard to quality and laryngeal size, in this
viewpoint. These confusions are not to be met with in the
current Italian School.

Summary of Register Categories

On the basis of what our ears tell us and what scientific investigation reveals about singing which utilizes legitimate
sound, we must conclude that chest and head qualities of the
male and female do correspond but without a relationship of
octave parallelism. Differences between the sexes with regard to vocal registration are due to differences of pubertal
change, laryngeal size, and laryngeal relationship to the
entire human skeletal structure. Additional room is required
to accommodate male cartilaginous development (consider his
vocal prominence alone); a longer chest-voice mechanism
exists in the male partly because of the larger physical mass
of his vocal folds as opposed to smaller mass in the female.
The mezzo and the contralto, possessing larger laryngeal
mechanisms than does the soprano, correspondingly have
somewhat longer chest registers than she. The soprano, in
all gradations of weightiness, followed by mezzo and contralto,
will sooner come to that laryngeal adjustment which brings
about the transition from chest to middle or lower head
voice, chiefly because she has not undergone the more

extensive pubertal increase in size experienced by the larynx of the male.

This discussion on vocal registration began with an indication that registration concepts extend from the no-register teacher to those who advocate as many as seven registers. Even those teachers who adamantly hold that registers do not exist, readily admit to the possibility of producing such sounds as female open chest and male falsetto, although they may believe that these and other recognizable registration qualities are unnaturally induced in response to misguided pedagogy. However, the no-register (one register) pedagogue may well be expressing hope for a unified scale throughout the voice by directing attention away from all register demarcations. Such teachers often stress that any change in the nature of laryngeal muscular action is so gradual that no sudden sensations are perceivable. On the other hand, it is frequently a human frailty to ignore or deny what we do not understand.

Advocates of two registers generally use such terms as "light (or thin) mechanism" and "heavy (or thick) mechanism," or chest register and falsetto register to indicate these qualities of registration. (Persons who designate the two registers as being chest and falsetto generally mean something more than just the imitative female sound of the Italian school known as falsetto, although some intend exactly that timbre.) Most two-register teachers also speak of a middle area in both male and female voices in which either mechanism can operate, generally in cooperation with each other. Thus it can be seen that the two-register advocate is often not far removed from the position of the three-register teacher; the latter simply provides a third term for the overlapping middle area.

Three-register teachers, it must by now be clear, generally speak of chest, mixed and head (or lower, middle and upper) registers. The Italian School is associated with the three-register concept and directs much of its attention to blending these registers as a means to an equalized scale throughout them. Herman Klein was closely associated with Manuel Garcia when Garcia lived with the Klein family for a period of ten years in his later life. Klein studied with the Maestro for a period of four years and assisted him in preparing his Hints on Singing. In Klein's The Bel Canto (1923), the approach of the Italian School to vocal registration is very well presented:

The provision of registers, with their three mechanical actions, enables the same vocal cords to produce a succession of sounds of extensive range.
They thus add to what might otherwise be a relatively limited compass and provide for an infinitely
greater variety of timbres.... [O]ne fact appears
--that we must not alter our manner of singing
because we feel the mechanism to be in some subtle
way altering its automatic procedure.

The solution of the problem lies in uniformity--
uniformity of breathing, or 'singing position', of
resonance--the last is perhaps the most important.
So long as the voice is securely reflected in its
ultimate forward position, and is sustained there
by the breath, supported from the diaphragm, the
vocal cords will enjoy the elasticity and freedom
essential for modifying their action, without that
sudden change or 'break', which is commonly heard.
Otherwise the modification cannot be made imperceptibly, and the abrupt transition from one register to another will become audible. The blending
tone, if properly graduated, extends over three or
at most four notes, to which the French give the
name of voix mixte.

With the aid of this voix mixte, the union of the
'chest' and 'medium', of 'medium' and 'head' tones,
proceeding either up or down the scale, the voice
can be brought into line throughout its whole compass. 16

(In addition to presenting a superb statement of the Italian
technique of vocal registration, Mr. Klein makes it eminently clear that Garcia's middle voice did not equate with an
effeminate falsetto timbre as some contemporary writers on
vocal pedagogy contend.)

Four- or five-register teachers break down one or
more of the other registers into sub-registers, such as lower middle, upper middle, etc. The typical Italianate teacher so divides the long middle register of the female voice.

Those teachers who admit to finding seven registers
usually add to the three main register divisions and their
sub-registers, such special areas of the voice as Strohbass
or Schnarregister (called the growl register by some English-

speaking teachers, consisting of a fourth or fifth below the normal male speaking voice), the flageolet register (bell register) in the female, and the falsetto in the male.

National and cultural preferences for specific qualities of sound result in opposing ideas on the existence of vocal registers and on the techniques of handling them. The areas of possible overlapping between pivotal registration points are the source of much controversy and of various "covering" and "vowel modification" theories which often sharply divide the schools. Although there is at times considerable theoretical agreement among some segments of the national schools on the subject of register blending, distinct variations do exist. To some extent these variants figure within the commentary which comprises the following chapters.

Chapter XI

REGISTRATION EVENTS
AND VOICE CATEGORIZATION

The pitches at which register transition is experienced
serve some teachers within the national schools as clues to
the vocal category of the singer. Those teachers who do not
believe registers exist cannot, of course, rely upon these devices for such assistance. The French School probably makes
the least use of such procedures, whereas both the English
and German schools frequently do. It is the Italian School
which has the greatest awareness of the relationship of registration events and vocal categorization.

In spite of individual variations within vocal instruments, there is a rather high degree of predictability as to
the location of register transitions within a particular category of voice. Physical structure of individual larynges,
while following the uniformity common to human structure
(for the most part), varies considerably depending upon vocal
type. Even a casual survey of the external appearance of
necks is enough to indicate great variation in the size of the
"Adam's apple" among both males and females. While this
evidence is immediately observable, it is but an outward manifestation of internal dimensions.

The terminal registration events in each category are
fairly predictable. The German word Fach has become a
standard term to indicate "specific category of singer"; chief
registration events will tend to occur in the voices of a given
Fach at identical pitches. The second register demarcation
will occur at a particular interval above the first register
termination, although the area between the two pivotal points
may occasionally be a bit longer in one voice than in another,
but rarely by more than a half tone.

Registration phenomena do not necessarily correspond
exactly to the pitches arbitrarily established for the uniform

tuning of instruments, sometimes falling midway between those arbitrary pitches. For example, a tenor voice may have registration points which lie slightly on the sharp side of d^1 (primo passaggio) and g^1 (secondo passaggio), but definitely lower than eb^1 and ab^1. Such location of pivotal registration notes may enter into the kind of registration problems encountered by some singers. (Shall he sing the note g^1 more openly, or shall it be treated as a pitch already more decisively a part of that timbre associated with the upper registration of the voice? To what extent will that note be modified in order to match the vocal sounds on either side of it?)

Although the Italian teacher keeps in mind the very real possibility of individual variants, the registration events of any instrument are considered better indicators of vocal classification than are such factors as range and timbre, both of which may be falsely disguised in an individual voice through compensatory methods of singing.

Approximate Passaggi in Male Voices

As can be seen from Chart A, the decision to train a male singer in one category or another, for example as a big lyric baritone or a dramatic tenor, must take into consideration factors other than merely the registration events, including the actual size of the instrument and other physical and psychological attributes of the individual singer. Nevertheless, the location of the pivotal points provides the most specific information for the teacher with regard to vocal categorization.

In addition to the categories indicated in Chart A, buffo counterparts can be identified. Although these buffo characteristics deal with timbre designations, the basso-buffo, the tenore-buffo, the Spielbariton and the Spieltenor (the latter two of the German theater, of course) generally indicate theatrical skill and specialization rather than vocal quality. Indeed, in the German theater, much of the leggiero literature belongs to the same singer who occupies the opera-buffa Fach.

Additional specifics of registration practices will be dealt with in chapters of this work devoted to vowel modification (XII) and to the tenor, baritone and bass voices (XV and XVI). However, it should be understood, with reference to Chart A, that the chest register extends up to the

A. APPROXIMATE PASSAGGI OF MALE VOICES

Primo passaggio	Secondo passaggio	Vocal Category
g	c^1	Basso profondo
$a\flat$	$d\flat^1$	Basso profondo
a	d^1	Basso cantante
$b\flat$	$e\flat^1$	Baritono drammatico
b	e^1	Baritono lirico
c^1	f^1	Baryton Martin (of French School)
c^1	f^1	Tenore robusto (drammatico)
c^1	f^1	Heldentenor (of German School)
$c\sharp^1$	$f\sharp^1$	Tenore robusto (heavy spinto)
$c\sharp^1$	$f\sharp^1$	Tenore spinto (more spinto than lirico)
d^1	g^1	Tenore spinto (more lirico than spinto)
d^1	g^1	Tenore lirico
$e\flat^1$	$a\flat^1$	Tenore leggiero (more leggiero than lirico)
e^1	a^1	Tenore leggiero
f	$b\flat^1$	Tenorino (similar to "Irish tenor")

primo passaggio, that the zona intermedia (which lies between primo and secondo passaggi) encompasses the middle register, and that the head register lies above the secondo passaggio.

Approximate Passaggi in Female Voices

As with the male, categorization of the female voice is in large measure determined by the location of registration events within the vocal scale. See Chart B.

Chart B indicates the possible overlapping of registers as well as determining the normal pivotal notes within the scale for the given categories. The passaggi of most assistance in determining vocal category among female voices are not those of the chest voice but those of upper middle and upper. For example, $c\sharp^2$ and $f\sharp^2$ are the pivotal points

B.   APPROXIMATE PASSAGGI OF FEMALE VOICES

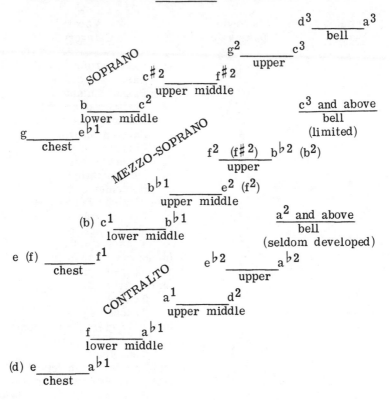

which mark the most frequently encountered soprano voice, b^1 and f^2 the mezzo, and a^b1 and d^2 the contralto.

The designation soprano includes a wide spectrum of vocal weight and timbre. These factors are reflected in the passaggi events which determine register definition, the heavier soprano approaching more nearly the mezzo-soprano pivotal points. The lighter-voiced mezzo will have pivotal points not far removed from those of the soprano, while the contralto passaggi in a more lyrical voice will not be much lower than those of the mezzo. Decisions regarding Fach must often be made cautiously in these cases, since it is possible the singer could go in either direction; the decision will partly determine the technical handling of the voice.

Vocal maturation figures importantly in the final

determination of passaggi as well. This explains the frequent happening of a change in vocal category sometimes in
mid-career, as for example some mezzo voices which then
become dramatic sopranos, or baritones who become dramatic
tenors.   It should also be remarked that a change in vocal
production in which a heavily-weighted voice learns a better
balance of resonances may permit a singer to change to a
neighboring Fach.   Often in such cases precepts of modification and "cover" had previously served to obscure the
actual passaggi events.

Chest, Mixture and Head in the Female Voice

Although emphases vary within the four major schools,
a general consideration of registration practices would seem
appropriate at this point.   (Occasional comment regarding
registration tendencies will be found in those sections of this
work which deal with individual vocal categories as they are
treated within each school.)

Open chest refers to a timbre which is almost entirely of the unmodified lower register as opposed to chest which
may have some elements of head quality within it.   When
truly open, chest voice in the female has a masculine directness about it which clearly sets it apart from middle voice.

Mixture describes that kind of tone which is neither
patently head nor chest; it is possible for either chest or
head timbre to predominate in this mixture.   Head mixture
indicates some considerable introduction of the lighter sound
into either the chest or the middle voice; chest mixture describes the carrying up of some of the chest timbre into the
lower middle voice.

The German School strenuously avoids any use of open
chest, an attitude which for the most part is shared by the
French School.   Indeed, very little is to be heard even of
chest mixture in the German School.   The Italian vocal
aesthetic enjoys the sudden employment of open chest, using
it quite dramatically for both musical and emotional effects.
Although the Italian must be able to carry head mixture to
the lower end of her vocal range, unlike the German she
does not use it exclusively.   The French singer generally
prefers the balanced head mixture in the lower voice.   English sopranos almost never use chest mixture or open chest,
but many operatic mezzos and contraltos in the English school

tend to do so.   In contrast, the English oratorio contralto can often be heard attempting to produce a dark quality of sound in the low voice while depending entirely on head mixture.

The preferences noted for open chest, chest mixture and head mixture within the schools must be understood as general practices, by no means without individual exception.

Most sopranos in general, regardless of national vocal tendencies, are capable of singing all but the lowest notes of the vocal compass without resorting to chest.   However, most sopranos (excepting the German) tend to mix some chest sound into lower middle voice as they arrive as $c^{\#}1$, c^1 or b in a descending scale, increasing the degree of chest sound on each additional half-step descent.   The extent to which this practice is followed is largely dependent upon the size and weight of the instrument.

In understanding the relationship of the register timbres in the descending scale in the female voice, it should be kept in mind that although lower and upper middle registers are not merely an extension of the head voice, they partake much more of its nature than they do of chest because they too involve a greater participation of the lighter than of the heavier mechanism.   As we have previously seen, the lighter mechanism finds its most complete action in head.

The classic passaggio in the Italian School beyond which a soprano should not carry up any of the chest mixture is $e^{\flat}$ above middle c.   Many dramatics and some spintos in this school carry some chest mixture up as far as g^1 on occasion, but the resultant sound is one of vulgarity to non-Italianate ears.   One must concede that the German, with her abhorrence of chest, does less violation to natural function than does her Italian counterpart who pushes up chest for dramatic purposes.   Open chest carried to the $e^{\flat}1$ point is also observable among a number of dramatic sopranos of the Italian School; while this phenomenon may thrill the Italian sensibilities, to many other listeners it partakes of the bizarre.

From the standpoint of healthy function, even chest mixture should approach the cessation point very early in the lower voice, at least by d^1, and be totally absent by $e^{\flat}1$.   Of course, a sizable soprano can sing a tone heavily weighted with chest up as far as $e^{\flat}1$, but then the transition which follows to lower-middle voice would be so drastic as to indicate some special interpretative effect.

For the Italian mezzo-soprano, $e^{\flat 1}$ should normally begin to be predominantly timbre of lower middle voice, with f^1 or $f^{\sharp 1}$ as the termination point for any chest mixture. The French mezzo will have eliminated any of the chest mixture timbre considerably earlier, as will the German. Again, if fairly open chest is maintained through f^1 or $f^{\sharp 1}$, it will be of a stark and dramatic nature; the next note simply must sound like a sudden switch of registration. There are mezzos who now and again take the chest voice up through the pitch a^1 for special coloration. Few teachers endorse such a practice, considering it vocally dangerous. The character alto, frequently an older singer whose registration mechanism is no longer flexible, may carry chest up as far as any gospel or soul belter, but only as a device utilizing comic elements inherent in female register shifts.

A contralto often prefers to use no middle voice mixture whatsoever until $e^{\flat 1}$ or even e^1. Because of her larger laryngeal structure, she does not do the violence to her instrument that the soprano would do were she to carry the same timbre that far up the ascending scale. Needing additional weight and volume in the low voice, she tends to sing all the notes in her lower register with a preponderance of chest quality. She begins mixing quite late and often very slightly, delaying the transition into middle voice until around g^1 or $a^{\flat 1}$. This means that she frequently neglects using the lower-middle register, or at least overweights it in the direction of chest mixture, up to the upper-middle sub-register demarcation. Naturally, the larger the voice the more appropriate the continuance of chest. For a highly dramatic effect the contralto may on occasion use a fairly open chest sound as high as $b^{\flat 1}$, but again, not without risking a note of comic vulgar masculinity.

It is true that there are female singers of good vocal repute who carry chest up a note or two higher in their particular category than is generally thought desirable, in response to the demands of specific operatic roles. When this practice becomes habitual, so as to produce sound startling in quality or impressive in size, the voice inevitably begins to sound as though it hangs in segments. When the chest voice becomes standard practice beyond its normal range limitations, the middle voice will no longer respond well, because the heavier mechanism of the vocalis muscles (internal thyroarytenoids) has won a permanent victory over the lighter mechanism (the predominantly cricothyroidal action).

Carrying female chest well up into middle voice is a pernicious technique sometimes used by entertainers, singers of musical comedy, rock, soul or belting (techniques similar to out-moded torch). Such singers often lose the facility to pass into head voice and must rely in time entirely on the heavier mechanism. This practice is totally removed from the kind of register consideration found among students of traditional serious music in Western culture. Even though tastes regarding the uses of chest vary nationally to some extent, all of the schools are aware of the danger of making use of the chest mechanism outside of the low range of the voice.

Open chest carried beyond normal register demarcations occurs in response to a demand for purposeful register violation, the aim being to produce sound of a primitive or highly emotive nature. The natural coordination of laryngeal and resonator action is upset. Physiologically, this vocal act approaches the animalistic shriek of pain or terror, or the shout. As part of the current drift of popular culture, open yelling of emotional texts is prevalent. Its frequent use precludes any unification of the registers of the voice, producing muscular and even cordal imbalance, vocal nodules, and irreparable damage to the speaking as well as the singing voice.

A healthy voice must learn the art of register blending, much of which is determined by the skill with which middle voice is executed. In most sopranos, the middle register extends from $e^\flat 1$ (above middle c) to $f^\sharp 2$ (top line, treble clef) or g^2; it can comfortably descend about the distance of a fourth below the head-chest pivot point ($e^\flat 1$) to $b^\flat$. In most cases, a division of this long middle register occurs around $c^\sharp 2$ (or at c^2 in a somewhat heavier soprano voice). The area below this point makes up the lower-middle voice; the area extending above it (c^2 or $c^\sharp 2$) comprises the upper-middle voice on up to $f^\sharp 2$ or g^2. (See Chart B showing the approximate passaggi of female voices.)

The area of the soprano voice which lies above the $f^\sharp 2$-g^2 pivotal point (which pitches designate the secondo passaggio transition, concluding the long middle register) perhaps more accurately should be termed upper voice,

although head is the term in general usage. "Head" seems
to imply that the mechanistic function which it represents is
present only beyond the secondo passaggio, which is not the
case, as we have seen. Much of the muscular action which
produces head quality and sensation may be present in the
lower, long middle voice. However, to term head (as some
do) the entire area of the voice which lies above chest is to
ignore three recognizable registration areas; to lump them
together (as is the case with the two-register teacher who
fails to see an overlapping area) is to skirt issues of registration which are very real to the singer who attempts to
accomplish a unified scale. Even in the Italian School,
which recognizes the subdivisions of the middle voice, one
often speaks of head when meaning any sound not executed in
chest. Perhaps many confusions would be resolved were the
expressions chest and head supplanted by low, lower middle,
upper middle, upper, and bell register designations.

Chart B indicates a range of notes referred to as the
bell register, lying above high d^3 (approximately) for the
soprano. In producing notes within the compass of this
range, the French and the Italian schools often find a key to
the brilliant development of the upper voice. The shape of
the mouth is drastically altered by extensive buccal closure,
exaggerated smile and elevated maxillaries. There is a
heavy concentration of upper partials, and unless modified,
the sound becomes brittle and dry. This sound then is
brought down into the neighboring tones of the upper register.
This practice is not common among German teachers nor
among teachers of the English School. (See Chapter XIII,
The Soprano Voice.)

The mezzo-soprano frequently experiences a kind of
transition feeling at b^b1 or b^1 (above middle c), midway in
the long middle voice, comparable to what the soprano experiences about a whole tone above. (Although noticed by
most sopranos of considerable size, for a coloratura or
soubrette there may be very little or no awareness of this
sub-register transition.) The mezzo's transition into upper
voice, as indicated in Chart B, is also about a tone lower
than is the soprano's. Bell register exists for her, but she
seldom develops it in any usable way. However, French
mezzos tend to vocalize in it rather extensively.

The contralto voice is a truly rare instrument, although the term is often misapplied to limited mezzos who
have not discovered how to sing above the secondo passaggio.

(As has been noted, its registration phenomena correspond to those in the higher female voices, but at lower pitches.) The contralto generally possesses the bell register to a very limited extent, if at all. This is because the larger the larynx, the less likelihood that the development of that register will be fruitful, and because the literature does not demand the kind of brilliance which can result from exercising that register.

Chapter XII

VOWEL MODIFICATION

Before turning to some tendencies which prevail within specific vocal categories among the national schools, a
word must be said about the technical practice known as
vowel modification. This term embraces any consciously-
learned adjustment of vowel formation as a means to better
resonance balance at any pitch in the entire singing range.
However, its chief pedagogical function is to assist in negotiating smooth register transition by inducing certain kinds of
muscular coordination among the intrinsic muscles of the
larynx, which when coupled with breath management techniques ensures successful laryngeal action at the passaggi.
Vowel modification also is closely related to other technical
aspects of singing already discussed in this work, such as
resonance balance and resonantal adjustment in general,
vowel formation, vibrancy rate, and laryngeal position.

As pitch ascends, the preponderance of upper partials
increases, especially in the closer vowels. This phenomenon
will result in strident, white, open or excessively bright
vowel sounds, unless means are devised for avoiding them.
It is at the passaggi points, particularly the second registration terminal, that this tendency is most marked. Were
the vowel to be sung with the same acoustical formation as
at a lower pitch level, the resultant sound would not match
the general timbre of the ascending scale. Cultural preferences are clearly discernible in pedagogical attitudes toward
vowel modification.

The German School

The German-schooled singer typically prefers vowel
modification of a somewhat extreme nature commencing at
the first register point in the male voice. Deckung (cover)

137

results from darkening the vowel by altering its acoustical
shape through increased laryngeal depression and pharyngeal
enlargement; the vocalis muscles are encouraged to greater
activity as a result of escalated muscular antagonisms in the
torso and neck. Within the area of a fourth above the first
pivotal register point, the vowel will have been altered to a
high degree of neutralization, regardless of its actual phonetic shape. (This area is the zona di passaggio of the Italian
School, beginning at the primo passaggio and concluding a
fourth above, at the secondo passaggio.) Tones above the
second terminal point are thought to approach a single vowel
color, generally (u) (oo), or, with some teachers, the schwa
(ə) ["uh']. In this pedagogy, the tendency may be so marked
that an arpeggio (1 - 3 - 5 - 8 - 5 - 3 - 1) executed on
(a) ["ah"] in the key of F will sound to an uninitiated ear as
though it were (a - ɔ - o - u - o - ɔ - a) ["ah-aw-oh-oo-
oh-aw-ah"], although the same vowel is indicated throughout.
This is the familiar sound of Deckung, so characteristic in
the middle and upper voice of the German-schooled singer.

A word should be added about the expression gedeckt,
as it is used in singing. At times it serves as a register
designation, indicating the sound of Deckung above the first
pivotal registration point. Given another usage, gedeckt refers to a character of sound throughout the entire singing
voice, not unrelated to the Italian voce chiusa, being the
avoidance of an undesirable character of openness in the
vocal quality.

It is appropriate that extremes of vowel modification
and concepts of cover should be considered desirable in the
typical German School, inasmuch as these factors have much
in common with the convictions of that school regarding other
technical facets. Indeed, without the rubric regarding modification and neutralization of the vowel, much of the aesthetic
ideal regarding vocal timbre would not be possible. Vowel
modification is used as a device to induce many of the functions which characterize the physical processes that occur
within the Germanic techniques of singing.

The Italian School

The Italian-trained teacher almost never requests any
specific coperto quality at the primo passaggio. For the
most part, vowel modification is induced only near the secondo passaggio point, becoming somewhat more complete in the

very uppermost part of the voice. Moreover, in the Italian
School it is sometimes held that this modification, designated
as voce coperta, will happen automatically, given the increased
buccal aperture for ascending pitch and accompanying increase
in breath support.

    With some other Italian teachers, an almost impercep-
tible vowel modification (voce coperta) begins at the primo
passaggio, continuing gradually throughout the zona intermedia,
with somewhat more intentional modification occurring above
the second passaggio in the upper extremes of the voice.
The working out of these passage areas, with regard to sequence of vowels in a given phrase, constitutes much of the
skilful registration unification methodology of the Italian
School. Any variations in this technique of voce coperta (also suono coperto) are dictated by individual idiosyncracies as
expressed in the location of the passaggi and in the weight
and size of the voice.

    To the Italian-trained ear, the German technique of
Deckung produces a tono sporco (dirty tone). The Italian
takes exception to statements which equate Deckung with the
voce coperta, and the two processes involve dissimilar laryngeal events. Without doubt, the Italianate singer introduces
vowel modification much less drastically and considerably
later than does the Germanic. The physiological alterations
within the vocal tract which the German sees as concomitant
to vowel modification are avoided in the Italian School.
Pharyngeal distention, laryngeal depression and resonance
adjustments, which figure largely in techniques of registration and vowel modification in the German School, are not endorsed by the Italians.

The French School

    Registration matters are given less direct attention
among French-schooled teachers than in some other schools.
The typical male singer tends to sing throughout his voice
without introducing that kind of breath management and muscular balance more commonly thought to induce register
function. As a result, the general weight of his voice will
be lighter; range will be restricted to very little more than
those notes which lie just beyond the second pivotal point,
negotiable by slight register violation as in the voce finta,
or through resorting to falsetto. He finds little necessity
to modify his "natural" sound, and tends to apply the
principles of vowel modification hardly at all.

This search in the French School for natural singing produces in the female voice less obvious disengagement from the passaggi events because of the nature of the long middle voice and the French interest in developing the bell range. In larger instruments, where these factors are somewhat curtailed, vowel modification aspects are sometimes given more consideration simply because the need for them becomes more glaring. Yet the female as well as the male singer of the French School often suffers from voix blanche. This expression describes both an openness of the unmodified vowel during the course of a mounting scale, and a shallow production in general which is lacking in the support and resonance which produce the voce piena of the Italian School.

In spite of these tendencies, a distorted picture would emerge were one to suggest that French-trained teachers do not look for the even scale throughout the singing voice. In fact, the voce mista of the Italian School has its historical parallel in the important concept of the voix mixte of the French School; both terms include the gradual modification of the vowel, as well as resonance factors. However, it is fair to state that in France, with the exception of those teachers who consciously reject a national vocal aesthetic and imitate the neighboring Italian method, vowel modification as a means of inducing registration events is not given great priority. The heavy cover of the German School is decisively rejected as a viable vocal practice in France.

The English School

English tastes seem to dictate some middle ground between the less-modified ascending scale of Gallic habit and the drastically-modified Germanic one. As in many areas of vocal technique, the English cautiously adapt an Italian procedure to the national aesthetic. In the case of vowel modification, this means avoidance in general of the heavy alteration of the German School and the whiteness of the French School. Yet the ascending scale tends to lose some of the brilliance which always remains in the Italian scale, without doubt because of the English tendency toward vowel distortion as pitch mounts, as was earlier noted.

The English singer will not indulge in the complex physiological events Germans believe must accompany vowel modification, but he or she often chooses to modify vowels downward on the vowel spectrum as the scale ascends.

This frequently takes place beginning at the first register point in the male and at the midway pivot point in the long middle range of the female. The modified vowels would strike the Italian teacher as too dark, having about them a character of distortion.

The Even Scale

It would be difficult to devise a detailed vowel modification chart which would serve with exactitude for more than one individual singer. Vowel modification practices must ultimately rely upon the practiced ear of a highly-trained vocal technician. It has thus far been pointed out that the extent of modification considered desirable varies from school to school. However, within the schools, devices for achieving the unified scale are clearly related to vowel modification. Chart C indicates the principle of vowel modification; the unmodified vowel can be made closer or more open, generally by approaching a neighboring vowel on the spectrum.

C. VOWEL MODIFICATION GUIDELINES

Closed Modification (Higher)	The Unmodified Vowel	Open Modification (Lower)
(none)	i (ee)	I (ih)
i (ee)	I (in)	e (ay)
i (ee)	e (ay)	ɛ (eh)
e (ay)	ɛ (eh)	ə (uh) a (ah)
a (sat)	a (ah)	ɔ (aw)
a (ah)	ɔ (aw)	o (oh)
ɔ (aw)	o (oh)	U (foot)
ɔ (aw)	U (foot)	u (moon)
(none)	u (moon)	U (foot)

The schwa (ə) is the most neutral sound within the vowel spectrum, as it emanates from the larynx with the least amount of modification from the resonators. Significantly, (ə) does not exist as a legitimate vowel sound in the Italian language. The vowel (a) is probably one which strikes a number of singers as being somewhere in the middle of the vowel spectrum, neither high nor low (close or open). Some teachers use both (ə) ["uh"] and (a) ["ah"] as modifying centers toward which high, close vowels tend to modify in order to reduce brilliance, and to which the low, open vowels may modify to bring about an increase of brilliance. (Italians generally use (ɑ) ["ah"] as this central modifying vowel.) As indicated in the above chart, the singer can influence the relationship of fundamental and upper partials by proceeding either toward or away from neutralization.

If a singer believes that a tonal aesthetic must be based upon the most efficient physiological function in singing, the Italian School once again will come closest to satisfying that goal. It is the even scale, throughout the singing voice, which prompts the necessity for vowel modification and registration considerations. In the Italian School, the even scale is achieved through the chiaroscuro timbre, neither aperto nor cupo; the timbre must be chiuso throughout its range, but not inflicted with sudden vowel covering at specific registration points.

Chapter XIII

THE SOPRANO VOICE

The German School

The coloratura trained by typically Germanic techniques
is characterized by the flute-like quality of her velocity passages, nearly devoid of vibrato in both legato and staccato
melismas except for those occasional notes of longer duration.   This quality of straight tone is especially in evidence
at pianissimo level and in that area of the voice termed
Pfeifestimme (the zweite Höhe) by some teachers.   An ethereal, floating sound is prized as the ideal in the typical German coloratura.   She opens the mouth vertically as opposed
to the horizontal smile posture of some schools; minimal
consonantal articulation takes place.   The timbre which results from this buccal posture has about it much of the character of disembodiment to be found in the male voce finta.
Some German teachers believe it to be the female falsetto.

The German soubrette closely follows the same tonal
aesthetic, frequently being a voice of similar size and character to the coloratura, without having to utilize the extreme
upper range of the voice or to engage in frequent displays
of agility.   When of sufficient size to sing those roles which
can also be sung by lyric sopranos, and in roles requiring a
more coquettish nature, she tends to use less of the Flöten-
töne timbre, introducing greater warmth and brighter vowel
coloration; as the degree of breath mixture diminishes,
greater vibrancy emerges.

With both the coloratura and the soubrette in the
German School, outstanding examples of individual voices
which display brilliance and fire come to mind.   Such voices
are atypical, following pedagogical precepts which purposely
reject the German aesthetic in singing.   This fact serves to
illustrate the point that several strands of vocal ideal can

143

often be found running along with the typical, more general cultural tendency.

The lyrische Sopran, to whom falls the majority of those weiblich (womanly) roles of the lyric theater which intimately appeal to the sympathies and emotions of the opera-goer, appropriately displays more of the warmth the voice takes on when vibrato is present. Yet characteristically, her palette of vocal shadings leans heavily toward the kind of color and roundness idealized in the schwebender Ton. Clarity and brilliance are not emphasized. A German-trained Mimi appeals to our ears and sensibilities on the basis of her Weichheit (softness). As was earlier seen, the concept of Kopfstimme plays a major part in accomplishing this timbre.

The jugendliche dramatische Sopran (young dramatic soprano) possesses a larger instrument than does the lyric, requiring greater sustaining power and considerable dramatic thrust. (She need, incidentally, not be young; maturity is an essential to this Fach. She may later move into the literature of the hochdramatische Sopran, as her voice gains additional weight.) These qualities are wedded to a relatively high tessitura in the young dramatic literature. A voice of warmth and stamina is demanded.

Most singers in this category attempt to introduce the "round" quality so beloved in the German School. Pharyngeal enlargement and techniques of abdominal breath-management help assist this goal. On the other hand, the nature of the literature for this Fach demands a higher degree of frontal projection than does much of the lyric literature; the young dramatic singer in the German School often has more of this frontal quality than does her lyric soprano colleague.

The Zwischenfachsängerin (literally, a singer in-between categories) is a type of soprano voice in the German lyric theater which requires dramatic power and yet which must retain a quality of lyricism. A Zwischenfachsängerin might sing Aïda, Tosca, Sieglinde or Senta, but not Brünn-hilde, Isolde or Elektra, for example. Techniques of production tend to resemble those of the young dramatic.

The hochdramatische Sopran (dramatic soprano) is characterized by extreme weightiness, often accompanied by a slower vibrato rate. It is a stylistic earmark of Brünn-hilde to begin a sustained note totally devoid of vibrato,

introducing vibrancy only gradually as the phrase progresses.
The "holding" of the tone prior to allowing it to become vibrant is thought to give the impression of voluptuousness considered appropriate to the Wagnerian dramatic sound.   Because of the static weightiness of the vocal production itself,
this stylistic hallmark may well have grown out of vocal
necessity.   The vibrato is held out of the voice at the moment of onset because the kinds of muscular balance which
produce the vibrant attack are not present.   Lower abdominal support, upon which the typical hochdramatische Sopran
relies, not only stems the outward flow of breath but also
induces the kind of glottal closure which excludes vibrato at
the point of attack.

It is characteristic of the Zwischenfachsängerin as well
as of the jugendliche and the dramatische that even in moments of dramatic or vocal intensity in the lower range, of
which there are a number in the literature of those Fächer,
chest timbre is assiduously avoided.   Many times these
categories of the German School sound weak and without
penetrating power in low-lying passages; they seem unable
to deliver sufficient sound in dramatic leaps from upper to
lower voice.   This reluctance in the German School to make
use of either chest or of a chest-predominating mixture appears to be yet another manifestation of cultural conditioning.
The dramatic female voice in the German vocal aesthetic
must be noble, warm and ample, but never crude; there
must always be present a romantic concept of femininity, a
womanliness.   (Will the reassessment of feminine roles in
contemporary society influence the romantic concepts of
femininity as they have expressed themselves in the German
opera world?)   The uses of chest voice encountered in the
female voice within the Italian School are anathema to the
typical German pedagogue.

The Italian School

In direct contrast to the German-schooled coloratura,
the Italian coloratura voice is marked by brilliance and vibrancy, at times approaching a tonal color which strikes
many non-Italianate ears as shrill and blatant.   Melismatic
passages, both staccato and legato, are sung vibrantly at
all velocities.   Excessive rapidity of vibrato rate and a
bright edginess often mark the lighter Italian soprano voice.
The top voice is generally produced with an exaggerated
smile position; one grows accustomed to seeing a complete

row of upper teeth. This horizontal buccal posture increases
the upper partials in the sound to the point of painful imbalance in many instances.

   As will be seen shortly with the French coloratura,
the Italian coloratura makes much use of the quality of sound
known as the campanello (bell) timbre. She brings this timbre, excessively high on upper partials, down into upper
voice as far as possible, introducing an additional brightness
into voce di testa quality. Sometimes, on the uppermost
notes the teeth seem almost together, lips pulled laterally.
Though brilliant, the sound seems small and thin, giving the
impression of a chime or sharply-ringing distant bell. It is
the result of the peculiar relationship between the fundamental
and harmonics, set up by combining this particular buccal
posture with upper pitch extremities. Whereas an ethereal
flute quality is sought after by the Nordic coloratura and the
technical means developed by which to produce it, brilliance
is the traditional aim of the Italian coloratura.

   Similar tonal ideals are in evidence with the Italian
soubrette, becoming less prominent the closer her instrument
approaches that of the lyric in vocal weight and size.

   With regard to range, size and registration events,
the least specialized voice of the Italian School as regards
the female categories is the soprano lirico. The Italian
lyric soprano tends to be much less blatant than the coloratura singer, and avoids the typical shrillness of the latter.
She employs a better balance of fundamental and upper partials. When ideally realized, her technique epitomizes for
the female voice the ultimate appoggio concept of proper
breath-application, resonator adjustment, and equalized registration.

   The lirico spinto is required to support soaring lines
while maintaining the beauty of her lyrical tone. Her instrument is a larger version of the soprano lirico. Unlike the
Germanic jugendlich, she does not try for the roundness of
sound which overweights so many Nordic sopranos; as a result her quality is typically much more brilliant than that of
her northern counterpart.

   The soprano drammatico of the Norma or Turandot
type must possess greater stamina and volume than does the
lirico or spinto, but unlike her German neighbor she accen-
tuates brilliance in her singing. She has little interest in the

dark roundness or sumptuous warmth which her German-
trained counterpart finds so appropriate; her errors may well
be on the side of hardness and a driven kind of brilliance.
She, more than any other category of soprano in the Italian
School, plays upon the dramatic possibilities of sudden shifts
in and out of chest, and relies more heavily upon chest mixtures in general.

The French School

The French coloratura follows closely the same timbre
goals held by the Italian. The general avant concept of the
French School is very conducive to coloratura brilliance and
to vocal projection as well. Oftentimes the French coloratura voice is exceedingly white (the so-called voix blanche)
because of this; in producing the desired sound, the singer
experiences exaggerated sensations of resonance in the face
and the sinuses. Nasal resonance is often confused with
nasality. She is perhaps even fonder than the Italian of the
bell voice, and attempts to match much of the head voice
with it. This is accomplished by assiduously practicing to
bring the higher timbre of the flageolet voice down into the
entire range of head voice. (It is worth noting that all
types of sopranos in the French School vocalize rather extensively in the bell register; in the Italian School, generally
only the coloratura singer does so.)

The French soubrette is generally committed to lightness of vocal weight and brightness of tonal color. Physical
involvement in her singing seems lacking, with attention directed toward muscular relaxation and what she believes to
be natural breath production. In many respects, the general
technical tenets regarding voice production in the French
School seem more appropriately to apply to the coloratura
and soubrette categories than to many others.

The typical French lyric resembles the Italian in
most respects but frequently displays that lack of tonal depth
which characterizes much of the singing of the entire French
School. With the lyric, there is often a surface quality about
the sound which is appealing in its ease of production; it appears to lodge directly in the masque, with limited physical
activity in the body. Sweeping phrases which require dynamic
heightening and dramatic intensity often disappoint.

In the French School, spinto and dramatic voices are

less frequently encountered; both of these categories require considerable energy to maintain line and tessitura, and such involvement of the body is simply foreign to the singing aesthetics of the French. When these categories do emerge in France, they generally are the product of imported pedagogy, tending to follow their Latin rather than their Nordic neighbor. If this is not the case, seldom do they possess the physical energy to accomplish the repertory in a totally satisfying way.

The English School

Ideal soprano tone as a concept of the English School presents an interesting study in underlying national cultural factors. Leaving aside the solo singer, for the moment, it is significant to note to what extent adult soprano choral tone in England calls to mind the boy treble voice. The unchanged boy soprano of cathedral and chapel choir with its straight, vibratoless quality, often tends toward the sharp side of the pitch. This "cathedral" tone still predominates in the adult soprano choristers; it is a tendency so readily discernible in both the small vocal ensemble and the large oratorio chorus that one wonders if English ears any longer take note of the pitch vagaries which result.

In addition to this phenomenon of the adult female soprano, the adult male treble voice, joining with the unchanged boy treble in liturgical groups, produces a decided prominence for the soprano line in all British choral singing. This same prominence of the soprano line pertains in most mixed English choruses; tenors and altos are frequently the forgotten people chorally, while basses fare little better. The notion of building sectional balance upon the basses as the foundation, which is true of much American and German choral singing, is not encountered among the English. To many non-British ears, English choral singing is disturbingly top-heavy.

The impact of choral tone on the general vocal aesthetic is greatest in England; even including Germany, where a final choral tradition exists, no other nation can claim the extent and quality of choral activity which takes place in England. The involvement of persons in small vocal groups and in immense oratorio and symphonic choruses is nearly overwhelming in its magnitude. (It is perhaps kindest to pass over choral activities in France in silence, while Italian choral

sound is almost totally typified by a number of ill-matched
solo voices gathered together on Sunday morning to best each
other in all-out vocal combat.)

There can be little doubt that the sound produced by
the English female soprano chorister is determined by certain
vocal aesthetics indigenous to the island. Of direct interest
to this study is the extent to which that same aesthetic is at
work in the English solo soprano voice. This native quality
is often prized by English critics who comment on the purity
and the "chaste," "ethereal" qualities of some soprano voices.
This is especially the case with the solo oratorio singer,
even in a day when the former division in England between
oratorio and operatic artist is diminishing.

The view could well be supported that considerable
influence from this kind of tonal preference drifts over into
the English lyric theater as well. Certainly the typical
English coloratura sound does not bear a close resemblance
to the French or Italian coloratura productions. Rather, the
flute is her model. In this she resembles the German singer
of this Fach, demonstrating the soft, dulcet aspects of coloratura singing as opposed to the brilliant edge which so often
is found in the French and Italian coloratura voices. Once
again, it must be noted that some outstanding exceptions to
the typical approach to the English coloratura sound can be
cited.

The English soubrette, generally in need of more
sauciness of character portrayal than such flute-like tones
can manage, often has a more direct frontal sound than has
the average English coloratura.

English lyric sopranos fall into two distinct categories
related to literature and style. The first of these is made
up of sopranos who seem typically to embrace the boy-treble
quality as the essence of good tone. They are devoted chiefly to early music and the literature of the oratorio. Many
English sopranos seem convinced that when a sacred text is
to be sung, the tone can only be appropriate if it appears
removed from the physical world. Although Handel was a
direct outgrowth of the Neapolitan Opera School as a vocal
composer, and although he made no appreciable differences
in the vocal writing between his operatic and oratorio works,
one continues to hear Handelian oratorio sung in England as
though large numbers of disembodied spirits have convened
for vocalizing. The English lyric soprano sings her oratorio

arias accordingly. Teachers who advocate this approach often speak of the "purity" of vocal tone essential to the proper performance of the music of the Baroque, of the oratorio and of much of the song literature. They find a more vibrant sound to be "operatic." As a result of this conviction, many teachers in England believe that a distinct pedagogical approach must be chosen to train specialized singers in the oratorio and song literature fields. (Some prominent Scottish teachers of singing recognize this sound as uniquely English, naming it "the London sound.")

An interesting aspect of the "pure" English soprano sound is that, in point of fact, it is in its very tonal im- purity that its appeal lies; the "purity" is the result of a large admixture of breath in the tone which serves to vitiate the natural vibrato phenomenon. Because of the minimal activity of the vocal valve in its breath-retention capacity, a lower percentage of the breath which passes over the cords is turned into tone; breath escapes rather freely and the tone thereby becomes straight and "pure" (actually, impure).

This predilection for "purity" which marks the adult female soprano in this portion of the English School, stems directly out of the same aesthetic that produces the English boy-treble timbre.

Although the pure timbre of the boy chorister continues to reign, some English choirmasters are beginning to question its appropriateness to all choral situations. The Continental approach to training the unchanged adolescent male voice is beginning to make some inroads into the traditional English concepts of what constitutes good male treble vocal quality. The Continental approach differs from the typical English boy- treble sound by introducing some chest mixture into the pure head timbre. As can be deduced from earlier discussions in this work regarding laryngeal function, breath application elements must be increased when breath mixture is eliminated, permitting a more efficient cooperation of the intrinsic laryn- geal musculature. The English choirmaster who introduces the Continental sound to his youthful charges, requires from them greater physical involvement in singing. Traditionalists find that he loses "purity" and much of the spiritual quality of the sound, although adding power and a wider range of expressiveness. Several prominent chapel and cathedral choirs are now admittedly committed to the Continental ap- proach to the treble voice as opposed to the traditional British treble ideal. What the final impact on British liturgi-

cal music will be remains to be seen. It is doubtful that
the national tonal aesthetic will undergo any fundamental change
in this regard for many years to come.

Surely the wide-spread use of the male falsettist,
both in liturgical singing and in the burgeoning counter-tenor
literature, is but an extension of the predilection for a specialized sound such as the boy treble provides. Only in the
English School must one give serious consideration to the
male soprano as a frequently encountered performer. It
should be noted that although some teachers associated with
certain Germanic techniques make similar attempts, acceptance of the adult male soprano or alto (the falsettist)
is far less in Germany than in England.

The second category of English lyric soprano, whose
tonal ideals do not mirror the traditional English soprano
timbre, is generally associated with operatic and non-period
vocal literature. At her best, she reminds one of that admirable tonal balance many times found in the Italian soprano
lirico. However, even in this group of English sopranos,
two factors militate against achieving this balance: support
inadequacies and vowel distortion. The tendency of the English lyric soprano, as among English singers in general, is
to hang the jaw to the point of timbre distortion and to the
detriment of diction. In addition, high-chest methods of
breathing, with shoulders often raised for the production of
the top voice in particular, frequently work against the lyrical quality which should be present in this vocal category.
As was earlier mentioned, such techniques are not merely
the result of errors of physical coordination, but are pedagogical aims set forth by numerous English teachers.

The weightier soprano voices in the typical English
School have a remarkable tendency toward noisiness in the
upper range. These disturbing by-noises result from inefficient breath techniques and from the resonantal imbalances
which accompany them. They become more marked in
heavier voices because of the increase in energy and volume
which these categories demand. (The larger the instrument
and the higher the dynamic level which often accompanies a
mounting vocal line, the more audible the presence of breath
mixture.) However, the spinto and the dramatic sopranos
of the English School do not lean toward Germanic techniques
unless trained specifically in its precepts. When not hindered
by the above-mentioned national adaptations to tonal ideals,
these English singers tend to parallel the more dramatic soprano voices of the Italian School.

Chapter XIV

THE MEZZO AND CONTRALTO VOICES

The German School

Among female voices of considerable size and among
those with lower passaggi events there is a clear tendency
in the German School to enrich the sound by altering the
acoustical arrangement of the resonators to an even greater
extent than with other female categories. The widest pharyngeal distention of the entire school often occurs in the mezzo
and the contralto voices.

However, it is noteworthy that German-trained mezzos
who must sing the high-lying roles of standard operatic literature, especially the Italian repertory, cannot in actual practice maintain such postures of the mouth and pharynx as their
nationally-oriented pedagogy would seem to dictate. They must
of necessity modify the Germanic buccal-pharyngeal posture
as they negotiate the higher tessitura of that literature; the
exaggerated vertical buccal posture which pertains in the
performance of much of the literature sung by the German
mezzo must be drastically altered in the upper range to a
more horizontal position. In so doing, the German mezzo
Italianizes her Nordic production to some extent when she
confronts the demands of operatic literature.

Previous references have been made in this work to
the German penchant for relying almost entirely on head
voice to negotiate the lowest extremities of the range. The
disadvantages of such practices are most evident in the lower
female categories. Instead of achieving a unified scale, the
German mezzo and contralto often produce a scale which
sounds sectionalized in its registration aspects by the very
avoidance of chest. The head timbre simply is not adequate
to the demands which the standard repertory makes in vocal
writing for the lower ranges of the female instrument. The

152

bottom seems to fall out of the sound and we are left with
a thin head timbre at exactly that moment when the literature seems to cry out for a more visceral quality. Yet it
is precisely because the German wishes to avoid the appearance of register shifts within the scale that she avoids the
introduction of chest. Obviously, to the Germanic ear the
loss of dramatic impact which such practices achieve is not
aesthetically disturbing.

The French School

Song literature and those operatic roles which concentrate on lightness and brilliance are most adapted to the
typical French-trained mezzo voice. Her most successful
operatic accomplishments are to be found in the mezzo-
coloratura literature of the nineteenth century; in this literature she excels, outdistancing the typical German mezzo and
rivaling her Italian counterpart in vocal facility. On the
other hand, she seldom manages the late nineteenth-century
dramatic mezzo-soprano literature with much ease.

Not infrequently in the French School the term mezzo
is misapplied to a short lyric soprano voice which has not
acquired comfortable negotiation of the full compass of the
upper register in the lyric literature, or to a lyric soprano
voice which cannot maintain the high-lying sostenuto of the
lyric soprano repertory. Timbre differentiation between the
lyric soprano and the mezzo are of less concern in the French
School than elsewhere. If the female voice is short on top,
it is taken to be a mezzo. Such a singer is restricted to
singing those secondary roles often assigned to a utility singer in major houses, because in such roles register extremes
are avoided. On the other hand, it should be stated emphatically that the distinctive light timbre of the typical well-
trained French mezzo is highly pleasurable with its grace
and ease, never clouded nor muddied with attempts to darken
or enrich.

It is difficult to clearly identify attitudes of the French
School toward the contralto voice. Among the French, this
category of singer is not readily differentiated by ear from
the French mezzo, the term being generally applied to a
female voice which can sing low pitches while lacking a well-
developed upper range. The French ear, cultivated by national attitudes toward vocalism, is willing to accept a much
lighter timbre in the lower female vocal categories than does

any other national ear. Let it once again be indicated that notable exceptions exist; such exceptions usually lie outside the general cultural influences, and have been trained by non-French-schooled teachers.

The Italian School

Mezzo-soprano training in the Italian School diligently strives to avoid the thicker sounds of the German. More than in any other school, the Italian mezzo closely resembles the dramatic soprano voice. An Italian-trained Eboli or Azucena thrills with her brilliance and ringing timbre. Her dramatically powerful top voice and exciting focus of sound distinguish her from the kinds of timbre preferences which pertain among mezzos in the other schools. Frequently the Italian dramatic soprano emerges from this vocal category as her instrument matures; she may then continue to sing both dramatic mezzo and overlapping dramatic soprano roles for a period of years. With much less frequency does such a change of vocal category occur among mezzos of other schools.

Among all the schools, the Italian contralto is the sole exemplar of this vocal category who retains both brilliance and depth throughout the vocal range. She has nothing to do with the hollow sounds associated with the typical German and English contraltos, and she avoids that lightness of timbre which characterizes the French contralto. The Italian relies heavily on chest coloration in the lowest ranges of the voice; she does not permit this participation of chest and chest mixture to thicken the entire scale to the detriment of the upper range. As a result of this utilization of chest and chest mixture, and of the skilful transition of those timbres into head, she avoids the hootiness which is often to be heard among the English and the German contraltos and the thinness which distinguishes the French.

As she matures, the Italian contralto may move into the mezzo-soprano category, which offers a far more extensive repertory for her; as a contralto she must be content with character roles in the theater, because much of the Italian operatic literature for the lower female voices is not geared to the duties of the heroine. It is also not uncommon for an Italian mezzo as she ages to undergo a reverse direction in category change--she undertakes the typical character roles which avoid the high-lying passages of much of the

mezzo-soprano literature. As the voice thickens with age
and loses its brilliance, she moves into the contralto buffo
literature, or to the small serious character roles for low
female voice.

The English School

In the vocal categories of mezzo and contralto, the
English vocal aesthetic produces a specialized sound. The
characteristic timbre results from the demand of the ear for
a muted quality of vocal sound, produced by the unique buccal
resonator adjustments of the English School. The sound of
the English-trained mezzo or contralto is very unlike that
of the Italian or French mezzo, nor can it be mistaken for
that of the German. Because this peculiarly English mezzo-
contralto timbre is the result of the sagging British jaw, the
sound might best be described as mandibular. It appears to
issue from the unhinged mandible, avoiding much of the
frontal timbre which characterizes many other mezzo voices.

The English mezzo is generally incapable of negotiating either the mezzo-coloratura or the dramatic mezzo literatures with any degree of skill. Her high torso breathing,
upper-back spreading, and frequent vowel distortion, militate
against the most efficient breath management and resonantal
balance. She is at her best in the slow-moving roles often
written for the oratorio mezzo, or in the song literature
which plays upon the darker emotional hues.

What we have termed the mandibular mezzo sound
is eminently British in its tonal characteristics, but it is not
the only mezzo sound to be heard among English-trained
singers. A quite contrasting tonal ideal is offered occasionally by some singers who perform the dramatic mezzo operatic literature. Among this minority group of singers there
is little or no interest in the somber, remote, sepulchral
quality of sister mezzos, and they rival their Italianate
colleagues in the ability to handle mezzo-coloratura and
dramatic mezzo literature. Technical devices approach those
of the Italianate-oriented singer.

Once again within a category of voice in the English
School one notices that the demands of vocal literature tend
to modify general national timbre preferences.

Chapter XV

THE TENOR VOICE

The French School

     Earlier in this work it was remarked that the French
School tends to ignore many aspects of registration in the
male voice, partly because of the philosophical commitment
on the part of the French singer to the preservation of linguistic subtlety, and partly because of the search for "natur-
alness" of vocal production.

     The inclination to ignore registration events is less
detrimental with the ténor léger than it proves to be with the
lyric or heavier categories of tenor voice. The registration
events of the true ténor léger occur so high in the voice that
the pivotal registration points can easily be stretched to accomplish the range requirements of the literature. In addition, the vocal quality itself is so light that to merge it with
falsetto requires no major adjustment of timbre. Generally,
in the ténor léger there is almost no vowel modification
throughout the scale, the tone retaining a recognizably open
sound from the lowest to the highest pitches. Only the open
Celtic flavor of the light, amateur Irish tenor can rival the
French léger in the aperto timbre of his vocal quality. This
classification of voice, the ténor léger, is the French tenor
par excellence. His is the norm for the tenor sound in
France, whereas the lirico or lirico spinto is what the Italian
has in mind when he thinks of the tenor voice.

     Although there are systems for vocal classification
which are based upon the length of the cords, the degree of
the excitability of the recurrent nerve, the shape of the
sternocleidomastoids and their relationship to laryngeal positioning, or other physiologically observable factors, vocal
classification ultimately does not depend on such phenomena.
It is determined by the kinds of sounds preferred by a cultural

156

milieu which surrounds the singer. By no means is this to say that a singer of one physical construction may choose any vocal category which appeals to him or her. However, it does explain why within near categories one national school will produce more voices of a specific type than will another. One would be hard-pressed indeed to prove that differences in physical structure explain the presence of a higher number of Heldentenöre in Germany than elsewhere, of a larger supply of the tenore lirico spinto in Italy or of the unusual number of the ténor léger in France.

The French ténor lyrique is characterized by a short top voice, the result of the hesitancy on the part of the French School to fully utilize muscular antagonism and sub-glottal pressures during the act of singing much beyond the requirements of speech; body and voice simply do not get together in sufficient degree to accomplish the proper ne-gotiation of upper voice. This physically disengaged tech-nique which may have some virtue for the ténor léger (or at least produces fewer audible dire consequences), proves to be the down-fall of other categories of French tenor. Typically, the upper voice of the French lyric tenor is marred by a tendency to be "wide open" and shrill. With regard to heavier categories of French tenor, it is difficult to generalize because their number is not great; potential tenor voices of any weight in France are generally consid-ered to be lyric baritones and are handled accordingly.

Too apparent to require detailed comment is the ob-servation that the French predilection for a less than fully energized sound and the vocal demands of much of the French song literature complement each other.

The Italian School

Tenorino is a term used pejoratively in the Italian School to designate an instrument too small for serious professional development. Sometimes the term may also refer to a high light tenor voice which is suited to chamber literature with limited vocal demands or to the literature of the popular idiom.

A voice of greater size than the tenorino is to be found in the leggiero. To him often fall such roles as Nemorino, Ottavio, Fenton and Almaviva (although these roles may also be sung by some lyric tenors as well). The tenore leggiero

is distinguished by lightness of vocal timbre and above all
by the manner in which he approaches the upper voice above
the secondo passaggio. Of all the Italian male categories of
operatic suitability, only the leggiero dare sing at times
without taking into account the events of the upper passaggio
which are generally considered essential within the national
vocal aesthetic. Indeed, in his voice this event occurs so
late (frequently at a♭1 or even a bit higher) that his middle
voice is so long that he may not need to concern himself at
all with voce coperta. That is to say, his middle register
concludes on such a high pitch that he scarcely need observe
any of the vowel modification aspects of the secondo passaggio nor the registration events to which modification contributes. A small amount of register violation will bring him
into the highest pitches of the voice without his ever having
entered legitimately into the upper register.

The Italian leggiero is the one male singer of the
Italian School whose head and neck postures may at times
resemble the typical singer of the French School, in some
areas of the voice. Because he wishes to avoid the application of power which so characterizes the typical energized
singer of the Italian School, he minimizes the connection
between body and voice; dropping chest and slightly elevating
chin and head, he thereby avoids the kind of additional sub-
glottal pressures which are required to effect registration
events at the passaggi points. In so doing he produces that
kind of timbre much associated with the French ténor léger.
The Italian vocal aesthetic permits the mild register violation which results in this quality only in the lightest category
of the male voice. However, any opera buff will recall that
following the cavatina section of a typical leggiero aria, with
the commencement of the cabaletta where more dramatic
power is needed, the leggiero's chin is no longer elevated,
the relationship between torso and neck is re-established,
normal male passaggi events are taken into account and
greater energy is introduced into the sound.

This timbre, peculiar to the leggiero, should not be
confused with voce finta, which also results from the elevated
larynx and from the lack of muscular involvement, as was
earlier mentioned. Voce finta suggests a timbre of muted,
introspective nature, whereas the standard leggiero quality
is frequently of a more open, brighter nature. Indeed, the
leggiero may make use of voce finta as well. Unlike his
French or German counterparts, he does not resort to the
use of falsetto.

The Italian tenore lirico is the high-voiced male version of the soprano lirico, so far as tonal ideal is concerned. Lying midway between the leggiero and lirico spinto categories, his passaggi events occurring classically at d^1 and g^1, he combines the qualities of lyricism and vital masculinity so beloved by the Italian opera-goer. His is the Rodolfo voice, the epitome of romantic male vocalism, bringing together into one sound, power, grace and emotion. In the ideal singer there is no tendency to falsify the vocal quality in order to meet the demands of either a stilo grazioso or a stilo drammatico. His chiaroscuro tonal ideal is seldom modified by technical aberrations which plague some other categories of tenor. The tenore lirico is the unspecialized tenor voice of the Italian School and is in some ways its best male example.

The lirico spinto partakes of the best of the traditions of the Italian School the more nearly he remains lirico and the more restraint he exercises regarding the spinto aspects of his production. Increasingly, the current search for the Verdi tenor induces lyric tenors to forsake the balanced proportions described above, and spingere la voce in the hope of producing a more dramatic sound than the natural dimensions of the instrument indicate. An attempt to enlarge the voice in the middle register through a higher degree of chest registration, increased sub-glottal pressure and darkened vowel has contributed to the rapid demise of a number of beautiful Italian lyric tenor voices in recent decades. In spite of the literal meaning of the verb spingere, the lirico spinto is not a "pushed" lyric tenor. The true lirico spinto tone should be as free-flowing and unimpeded at the laryngeal exit as any lirico. Any addition of the heavy mechanism, retention of an excess of chest timbre in the middle register, or an unnatural covering of the upper voice can only be injurious and lead to an early vocal collapse.

It must be acknowledged that a greater degree of energization must be present throughout the lirico spinto instrument in order to maintain the intensity of line and tessitura as well as amplitude, but there is no need for excessive breath pressure at the glottis. The instrument itself, if truly spinto, will provide the necessary timbre without technical falsifications. However, even when the Italian tenor sings troppo drammatico, his errors are not those of the German Held, which will be considered in a moment. The exaggerated spinto quality is produced by a sternum incorrectly elevated to the point of tension, and an increased level of breath compression within the lungs; the upper torso appears to be in a high state of muscular antagonism.

The robusto (tenore drammatico) is the Italian vocal category nearest in size to the German Heldentenor. Because of the great energy required to support amplitude, tessitura and general dramatic impact, the tendency for the performer of this Fach is to darken the voice excessively, substituting brute force for the flexible breath support more generally characteristic of the Italian School. Yet the robusto who can combine lyricism with power produces what to many listeners is the ultimate in satisfying male vocalism.

The German School

As regards timbre and technique, the Spieltenor of the German School exhibits some of the characteristics of the tenore leggiero and the ténor léger, yet he illustrates that cultural differentiation one has come to expect of the German-trained singer. Not infrequently he partakes of a Knödel, the characteristic sound produced by spreading the pharyngeal wall. However, this particular Fach tends to avoid the heavy production aspects of the typical German School. His is a tenor timbre described as ingolato by the Italians and dans la gorge by the French (meaning in the throat, in both cases). Small in dimension, the Spieltenor has greater carrying power than many other categories in the German School because he is less intent on producing the Kopfstimme and the duftige qualities generally demanded of larger voices by that school.

The Tenorbuffo, as his category designates, must concern himself to a large extent with buffoesque characterization. In this lies his chief differentiation from the Spieltenor. In fact, in some instances, the term Spieltenor is but a more palatable Fach description for the singer who is hired to do chiefly buffo roles. In other circumstances, Spieltenor is a term indicating a voice of sufficient timbre to be appropriately cast in roles of more substance, including some of the lyric literature, not unlike the sizeable tenore leggiero. He may be given such assignments as Ottavio, Pedrillo or Shuisky, while the Tenorbuffo might more logically be cast as Monostatos, the Figaro Basilio or Goro.

A distinct category of light tenor, prized as a singer of Bach and of early music, is much in evidence in the Ger-

man School and is exemplary of the pervasiveness of Kopfstimme timbre within the school. Singers of this particular
Fach often practice the conscious introduction of breath into
the sound ("commence the breath and add the tone") so as to
reduce brilliance and focus to a minimum. Straight tone,
nearly devoid of vibrato, is mistaken for purity of sound just
as it is in some soprano categories and in some segments of
the English School. Divested of vitality, the tone seems to
be without kernel or center. The construction of the entire
voice on the breath-mixture principle serves to iron out the
scale with a certain kind of uniformity. Notes above g^1 or
$g^{\#}1$ are produced in gemischtes Falsett (falsetto reinforced
by considerable breath energy). Because of the small size
of the instrument, the singer, without apology, has the ability
to go into and out of falsetto without the discernible shift of
register often present in the larger, well-proportioned male
voice. Within Germany, and among adherents of Germanic
vocal techniques, many minor careers have been built for
singers of this Fach upon these principles.

Not all German pedagogues endorse this category of
singer (who bears some resemblance to the tenorino of the
Italian School with regard to the size of the vocal instrument),
believing him to rely upon the Fistelstimme. Fistelstimme
indicates, to some German teachers, the recognizable Falsettierung of those singers who obviously resort to falsetto
usage in performance. Another group of German pedagogues
uses the term to connote a sound corresponding to the Italian
voce finta as well as to the falsettto timbre. Yet another
group uses Fistelstimme interchangeably with the term Schwin-
delstimme to denote either falsetto or voce finta, disapprov-
ing of them both. These latter teachers stand outside the
mainstream of the national vocal aesthetic. However, Fistelei
or Falsettierung may be put to good purpose by the Tenorbuffo,
as the demands of caricature and jocundity dictate. But
these sounds are not considered by a number of German
teachers as appropriate for any serious music, even Bach
or the liturgical music of the past. Within the operatic literature, the same viewpoint would prevail among this group of
teachers with regard to the Spieltenor Fach; the Spieltenor
will be expected to have sufficient vocal resources so that he
will not have to rely upon either Fistelstimme or Schwindel-
stimme.

The German lyrischer Tenor shares with the jugendlicher Heldentenor (in size comparable to the lirico spinto of
the Italian School) and with the schwerer Heldentenor (com-

parable in weight to the tenore robusto or tenore drammatico
of the Italian School) those tonal ideals which are realized
largely through the low-breath devices and vowel and resonance adjustments common to most singers of the German
School. The more lyrical nature of his repertory makes
some of these typical national tendencies less marked than
they may be in the heavier categories. Depending on the
weight of the individual instrument, the singer may be trained
in the direction of strong reliance upon the Kopfstimme, or
conversely, toward the Verbrustung (heavy reliance upon an
increase of chest mixture) which is so much a part of the
technique of the Helden Fächer.

The quality of chest (the heavy mechanism of the
voice) predominates more completely within the schwerer
Heldentenor than in any other category within the German
School. Indeed, no other vocal category in the entire field
of singing makes such reliance upon the function of the heavy
mechanism. (One can only speculate as to what Wagner
would think of the vocal sounds heard today from the typical
Heldentenöre of the German Theater, especially when one
recalls his comments about the necessity for lyricism in
singing.)

Along with the application of low-breath techniques in
the German School, premature Deckung (cover) occurs in all
German male vocal categories but especially with the dramatic singer. Spread pharynx, lowered larynx, darkened vowel
formation and low-breath management all contribute to the
unique sound which strikes the German ear as one of power
and dramatic impact appropriate to Florestan or Tristan.

With the jugendlicher Held, this combination of national vocal techniques is applied less drastically than with the
schwerer Held but still quite recognizably. As was previously mentioned, tension may plague many lirico spinto tenors
and the more dramatic voices of the Italian School as well
as of the German; it should be noted, however, that whereas
the over-weighted German-trained instrument will frequently
oscillate (wobble) in the upper range, the Italian spinto when
too intense will generally show an increase in vibrato rate,
to the point of a fast tremolo. These unrelated sources of
tension produce dissimilar results and underscore the hypothesis that opposing aesthetics and pedagogical techniques can
be identified among the national schools.

The English School

The most typical specimen of the English-trained tenor voice is recognized by that timbre earlier noted as "pure," but which actually is produced with at least some slight admixture of breath. It is marked by frequent straight-tone usage as an expressive device. Thus even in the professional male tenor voice one finds much of the characteristic cathedral tone so evident among English male chapel choristers. As compared to tenors of the Italian School, this tenorial timbre is dull and opaque. Nor could it be mistaken for the typical French tenor sound, although its flutiness may in some respects call to mind the German oratorio or Bach tenor.

Running concurrently with this very indigenous vocal sound is another English tenor timbre sometimes associated with the lyric theater but quite removed from the cathedral tone. Without doubt, the Italian School here shows its influence, while the German, almost none, and the French, relatively little. Yet even the operatic tenor trained in the English School shows some distinct national tendencies. His upper register is marked by a quality of openness not encountered in either the Italian or German Schools. Although open, his upper register does not resemble the thin, bodiless quality of the French tenor; it is fully energized, ringing and vibrant, often exceedingly dramatic in character, being the product of increased breath pressure at the larynx, along with the typical high posture of the torso, raised shoulders and drawn-in epigastrium. This production shares some of the same tendency toward tremolo which is in evidence with the Italian _spinto_ who over-energizes the sound; however it lacks the Italian's resonance balance, being considerably more strident. This English tenor operatic timbre is frequently accompanied by audible by-noises, a national vocal condition previously noted when English soprano voices of the lyric theater were considered. This big, open quality is to be found in both lyric and dramatic tenor voices of the English School; the element of size simply makes it more obvious with the dramatic tenor.

Of increasing interest in the English School is the position of the "counter-tenor." While occasionally in England a _leggiero_ or _tenorino_ is chosen to perform the counter-tenor literature, most of the singers who are currently termed counter-tenors are patently male falsettists, whether they admit to it or not. Training the counter-tenor in England

164 / The Tenor Voice

is thought to be a highly specialized art, frequently undertaken with a kind of chauvinism seldom encountered in vocal circles outside the training of the lirico spinto in Italy.

A counter-tenor is taught to carry the falsetto downward below the primo passaggio, continuing if possible throughout the range. Not infrequently he has difficulty in avoiding his normal male sound near the low range extremities; when he fails to manage falsetto in his lowest notes, he reveals the entire scale for the registration falsification it actually is. His British audiences often seem to accept this failure to incorporate the lowest notes into the over-all falsetto scale with a kind of philosophical acquiescence.

Such voices may be made out of the material of the normal tenor voice, but more frequently they are produced from the normal baritone instrument. It is sometimes amusing to hear the low speaking voice of the so-called counter-tenor juxtaposed to the cultivated singing voice he employs.

Mastery of the technique of counter-tenoring entails the skilful use of calculated violation of the registration events of the normally-produced male voice. Such control of the instrument is brought about by procedures which avoid laryngeal muscular involvement; structural support of the larynx offered by the extrinsic muscles is reduced through postural modifications. The intrinsic muscles of the larynx which assist in bringing about the legitimate registration of the male voice are not permitted to accomplish their coordinate function. However, through systems of breath reinforcement of the falsetto, the counter-tenor sound may be quite full, especially in the upper range.

When the tenorino sings the counter-tenor literature (which is very rarely the case currently in England), he tends to avoid all register phenomena, negotiating the scale without any perceptible vowel modification, approaching in timbre the pre-pubertal male. He generally lacks the ease of production evinced by the accomplished falsettist, and therefore appeals less to the emerging tastes associated with the literature of the counter-tenor within the past few decades. Although a relatively small group of German pedagogues teaches the counter-tenor voice through the falsetto route, there is little actual support outside of England (and of course New York studios) for this vocal aesthetic which seems so patently to violate normal function.

Chapter XVI

THE BARITONE AND BASS VOICES

Given the scale of structural variations possible within the male larynx, the lyric baritone voice probably occupies
the most central position, qualifying as the normal male
voice. Dramatic baritones, bass-baritones, basses, and
the several categories of tenor result from structures which
are larger or smaller, thinner or thicker than those to be
found in the male mean, the baritone.

Concepts of ideal vocal tone, cultural influences, and
modes of instruction frequently contribute to the decision on
vocal Fach among male voices. As was indicated earlier,
laryngeal structure alone is not the sole determinant. It is
possible to find considerable variation in many areas among
singers within the same Fach. However, specific physical
types commonly indicate particular vocal categories; especially the structure of neck and chest are clues to vocal classification. The vocal prominence (Adam's apple) of a bass is
quite visibly located in a longer, thinner neck than that of
the tenor, whose smaller thyroid cartilage lies hidden in
his thicker, shorter neck; the flatter chest of the bass is in
clear-cut contrast to the thick, often compact torso of the
tenor. (At times obesity modifies the appearance of the
physical structure in the bass and of course there are exceptions as well.) Frequently, the heavier tenor instrument
and the big lyric baritone one are found in persons of similar
physique, both being stockily built. (Some persons contend
that the typical compact build of the Italian male accounts
for the high percentage of spinto voices to be found in Italy;
does it follow that the typical baryton lyrique is the result
of a particular French male physique?) The baritone, depending on how lyric or how dramatic, will tend toward either
the more compact or the more elongated build. The leggiero
and buffo tenor Fächer are frequently of much slighter physical build.

165

To designate the baritone voice as the normal male vocal instrument may seem to overlook historical evidence which indicates that the category itself did not exist until well into modern vocal history. Basses, tenors, eunuchs, and in some literatures falsettists did indeed perform the male vocal music of earlier centuries. However, it is equally plain that much of the literature of the seventeenth and eighteenth centuries for male voice was of medium vocal range, totally appropriate to the kind of voice we today term baritone. (Literature for castrato is, of course, not here under consideration.) Further, it is doubtful that the kind of vocal timbre we term bass was any more prevalent in the eighteenth century than currently; the actual bass voice is not, by comparison with the baritone, a common phenomenon. The term bass as found during the Baroque obviously included the kinds of voices today termed baritone as well as the very low-ranged male instrument. To insist that the baritone voice is a late eighteenth-century creation is to read narrowly the meaning of the term bass as applied to Baroque literature. Indeed, it is still common practice to refer to low-voiced male choristers as basses, although few actually are, and it can easily be documented how often operatic roles marked bass overlap those marked baritone in both range and tessitura.

The vast majority of male speaking voices are marked neither by an excessively low nor a remarkably high pitch level. Those persons who are potential tenors frequently speak on a pitch level about a minor third above the mean, those who might be potential basses about a minor third below. The baritone speaking voice is the normal male voice and consequently the normal male singing instrument.

It has been previously noted that the pivotal pitches of register demarcation help one to determine the vocal category of a singer. It has been argued further in this study that the national pedagogical viewpoints regarding categories produce considerable variation in the actual timbre within those categories. These pedagogies have developed in response to certain tonal ideals, specific cultural emphases, and national preferences in vocal sound.

The French School

The French baryton lyrique is of special interest to

any study dealing with cultural influences on the pedagogical approach to the singing voice. Based upon the extent to which one encounters lyric baritones among French male singers, it would be tempting to say that there are more males who meet the specifications of this <u>Fach</u> in France than in any other country of the Western world. Obviously this phenomenon cannot be related solely to physique, although such an analysis applied to a sizeable sample of French male singers might offer interesting results. It is probably only when viewed within the aesthetic-technical approaches of the French School of singing that such a preponderance of lyric baritones becomes logical.

What are the factors of vocal technique which are responsible for this high percentage of lyric baritones among French singers? Unless the French male voice is clearly <u>léger</u>, the French penchant for <u>laisser faire</u> in singing seldom produces the necessary energy factors for the emergence of tenor voices. Thus, many so-called French baritones are short tenor voices which stop at f#^{1} or g^1, simply because the necessary physical involvement to permit entry into the upper register is not called into play. Conversely, many Italian singers trained as <u>lirico spinto</u> tenors on the southern side of the Alps would have been trained as lyric baritones had they chosen a more northerly birthplace.

In France, a considerable gap exists in categories lying between the <u>ténor léger</u> and the <u>baryton lyrique</u>; there are fewer heavier tenor voices in France than are to be found elsewhere in modern Europe. One suspects, again, that this is not because of physical or structural factors but because the national ear and an accommodating pedagogy so dictate. It is particularly worth noting that the medium-voiced French male is perfectly well-suited to the kind of upper middle tessitura demanded in much of the French song literature. How often evident it is that the songs of Fauré in the original keys are maddeningly uncomfortable for the German or Italian baritone of any considerable size, and ungratefully low for the German and Italian tenor voice.

The registration principles of the French School have been discussed sufficiently in this work to make it clear that the baritone voice as it emerges in the French School often is characterized by an avoidance of registration events as they tend to occur in the well-supported voice elsewhere.

When the <u>basse</u> occurs in the French School, his

production is often marked by a clarity and resonance which stand in direct contrast to the cavernous, barrel sound of the German Bass; further, the French basse is frequently characterized by a far more rapid vibrato rate than is the German seriöser Bass. (See Chapter IX, Vibrato and National Tendencies.)

The cool delight of a French basse, with his light, fresh timbre coupled with the masculinity of the low male range is difficult to exceed in much of the literature. The lyricism of a well-schooled baritone voice of the French School pleases in its subtlety, grace and ease of production. Unfortunately, neither category in the French School can produce the necessary power and dramatic force required in much of the operatic literature for baritone and bass.

The German School

Clearly set apart from the French and the Italian bass, the German must introduce into his timbre the weight, the thickness, the roundness expected of him as a singer operating within the tonal aesthetic prevailing in his national school. Exactly those concepts of pharyngeal enlargement, laryngeal depression, and early Deckung which flourish within the German School work against clarity and focus in his sound. The seriöser Bass (or Stehbass as he is often called because he frequently remains in one place without dramatic movement to deliver his impressive pronouncements) believes that he above all vocal categories must deliver the dark, rich sound so much in demand by the Germanic ear. Ein schwarzer Bass (a black bass) is a much-prized singer among the Germans; his timbre must be "black," the most solemn, the most sepulchral of all vocal colors attainable by the human vocal instrument. The elements of vocal production found within the Germanic aesthetic are able to produce this quality of blackness. As a result, his range is frequently very much limited in the upper voice, becoming a hoot or hollow straight-tone anywhere above his second registration point. His generally slow vibrato rate is often thought to contribute to vocal opulence, warmth and roundness. Flowing legato, ease of production, and lyrical line, so much a part of the French basse, are not among his vocal attributes.

The Spielbass and the Bass-buffo Fächer in the German Theater bear a relationship to each other not unlike that which the Spieltenor has to the Tenor-buffo. The Spielbass

tends to be more of a utility singer than does the Bass-buffo; good secondary roles which require quality voices often
fall to the Spielbass. Unfortunately for the favorable state
of vocalism in the German Theater, the Bass-buffo often delivers his parlando in near straight-tone fashion; he frequently pays more attention to histrionics than to vocal matters.
Both categories, Spiel and Buffo, observe the general technical precepts of the German School which have been examined
in this work.

The operatic literature of the Italian School forms
the central portion of the performance material of any opera
house in the Western world. A few houses in the German
theater more and more frequently perform these works in the
original language, although performances in German continue
to be expected. A common pattern in these houses is for a
German-language cast to alternate performances with an Ital-
ian-language cast; in such cases, vocal comparisons often
prove interesting. However, in all but the few international
houses of the German theater, German translations of the
Italian repertory still dominate. The provincial house remains largely unaffected by the trend toward original language performances.

The German School is not noted for producing baritones who easily sing the soaring, mounting vocal lines of
much of the Italian operatic literature; the technical tenets
of the German School do not permit that kind of vocalism.
Germanic vowel modification and registration techniques cannot easily be applied to the demands of high tessitura and
flowing cantilena.

This very point was admirably brought home to her
fellow German pedagogues by Frau Franziska Martienssen-
Lohmann who, while often clearly associated with many of
the tonal ideals of the German aesthetic, was inevitably directed by her own good ear and amazingly vast knowledge of
the singing instrument in all its categories to modify some
distinctly Germanic practices and to bring them more into
line with Italianate attitudes. Martienssen-Lohmann believed
that the rarity of a well-balanced high voice in the German
baritone was not due to some failure of inherited nature but
to false notions of weight and color, and to a misunderstand-
ing of the principle of Deckung. [1]

Several categories of baritone (Baritonfächer) exist
within the German theater, classification being determined

not by vocal timbre alone but also by theatrical skills and specialization. Der rein lyrische Bariton (the pure lyric baritone) should be able to accomplish the same literature undertaken by his Italian colleague, while the Charakter-bariton, a term somewhat interchangeable with Spielbariton, stands vocally quite near him, specializing in roles which require the skills of the gifted singing-actor. (An appropriate aside ought to be made regarding the high level of the general stage aspects of the German Opera; for a number of reasons, not the least of them being the impact from postwar legitimate theater in Germany, the standards in all phases of opera production have been exceedingly high. In general, German-trained singers of all Fächer are to be envied for their achievement in stage skills.)

The Heldenbariton finds the technical problems of the German-trained baritone augmented in his own production; the excesses of Deckung induce chest timbre in the middle voice, which makes successful negotiation into the upper voice almost impossible without register violations of a serious nature. This is similarly the case with the Zwischenfachsänger, a Fach identified by many German Intendanten and agents for those baritones who stop short of the heavier Wagnerian roles.

Any doubts one might entertain regarding the existence of national tonal preferences certainly must disappear when one juxtaposes the sound of the typical German Bariton with that of his French or Italian colleague.

The Italian School

The same ideals of clarity and vibrancy which prevail in the tenor voice are present in the Italian School in the lower vocal categories as well. The Italian lyric baritone does not see himself in need of darkening his timbre as a means of achieving the enrichment adjustments so dear to the German listener. Indeed, there are frequent moments in Italian operatic duets where the Italian-trained baritono lirico and the tenore spinto join their voices with remarkably similar timbre. Such a baritone quality would be considered entirely too light and bright in the German School. An Italian lyric baritone is expected to vocalize well into the upper voice, frequently with almost as much ease as does the tenor. What striking contrast this to the extremely limited upper range of the average French lyric baritone! While a g^1, or an $a^{\flat 1}$, from the German baritone may stir us through our

recognition of it as a feat difficult of execution, seldom do
we feel that physical joy has played any part in its creation.
Yet such sounds coming from the throat of a baritone trained
in the Italian School combine both lyricism and power in an
ideal resonance balance, being neither too open nor too
closed.

With the baritono drammatico and the basso cantante,
vocal timbre is darker only in so far as the events of the
passaggi occur at lower pitch levels in those categories.
The introduction of heavy chest and chest mixtures into the
zona intermedia are not considered desirable. As with the
French basse, the Italian basso profondo retains the direct,
focused character of tone so notable throughout the school.
The slower, more ponderous vibrato rate of the seriöser
Bass is inimical to both the French and the Italian ear.

The English School

An English baritone does not present us with the clear
indications of cultural preference that are to be found among
French and German singers. It does not therefore necessarily follow that his approach to vocal technique exactly parallels that of the Italian; he considers himself less specialized
than does the tenor or the bass of the English School, and
as a result of that conviction does not attempt to color his
sound. In pursuing that end his vocal production is bound to
approach the directness of the Italian baritone.

Furthermore, much of the standard oratorio repertory
for low male voice is best suited to the bass, less to the
more lyrical baritone voice; the general stylistic tendency of
the English oratorio singer to solemnize and intone does not
encroach upon the normal English baritone technique. However, the non-operatic English baritone, like other categories
in the school, finds it appropriate to color his vocal timbre
with that unmistakable, heavy British pallor when confronted
with any literature written prior to the late nineteenth century.

The English School, it has been pointed out several
times, generally tends to divide itself with regard to technical matters into operatic and non-operatic camps. This
division is clearly represented by the technical dichotomy
within the English bass category. Just as the English operatic baritone more nearly approaches the tonal ideals of the

Italian School, so does the English operatic bass. Yet even
here his timbre appears to be modified by the British desire
for a chaste, less brilliant vocalism. While not as thick as
the German bass, he seldom has the translucence of the
Frenchman or the vital vibrancy of the Italian. It is only
when we compare him to his English oratorio counterpart
that we see how much he has managed to escape from Angli-
cizing his timbre in accordance with the cultural aesthetic.

The bass oratorio specialist in England is outdone only
by the English oratorio contralto in the degree to which he
alters vocal production to correspond to notions of style and
tonal aesthetic. He combines within himself the most extreme tendencies of the English School, producing a sound
in the low male voice which does not find its equal for specialization in any other school. To many listening non-Eng-
lish ears it has the character of a dull hoot; to many English
listeners it is an expressive timbre totally appropriate to the
literature in question. Perhaps it is unseemly for a critic
not imbued with that particular insular aesthetic to judge it
by other vocal standards. However, from the standpoint of
functional efficiency such vocal timbre clearly does not rate
high marks.

Even in this category, it must be noted, now and
again basses are engaged to sing with some major oratorio
group on the basis of a reputation made in the opera house;
this is particularly more common in this age of singer agencies and personal representatives who sell singers by the
same methods as all modern hucksters. Thus, today one can
hear singers who have taken a long step from the opera house
into the oratorio hall. This raises the prospect that the
formerly clear lines of demarcation between operatic and
oratorio styles, as earlier maintained within the British
Isles, may be blurring.

Chapter XVII

THE ROLE OF LANGUAGE
IN NATIONAL PEDAGOGIES

Among teachers of singing, the nature of the several
languages is often assumed to be an indirect but major source
of the differences in tonal ideals which distinguish the four
national schools of singing. Only national temperament,
which is generally thought to shape every field of artistic
endeavor, is cited as being a more significant contributor
to the aesthetics of vocalized sound within the four schools.

Although these two intertwining influences may lie
subtly behind all national propensities in singing, it would be
impossible to irrefutably link each technical variance within
the several pedagogies or specific tonal preferences among
the schools solely to these causes. However, as an observer
of the vocal art crosses back and forth over the geographical
boundaries of Europe, there develops the inescapable conclusion that language and temperament undergird the existing
differences in attitudes toward the techniques of singing
among the four schools.

The systematic, comparative analysis of sounds encountered in the English, French, German and Italian languages comprises a major field of study in which phoneticians
continue to labor diligently. Singers themselves are seldom
concerned with the exacting nature of these linguistic studies,
yet they are expected to accurately negotiate vocal literature
in the four major Western European languages and increasingly in several others as well. That they do so with such
astoundingly good results should not be forgotten when the
singer mentality is subjected to the popular evaluations frequently made by fellow musicians. Most singers will admit
to language preferences in singing, finding it easier to negotiate the singing voice in one or more of them, not necessarily including their own. Inevitably, Italian is the favored
language for singing, among singers of all nationalities.

Two assumptions result from even a cursory glance
into the role of language with regard to the four national
schools of singing. First, although perhaps difficult to document, linguistic idiosyncracies partially dictate and color
aural perceptions which mold aesthetic principles out of which
national concepts of ideal vocal sound emerge. Secondly, certain languages are better adapted than others to the art of
singing because of the kinds of acoustical activity they engend-
er within the vocal tract. Both of these factors, national
tonal aesthetics and the mechanistic functions of language,
conjoin to produce qualities of vocal sound which vary from
school to school.

Italian as a Language for Singing

In even the most superficial of linguistic considerations, the Italian language emerges with certain vocal honors.
From the vantage point of functional directness, Italian sur-
passes English, French and German. It is oftentimes said
that the Italian language is ideal for singing because it is
chiefly a language of vowels; this popular impression is a
testimonial to the favorable condition of the Italian language
for singing, although probably somewhat inaccurate as to the
reason. It might better be affirmed that Italian is an easier
language for singing than any other because it contains fewer
possible vowel formations and because it presents a more
favorable condition with regard to consonants, requiring fewer radical acoustical adjustments of the vocal tract than does
either speech or song in most other European languages. Of
course, the frequency of such adjustments is relatively unim-
portant in speech, but is significant in song.

The Italian language contents itself with seven pure
vowels, the physiological execution of which does not entail
the variety of frequency in resonator adjustments which must
take place in singing in the other three major languages under
consideration. Those seven vowel sounds include (i) as in
prima, (e) as in beve, (ε) as in meglio, (a) as in camera,
(ɔ) as in morte, (o) as in non, and (u) as in uso. Although
in Italian more than one vowel may be incorporated in a
given syllable, the incidence of actual diphthongization is
infrequent in the language.

Equally important, the consonant clusters which are so
much a part of the German and English language sounds, do
not pile up on each other in Italian in difficult combinations.

Moreover, vowel sounds are not imperiled by the kinds of
consonant modification encountered in those two languages.
Consonants probably do not occur with less frequency in
Italian than in the other three languages; they simply exercise less influence on the language's vowels, at least in singing.

Italian as a language for singing is not encumbered
with the subtleties of French phonetic diversity nor with the
phonetic complications of German and English. No matter
whether one takes a broad or a detailed phonetic count of the
number of consonants within the several languages, Italian
will be found to possess a somewhat lower number of consonant clusters.

It is the limited number of vowel forms, the occurrence of few diphthongs, the lack of on-glides and off-glides
(transition sounds, which because of vowel purity in the Italian language are at a minimum) and the direct engagement
of lips, teeth, tongue and palate, which enable the flexible
and rapid production of distinct sound so characteristic of the
Italian language.

These physical phenomena within the Italian language
produce vowel sounds remarkable for purity throughout their
individual durations. Consonants, notable in their acoustical
precision, seem to be concentrated in the forward area of the
mouth regardless of their actual physical origins. Thus it is
not surprising that the tonal ideals of the Italian School stress
clarity, clean cordal approximation on the attack of all vowels,
tone free of breath mixture, and a natural balance of fundamental and upper partials which distinguishes sung vowels.
Clearly, vocal aesthetics relate to mechanical function in the
Italian School.

Having thus concentrated on this manifestly favorable
condition of the Italian language for singing, it may be surprising to learn that the Italian maestro does not accept the
notion popularly held outside the Italian School that his al-
lievo or allieva naturally enjoys an unimpeded speech which
leads him or her directly to functionally free song. This
is a point worth stressing: it is often hypothesized, especially among German and English pedagogues, that the basic pedagogical admonition of the Italian School--"Cantare come si
parla"--simply indicates a natural freedom of the speech
mechanism among Italians and is not really an instruction
which works for the non-Italianate singer as well.

An equally frequent and related argument finds itself in ready agreement that the Italian language is more conducive to singing than are other languages, but therefore concludes that the more complicated acoustical adjustments in the vocal tract necessitated by other languages demand a different basic approach to articulation and to placement. This argument is an illogical one because Italian vocal production is based upon the assumption that the resonating chambers must agree with the laryngeal shape of the vowel; the same principle of agreement between resonator adjustment and laryngeal shape (as opposed to distortion of that agreement through resonator setting) can be present in one vowel posture or in thirty differently constructed vowels. (See Chapter VI, Techniques of Vowel Formation.)

The teacher of singing who, when working on English diction, requests that English be sung as Italian obviously is not requesting an Italian accent in the handling of English consonants but is demanding pure, well-articulated basic vowel sounds. A greater variety of phonetic shapes is entailed in the singing of English (or German or French) than in the singing of Italian, but all can be realized through the same principles of execution.

The disadvantage in most languages is that the singer tends to slur phonemic discrimination because of the general linguistic need for rapid movement in the organs of speech to accommodate the many changes in vowel and consonant structure over short periods of time.

The advantages which it might seem would accrue to the native Italian-speaking singer are actual only if he or she can apply functional directness in matters of articulation no matter what language is being sung. From a technical standpoint, a well-trained singer who knows the languages ought to be able to sing them all equally well (he or she may feel a greater cultural affinity with some than with others, however). Although it may be true that the "naturally" well-produced voice is more commonly encountered in Italy than elsewhere, the same errors of coordination which can be made in thirty-five vowel sounds can unfortunately be managed in seven.

The Italian teacher of singing is as aware of regional, though non-dialectical, differences in schooled Italian as is the American or English counterpart with native-speaking students. Even today, speech habits vary greatly from one

region of Italy to another because of palatal elevation, nasality, freedom of tongue action or its hindrance, etc. In
addition, the degree to which the open or close vowel sounds
are characteristic of a given region in Italy influences the
approach the teacher will need to adopt in training the singing voice.

It is untrue that the Italian vowel sounds all are more
open (lower) than those of other languages and therefore more
vocal (a popular assumption among many teachers in the German School).   Indeed, in some geographical areas of the
Italian peninsula, the more cultivated the spoken Italian the
higher the degree of vowel closure.   Even the German close
(e) sound is not higher than the cultured Italian (e) in some
linguistic circles.   Neapolitans, Ferrarese, Bolognese and
Florentines are apt to use much more of the pronuncia aperta
than will Romans.   The cultivated language of Central Italy,
especially that of Tuscany, Umbria and Lazio, has long been
considered the prime example of properly-pronounced Italian.
But Rome, the political and religious center of Italian life,
has exerted its own influence on that model.   A discussion of
the relationship of these two poles is undertaken in the intro-
ductory chapter entitled "Firenze e Roma" of a book initiated
by Radio Italiana, Prontuario di pronunzia e di ortografia
(1949), authored by Giulio Bertoni and Francesco Ugolini. [1]
Regionalisms continue to exert an influence upon modes of
speech in Italy and to figure prominently in corrective techniques directed toward the perfection of the art of singing.
The visitor to Sicily will be struck by some delightful forms
of linguistic regionalisms which must be dealt with by the
singing teacher if his or her pupil is to master the commonly
accepted precepts of the Italian School.

It simply is not the experience of the Italian maestro
or maestra that the singer has but to open the mouth and
claim the singer's birthright.   Nevertheless, all historical
evidence regarding the development of the art of singing in
Italy can only be understood with reference to the nature of
the Italian language.   That Italian is the language of song
is difficult to refute, largely because of the phonetic reasons
cited above.   Identifiable technical procedures in the Italian
School are notable for the directness of Italian vowel formation and for the rapidity of the consonantal occurrences.
Concepts of cantilena, fioritura and parlando are inextricably
bound up with the continuously flowing sounds of the language
itself.   "Chi pronuncia bene, canta bene" is a firmly-held
dictum of the Italian School.

French as a Language for Singing

The quality and character of the singing tone in the French School is more directly determined by the sounds encountered in the spoken language than in any of the other major schools under consideration. It is true that speech habits directly contribute to techniques of vowel differentiation in the Italian School of singing as well as in the French, but it must be kept in mind that Italian speech is far less involved in subtleties of phonetic variation than is the speech of the French person. Carefully distinguished vowel gradations, nasals, and the important role of inflection and stress-- all must find fulfilment in sung French. French, generally acknowledged as the most "musical" of Western languages, with its expansive palette of vocal colors, makes greater demands that vocalized sound be closely bound to speech than is the case in any other European school of singing.

The French language already "sings" and the French-schooled singer has so much respect for the singing-spoken language that there is an avoidance of the technical means in the sung language which might in any way detract from linguistic concerns. Thus the full scope of the singing instrument with its attention to the flow of tone, to the application of power and to the sensuous sweeping line, is always kept somewhat in check by the demands of language. As was previously mentioned, the degree of energization so essential to the production of the well-balanced sung tone is at times less than optimum in the French School; this condition pertains largely out of concern for linguistic subtlety.

Pierre Bernac, eminent authority on the proper interpretation of the French mélodie, clearly stands in opposition to the common notion (by no means restricted to French-trained teachers) that French song literature cannot be "sung"; he would demand that the same attention be directed toward vocalism and musical factors when performing the French literature as the singer would direct toward the literatures of other languages:

> I have already insisted, and I would like to emphasize this again, that to consider the vocal line as 'quasi parlando' in style is to show a completely faulty conception of the French mélodie. Nothing could be further from the truth. To obtain the necessary beauty of sound, it is above all essential for the vocal line to be phrased with extreme smooth-

ness--sustained--'sung' in the fullest sense of the
word.   Naturally, the interpretation of the poem
is important!   But the first consideration should
be given to the music, as in any vocal work in any
language.   The vocal line must not be sacrificed
to the declamation of the poem, any more in
Fauré than in Schumann, in Wolf than in Poulenc. [2]

However, in spite of Bernac's admonition, the great
respect for language has shaped both the national literature
and the pedagogy of the French School.   Indeed, taking a
historical perspective, it cannot be gainsaid that early vocal
music in France, both in Languedoc-Provence and the Northern regions, was most probably more exactingly determined
by the evolution of poetic forms than was the case in either
Italy, England, or even Germany (where poetic influences
also exercised considerable influence upon vocal forms).

Truly an interesting historical case could be built,
beginning with the period of the troubadours and trouvères
and continuing through Fauré, Debussy and Poulenc, postu-
lating the constancy of linguistic restraint upon the singing
voice, out of respect for the spoken word which already
sings.   (It makes little difference that langue d'oc and langue
d'oïl did not share identical developmental influences; both
observed linguistic restraints upon musical forms as dictated
by poetic concerns.)   Martin Cooper indicates this historical
tendency toward the restraints of language within the French
song literature when dealing critically with Debussy's songs:

A beautiful voice is not the first requirement of a
singer of Debussy's songs; but good diction and
poetic sensibility are indispensable. [3]

Later he adds:

Debussy may in theory have admitted the presence
of 'melody' in the song, but his instinct for the
nature of the French language and the character of
his musical inspiration prevented him from exploit-
ing anything but a minute fraction of the potentialities of the human voice. [4]

In the interest of critical balance it ought to be remarked that the examination of a number of songs by Debussy
would seem to suggest that Cooper may somewhat overstate
his case with regard to Debussy's limited exploitation of the

potentialities of the human voice; one thinks of "C'est l'extase langoureuse" and other items in the "Ariettes oubliées," and of the songs of the almost orchestrally conceived "Proses lyriques" with their demanding vocal lines. Nevertheless, when the entire song literature from Debussy's hand is taken into account, Cooper's point remains valid.

Even the development of nineteenth-century French grand opera (and it should be remembered that during much of the nineteenth-century Paris was the operatic capital of the world, already so acknowledged by Beethoven and his contemporaries), with its expanding gamut of vocal demands, can logically be regarded as more imitative than indigenous, a foreign interlude in the French School of vocal writing.

Vocal pedagogical tendencies reflect the centrality of the spoken language in the French School of singing; textual communication has the highest priority. French pedagogical orientation can be understood only when viewed as part of a total cultural attitude among the French toward the merit of the spoken language. The character of the vocal literature of the French School serves to underscore both literary and linguistic heritages.

What of the actual sounds of the French language and the kinds of problems they present to the native French-speaking singer and to the non-French singer? What role do they play with regard to specific vocal techniques of the French School of singing? A detailed analysis of the phonetic possibilities of the French language requires the hand of the skilled phonetician. Restricting oneself even to a broad transcription of the language (making use of the minimal number of phonetic symbols necessary for a relatively accurate presentation of the sounds of the French language), we discover something of its complexity, with thirty-one vowel symbols (including those which indicate duration and nasality), nine diphthong and twenty-nine consonant symbols.

Tongue, lips, velum, jaw, cheeks and buccal resonator, accustomed to such mobility as that demanded by the complexities of the French language, can hardly be expected to forget such habits when confronting a sung text. Whereas an Italian speech mechanism (and the ear which controls it) concerns itself with seven vowel sounds, a French speech mechanism concerns itself with many more. Of course it could be argued that such a statement exalts many minor speech variations to a greater degree of importance than they actually possess. However, when one compares the kinds of activities undertaken within the vocal tract in the two languages and thinks of the elongation process which occurs in singing, it becomes obvious that the sung French language makes demands of acoustical adjustment far beyond those of the sung Italian language.

On the other part, the lower degree of consonant clustering may well set French favorably apart from German, and to some extent from English. In addition, the voiced sounds of the French mute (ə) vowel in singing and the avoidance of the back r (ʁ) somewhat contribute to an Italianization of the sung French language. These compensations of course do not essentially modify the linguistic characteristics of the French language.

Of interest to a consideration of the role of language in singing is the number of pedagogical sources which bracket the Italian and the French Schools under a heading of "Latin Schools" as opposed to the "Nordic Schools," meaning the German, chiefly. This oft-cited amalgamation of the French with the Italian School is more assumed than actual, based upon a popular view of the common Latin language heritage. However, such a shared linguistic heritage may indeed explain why some segments of the French School have more correlation with the Italian School than with any other. Perhaps this common linguistic root may also invite a glossing-over of the considerable disparity between the two schools.

It could successfully be argued that a French School of singing can be identified less obviously than can either an Italian or German (perhaps even less than an English). This is most probably because technical matters which grow out of concern for vocal sound are not of major consideration in the French School.

"How can I intelligently and persuasively present the text?" is a more viable concern for the typical French-trained singer than "How can I best present beautiful vocal tone?" The French singer, in general, is more interested in the beauty of the language and the way in which it can be shaped to phrase-structure than in the abstract beauty of the vocal sound. The language already sings!

German as a Language for Singing

When it comes to singability, German is generally

given low marks even by native singers. To a large extent, this reputation is actually quite undeserved. The bad reputation of the German language as a vehicle for singing rests largely upon a few sounds which strike the non-Germanic ear in particular as unnecessarily complicated in their formation: the ich-laut (ç), the ach-laut (x), the glottal plosive (ʔ) and the (ʃ) ["sh"], particularly as the latter occurs in combination with other consonants.

The high occurrence of cumulative consonant clusters further complicates the flow of vocal tone (as for example, ein Lichtstrahl, zum Streite, Ach! flüstern, Ich steche dich, Er lacht und schnaubt Wut!) when unskilfully handled by the singer. For many singers vocalization is vowelization; non-pitch consonants such as fricatives and plosives are viewed as impediments to the sung tone. A major goal of the singer is to establish a continual flow of vocal sound, seemingly unbroken by those consonantal noises which delineate syllable and word.

For all its bad reputation, the German language stands falsely accused of being a language of consonants. Vowelization forms as much a part of vocalization in the German language as it does in any other. However, special care must be taken to successfully handle those sounds so characteristic of the German language; many consonants in the German language, particularly as they accumulate in clusters, seem to be far removed from the forward position of the quickly formed and executed Italian consonants. This stems more from the duration factor than from actual phonetic formation; indeed, with the exception of very few consonants, most German language sounds can be sung with just as forward articulation as can the sounds of the Italian language.

The un-umlauted vowels in German must be sung with the same degree of clarity as when those same phonetic shapes are sung in Italian; to thicken these basic vowel sounds in singing German so that they emerge as Mischlaute is to distort the quality of both vocal tone and the German language. Good spoken German similarly avoids such Mischung, which is to be found among much dialectical speech. The presence of the Umlaut does bring an added dimension to the singer's vowel spectrum, providing possibilities for increased acoustical involvement. The (ö) as in öde, (oe) as in können, (y) as in Tür, and (Y) as in Schlüssel require certain audible resonance adjustments of the vocal tract, while the diphthongs (ɑo) as in Haus, (ae) as in Ei, and (ɔɸ) as in Leute must be given careful attention. (For the sake of clarity it must be noted that although a number of standard German dictionaries prefer (au) to represent the vowel sound in Haus, (ai) for the word Ei, and (oY) as the proper representation of the vowel sounds in Leute, and although a number of teachers and coaches of singers still advocate those phonetic spelling, current spoken language usage indicates (ao), (ae) and (ɔɸ) as the representation of those sounds. Increasingly, teachers and coaches of singers advocate these newer phonetic sounds when singing German as well as in speaking German.) Siebs deutsche Aussprache is the most essential source for a consideration of Bühnenaussprache (pronunciation of the theater) and for the new trends within the constantly evolving German language. 5

The vocal organs must assume a variety of postures in order to achieve the articulation of the large number of Vokalphoneme which are present in the German language; thirty-eight phonetic symbols are generally recognized for possible vowel sounds within the German language (several of these symbols being used to indicate foreign words taken over into the language), with thirty-nine possible consonant symbols (including several which indicate alternate possibilities). That some of these distinctive vowel shapes figure importantly in German singing techniques we have already noted in the chapter dealing with vowel formation. Who would doubt that the concept of a good singing tone within the German School and the nature of the German language itself are complementary factors which contribute heavily to distinctive techniques of singing in the German School?

Another segment of the German School, following a tradition different from the more common one, does not permit linguistic encumbrances to dictate tonal aesthetics in singing. For this second group of pedagogues, Vornesingen is just as possible and as desirable as it is held to be in the Italian School. Much technical work is directed toward minimizing the problems of singing in the German language through the most direct acoustical adjustments possible; the approach of the Italian School toward vowel formation and resonance balance is transplanted to German soil.

English as a Language for Singing

Occasionally some teachers of singing in the English

School claim that English is a more expressive language for
singing than Italian because it possesses twice as many vowel
possibilities and is therefore more capable of vocal coloration.   (Logically then, German and French would surpass
them both.) Certainly the fifteen or sixteen vowel sounds
(the number is expanded by some phoneticians depending on
whether a broad or an exact kind of measurement in used)
which are discernible in the English language, help determine
vocal coloration within the sung language.   Perhaps a more
pertinent factor lies with the presence of nine diphthongs
and the several triphthong combinations; these phonetic possibilities are further enriched by some twenty-five consonant
formations.

The English language in both its British and its North
American branches offers a series of problems in vocalized
sound which are not present in the other three major Western European languages here considered.   In some ways the
two strands of the common language offer separate challenges
and cannot be lumped together without blurring those problems; in other respects they share a similar condition.   Numerous comparisons of specific idiosyncracies could readily be assembled dealing with British and American speech
habits, but only a few generalities can be treated here.

Both British and American English are seriously
plagued by the tendency to alter any vowel sound as soon as
it has been born; tongue, palate and lips shift from one position to another without any distinct arrival or termination
points.   In any language, speech is a continuous, mobile
process, but among the Western European languages, English
is particularly so inclined.

It is true that the British singer may escape some of
the impediments to good vowel formation with which the
American singer has to contend, but the course of the English singer is not without its own built-in hurdles.   In spite
of television and radio, regional speech is by no means a
disappearing phenomenon in the British Isles, nor, hopefully
will it soon depart.   R. K. Webb discusses the interplay of
various determinants which underlie the diversity of English
life, citing as perhaps most striking, "the extraordinary
richness of dialects and accents which come so close to de-
feating foreigners who unwarily assume that the English they
hear from the B. B. C. or learn in schools is, as it is called,
standard. "[6] In many cases, a British teacher must give as
much attention to the elimination of regional speech habits in
singing as must the American.

Except in certain dialectical speech, the British singer does not have to guard against the retroflex action of the
tongue, the mid-Western (r), indicated phonetically as (ɜ),
and is seldom afflicted with the excessively low palatal posture which so often marks American speech, producing the
nasal twang. While free of these two major hindrances to
good vocalization, the typical English singer has his or her
own set of speech habits which are highly disruptive of good
singing quality.

One such habit is the tendency to manage the diphthongization of every vowel with a degree of accomplishment
not to be matched even by American-Appalachian speech;
"Oh, I do hope you enjoy your holiday!" on most British
lips today becomes a florid exercise in diphthong and triphthong practices. A second notable inclination is to treat
both the vowels (a) and (ɔ) as though they were the vowel
(o). (If Joan Hokins [o - o] is paged at Heathrow Airport,
you should by all means respond if your name is John (a)
Hawkins (ɔ)!)

Furthermore, the character of the spoken English
(o), at least in its current state of execution, is certainly
one of the most involved language sounds ever devised by
the ear of man. George Baker, a well-known figure in
British musical life, commenting on the British (o), once
observed, "It is impossible to give a phonetic illustration
of the pinched sound adopted by professedly cultured people."[7]
The degree of vowel distortion, that is to say, the extent to
which transition sounds occur during the emission of a vowel,
is probably at least as prevalent in British as in North American English.

It is fair to say that the English voice student tends
to devote much less attention to the phonetic realization of
sung texts than does the North American singer; the latter
is convinced that standard stage-English must be consciously
learned, while the British singer very often makes the false
assumption that he or she already speaks the King's English.
The American student of singing strives to eliminate regional
excesses from sung English with almost the same degree of
care he or she devotes to the singing of foreign language
sounds. It is interesting to note that English diction is part
of the standard curriculum in most American conservatories
and schools of music. An excellent rule for determining the
proper handling of sung English diction might well be the
following: if the nationality of either the British or the

North American singer is recognizable on the basis of sung English diction, neither is handling it properly.

Although a comparative study of American and British speech characteristics reveals many fascinating differences, such differences do not directly pertain to this particular study and must go unmentioned. Differences between the two strands of a common language are entertaining to recount, but all too often these small matters cloud the fact that in singing no disparity between the languages should be discernible. A most significant fact emerges so far as national tendencies in singing are concerned: language alone cannot explain the existence of differing tonal ideals in singing.

Historical events established English as the major language of North America as well as of Great Britain, and in spite of a number of dissimilar practices, the English language on both sides of the Atlantic is one language. However, there exists a distinct English School of vocalized sound based upon certain identifiable aesthetic principles. Were these tenets related to language only, one could expect to find similar tonal ideals predominating among singers in North America; they in fact do not. (The relationship of the North American singer to the four major European schools of singing is given some consideration in the concluding chapter of this work.)

Some English teachers, not unlike many German pedagogues, assume that their native language is ill-adapted to singing and that special technical means must be devised as a corrective. Such reasoning explains, for example, the belief that the jaw must drop lower with the English singer than is necessary for the "Latin" singer.

Prior to concluding this consideration of linguistic attitudes about English as a singing language, it should be noted that some atypical English teachers attempt to apply the same general acoustic principles to singing in English as in Italian, avoiding compensatory adjustments for the linguistic complexities of the English language; this group of teachers clearly espouses an Italian-oriented pedogogical attitude.

Singing Foreign Languages

The habitual activities involving the speech organs

prove significant not only in the singing of one's own language, they also influence the way one sings foreign languages as well. Obviously, a singer cannot use one vocal technique while singing English or German and yet another when singing Italian and French. The articulatory events, as seen from a functional viewpoint, cannot be built upon a shifting technical basis; a physiological basis for singing results from routining and from conditioning. Lifelong language habits will determine some of the problems a singer encounters in any language, native or foreign; no matter what language is being performed, the sounds must lend themselves to an exact phonetic transcription.

In the singing of any language, if the vowels are exact in their formation (not being victimized by transitional sounds) and if consonants are allowed to occur within the vocal line without influencing neighboring vowels, it will not matter whether vowels and consonants are few or many. The manner of their exact execution will vary from language to language, but their presence need not so complicate a given language that it becomes unfavorable for singing. Only by carrying over into song the retention of speech habits that include on-glides, off-glides, nasality and gutteral production does the singer allow one language to be less singable than another.

Concepts of the ideal tone and actual physical function are closely allied in the Italian School of singing. This principle of functional directness is equally applicable in singing languages of greater phonetic complexity than Italian. When the same principle of functional directness is applied to singing other languages, the tonal aesthetic then closely resembles that of the Italian School.

No teacher of singing is likely to request that any language be sung "like English," "like German" or "like French"; frequently teachers of singing request that non-Italian languages be sung "like Italian." It is significant that within each of the non-Italian schools there is to be found a sizeable group of teachers who strive for an Italianate approach to vowel differentiation, although dealing with other language sounds. It is universally acknowledged that the sung Italian vowels serve as models of phonetic clarity for all other schools.

The sounds of language and the vocal techniques for accomplishing them with the greatest degree of efficiency meet most compatibly in the Italian School of singing.

Chapter XVIII

NATIONAL TEMPERAMENT AND VOCAL IDEALS

In approaching the subject of national temperament one
enters the realm of dangerously subjective evaluations, un-
verifiable impressions, poetic-mystical concepts, and a kind
of popular folk wisdom.   Teachers of singing in all four major schools uniformly attribute many national tendencies in
singing to language and national temperment factors.   Linguistic influences can more readily be established than can
those more nebulous tendencies thought to evolve from national temperaments.

National temperament is often revealed through the perceptions of the outsider; the Northerner frequently idealizes
the uninhibited nature of the Latin singer, citing physical
strength and athleticism as attributes of the Southerner.
These temperamental factors are sometimes presented as explanation for variances in vocal techniques which work south
of the Alps but not north of them.

With reference to the Italian School a number of sources could be cited from the pedagogical literature of the
north to prove that the sun, the sea, the wine, the church,
physique and the romance of it all, produce gondoliers and
stevedores who skilfully break forth periodically without for-
mal training into the most difficult operatic repertory.   The
implication of the northern critic is clear: the technique
of the Italian School is sub-intellectual, acquired through
heredity and physical environment by a kind of cultural osmosis; northern minds and bodies must arrive at technical
skills in singing by more strenuously intellectualized systems.

In comparing the temperaments of the southern and
northern European singer, H. Egenolf enunciates a familiar
theme:

188

In Germany we find such faultless voices only seldom, but in Italy in large numbers. Let us draw
a comparison between the tenor of a German choral
society and the unrestricted singing beggar from
the gutters of Naples! There we hear the difference exactly. We suppose--and this is still to be
heard--that these Italian throats have even a different structure from a German throat. The throat
is the same, but the vocal function is an entirely
different one. Why? Well, the Italian is more
relaxed, inwardly looser than we are. We live,
who would want to deny, in a permanently cramped
condition, which hinders a free vocal development
and free vocalism. [1]

Additional comment indicates that the Germanic and Italianate
temperaments produce varying physical responses in singing.
"In comparison, the bodily flexibility, for example, of the
Italian singer is completely adequate to the agility of his
vocalism. "[2]

On the other hand, the Mediterranean singer tends to
view the northern colleague as an uncoordinated analytical
giant of profound intellectual abilities; the literature of the
Lied inspires the southern singer with awe. The Southerner
tends to view his or her vocalism as intuitive, that of the
Northerner as something acquired. Even the Italian pedagogue
appears somewhat defensive that most of the literature on the
technique of singing (in this century) has not been produced
by Italians but by Nordic authors.

The collector of publications dealing with vocal pedagogy strikes a gold mine in bookstores throughout Germany
and England; the same search provides meager reward in
Italy except for collections of practical esercizi, and very
little in France. A bookseller in Naples volunteered a
chauvinistic explanation: "The Germans who don't know how
to sing write books for each other on how they think it happens; in Italy, we all know what good singing is and no one
wants to write or read about it. "

Although the Neapolitan shopkeeper may not convince
with his explanation, it may well be that the uniformity of
vocal ideals in Italy has indeed obviated technical apologies
in the form of vocal treatises. Opposing notions of vocal
production do not abound in Italy as they tend to do in England and Germany. The Italian student of singing may look

for a teacher who can clearly articulate the generally accepted technique, but a change of teachers seldom involves
a change of the basic techniques of singing.

When pressed as to technical allegiance, the French
singing teacher believes the national French School of singing
is identifiable because of its adherence to natural production;
nevertheless, this position is often seen as lying somewhere
between Italian and German pedagogies. Some French teachers like to think that the French School emulates the techniques of the Italian School and the musicianship of the German. Thus far, interest in scientific investigation into the
physical processes of singing has made no appreciable impact on practical pedagogy in France (in spite of Raoul Husson and his associates).

In Germany, and probably to a lesser extent in England, scientific studies dealing with vocal production tend to
have a direct impact on studio teaching. These studies are
interpreted in a number of ways and contribute directly to
the diversity of vocal methods in those countries.

A non-European observer, somewhat removed from the
ancient assumptions and local prejudices which tend to lie
on opposite sides of river valleys and mountain ranges, finds
little substantial evidence to support many of the more spectacular popular notions about the differences in national temperament as they relate to singing. But an objective observer may very well see cultural and vocal traditions which
stem from racial sources.

Indeed, racial history (in a loose sense of that term)
underlies all national culture. Any practicing artist is en-
circled by a psychological web of nationalism; his vocalism
has been formed by the sounds which surround him. (Additional consideration of this topic will be undertaken in
Chapter XIX, International Tonal Ideals.) While it would
be non-productive to speculate as to the nature of the Latin,
Gallic, Germanic or British "spirit" in general, perhaps
because of the immediacy of that unique emotive power which
resides in the human voice, the essence of national temperament may be most manifest in singing. Certainly, tonal
concepts indicate temperamental proclivities as emphatically
as do the fields of literature, architecture and painting.

The nature of the vocal literature associated with
each of the schools is instructive on the topic of national

temperament. A nation whose output reaches from the early development of opera through the verismo school, culminating in Puccini must possess a kind of emotive quality different from that which could produce the subtle, intimate vocal literature represented by Schubert, Schumann, Brahms, Wolf and Strauss. The literary orientation of the vocal literature of these schools reflects their respective cultural heritages.

English vocal music and French vocal literature, with geographically nothing but a channel of water between, are temperamentally worlds apart, as are the two cultures in general. Can one, for example, imagine the vocal music of Ralph Vaughan Williams, Gerald Finzi or Benjamin Britten emerging from a Parisian school of composers? (Or, for that matter, could a Fauré or a Mascagni have come out of Berlin or Manchester?) Vocal literature and the singing techniques to perform it are shaped by those same subtle influences of national culture which have produced all art.

Certainly the choral traditions which exist in England and Germany, each with its own distinctive tonal quality, have evolved in response to cultural demands of church and state which are decisively different from those in Italy and France. To listen to choirs at San Marco and Westminster Abbey within a brief period of time is to experience shock at the juxtaposition of two entirely different spheres of choral sound. Such vocalism does not exist in a vacuum; it proceeds out of an underlying aesthetic which can be explained only on the basis of national culture.

Although the Italian may not be the Naturmensch northern colleagues assume, giving audible and visible vent to emotions continues to be a daily happening not likely to produce inhibited vocal sound unless non-cultural pathological reasons are present. A quick, energetic physical metabolism is discernible in the vitalized, direct vocalism which the Italian tends to produce. It is this national trait which leads some commentators north of the Alps to assume that the physical structure of the Italian vocal instrument produces certain advantages for singing. Italian-schooled singing is often uncouth, lacking in subtlety and dynamic variation, but it will seldom suffer from a lack of visceral involvement or from a lack of externalized emotion.

The dynamic sound of the finest Italian singing results from high efficiency of physical coordination coupled to freedom of emotional expression. It is this temperamental factor which permits the Italian to bring the natural physical vitality of the body into the act of singing. Among Italians, singers and non-singers, émotion is outwardly projected; the result among Italian singers tends to be that joyous lyricism which prevails in the best of the Italian School.

Italian voice lessons can be exciting occasions. A relationship often exists between teacher and pupil with something of the athletic event about it; it is a field for personal interaction. An Italian maestro may shake his fist at the pupil while shouting, "Ma perché canti così?" (Why do you sing like that?), when the tone is not to his liking. Can one really picture that happening in London or Hamburg? Or Paris?

The German, in spite of interest in technical matters, in matters musical remains the mystic, the philosopher, the incurable romantic. He or she uses the voice to express something of this inner life and in so doing searches instinctively for ways to enrich and color vocal sounds. Paradoxically, in the desire to communicate intimate experience, the singer may often internalize the sound rather than give it outward projection. The tendency is to analyze why and how one does what one does; Germanic methods incorporate both this technical curiosity and the urge toward romantic communication. German books on vocal technique generally begin with philosophical speculation as to the nature of man, proceed to diagramatic studies of the breath mechanism and the vocal apparatus, and conclude with highly technical explanations on how to produce a wide spectrum of vocal sounds.

The French person, with typical commitment to proper proportion and balanced perspective on matters aesthetic as well as practical, presents a somewhat mannered vocalism, encumbered neither by body nor emotion, which will not compete with the finesse required by an already musical language. In the French School, caution generally dictates that the physical aspects of singing not become accentuated; vocal sound per se never usurps the place of the word. Moderation and the control of lyrical elements must always be maintained. Once again Pierre Bernac may be called upon to present this marvelous doctrine of moderation prevailing within the French School:

> To sum up: in the French mélodie the singer and
> the pianist must succeed in combining precision

with lyricism. But it must be controlled lyricism,
for just as the French composer never gives way
to sentimentality or emphasis and abominates over-
statement, so in the same way his interpreters
must have a sense of moderation of expression, a
critical capacity, which after all is no more than
one of the most vigorous forms of intelligence.

There can be no doubt that it is easier for performers to give themselves up to the sentimental
outpourings of German music and poetry than to
re-create the subtle poetic climate, the intellectual
refinement and the controlled profundity of French
music and Poetry. [3]

The kind of vocal intensity and obvious emotional ex-
ternalization that the French person's southern neighbor finds
totally appropriate (and which incidentally also can be highly
mannered) is offensive to the Gallic spirit in general. A
French man or woman, in matters of the heart, finds it difficult to seriously sing the kind of "Gran Dio, pietà di me"
sort of sentiment which the Italian delivers with such visceral
relish. In general, the urbanity of the French-trained singer
simply does not permit that kind of naked sentiment to be
present in his or her vocal quality. Nor does the French
singer care to reveal in song the introspective interior aspects of the personal psyche, so much admired across the
Rhine. Bernac well expresses this intellectual objectivity
in his critical comparison of the stylistic aspects of the Lied
and the chanson:

A French mélodie is a musico-literary work in
which the heart plays its part, but which, in its
poem and its music, is an art infinitely more concerned with sensitive perceptions and impressions,
more intellectual and more objective, than a German Lied, which is almost always subjective, both
musically and poetically. [4]

Journeying across the Channel, we encounter yet
another attitude toward direct emotional involvement in the
art of singing. With the English singer, emotional displays
in singing remain anathema; he or she is chiefly concerned
with skill, with the craft of singing. Good management should
apply in singing as it does in any other activity. One ought
to be able to sing high and low, loud and soft, fast and slow,
with a high degree of efficiency made possible by the per-

fection of a craft. The English singer directs less conscious attention to the realization of the emotional content of vocal literature than does any other typical singer emerging from a national cultural environment. The public revelation of an interior, private world would appear to the English singer as an unnecessary bit of personal exhibitionism. Voice recitals in England tend to be exercises in propriety. (In Italy we may be embarrassed by the display of personal sentiment.) For the English singer, beauty of vocal sound is best represented by musical and technical control.

Such generalities regarding national traits of temperament no doubt suffer the error of all generalities. Yet there are compelling reasons for associating varying national attitudes toward vocalism with overall cultural attitudes. Throughout this study those differences have been examined as they express themselves in technical, pedagogical ideas about singing; vocal techniques are but the means for achieving certain sounds which most please a particular cultural unit. Specific kinds of vocal literature and specific kinds of vocal sounds have evolved which directly correspond to national temperaments.

Above all, the Italian singer wants to make beautiful visceral sound which will excite and thrill both the ear and the heart; the French singer wants to present the inherent beauty of the spoken word in sung tone; the German singer wishes to express his or her inner emotions and sentiments to a listening world through poetic insight and the use of illustrative vocal colors; the English singer wishes to perfect the vocal craft itself so that he or she can deal as effectively with musical demands of the literature as can any other instrumentalist.

Chapter XIX

INTERNATIONAL TONAL IDEALS

We live in a day when national idiosyncracies in the arts tend increasingly to become blurred by the technological condensing of distances.   While it is certain that the nations of the Western world are currently swept along by a some- what uniform cultural drift, partly effected by the age of satellite communication, regional elements in the arts con- tinue to persevere.

Much of what contributes to the personal vision of any performing artist stems directly from the local, regional and national influences which mold him or her.   Those personal experiences must be drawn upon when artistic communication seeks realization.

The advent of broadcast, televised and recorded per- formances, often centering around a relatively small band of international artists who fly from place to place to perform and record, has smoothed away some of the distinct national edges of singing styles.   Although it would be difficult to offer more than conjecture, it may be that a greater degree of internationalism prevails among well-known singing artists today than at any time since the widespread dominance of the Italian School in the later decades of the eighteenth century.

However, it should be noted that even a member of this international coterie has been surrounded by the immedi- ate influences of place just as assuredly as has been the poet, the novelist, the painter or sculptor.   In fact, seldom does the singing artist leave us in doubt as to which vocal tradition has been followed.   He or she did not emerge ar- tistically full-blown upon the international scene.   The artistic training-ground has been experienced within a specific region, surrounded by other singers and by audiences steeped in a particular vocal tradition.   Although the internationally rec- ognized artist may have shed many excesses of a particular national tradition, yet by the very eminence which that artist

has attained, some of the tonal traditions of his or her school
will be perpetuated.

A false picture of internationalism in singing would be
painted if it were contended that international singing artists
all tend to sing by identical techniques or that they share
the same tonal ideals. In metropolitan vocal centers (London, New York, Vienna, Tokyo, Hamburg, Paris, Milan) a
catholicity of taste prevails among public and critics. The
sophisticated listener learns to accept many varieties of vocal
sound, judging them with a shifting set of criteria.

This situation is especially the case in a city such as
London where the variety of vocal productions even within the
same public performance must be obvious to the most unsophisticated ear. However, this leniency toward vocal diversity
does not negate the existence of distinct national tendencies
in tonal preferences among the British. The British listener
may very well admit the possibility of singing styles foreign
to the British ear while reserving highest applause to the
more indigenous vocal sound. Such vocal variety, which
bespeaks a kind of British broadmindedness, is also indicative of the various routes through which performing artists
"arrive" in Great Britain. In England there is great activity in
all forms of vocal music, be it opera, oratorio, symphonic song
literature, the song recital, early music or contemporary British idioms. The frequent appearance of foreign artists adds considerably to this wide panorama of vocal techniques and musical
styles. Anyone who wishes to study the many facets of vocalism
should experience the astounding offerings of contemporary London. (Nothing comparable can be encountered in New York, Berlin, Paris or Rome.) Without doubt, this situation is at least
partially due to that generally flexible British ability to accept
the slightly eccentric in all areas of modern life.

Such acceptability of the diversity of vocal production
will not be met with either in Italy or in France; cultural
dictates are far less broad and all-encompassing than among
the English. Beyond that consideration, it must be remarked
that a limited number of musical performances take place
currently in either Italy or France. Neither of these countries can manage the kind of musical renaissance which England is currently enjoying. (Empire may have diminished,
but artistic interests have become paramount in contemporary
England.) Foreign singing artists have long been welcome
in England; this is not the case in Italy or France, but Germany has been equally hospitable.

If one wishes to find the typical national sound in any

of the four schools, one will probably discover it more clearly demonstrated in the Academy of Music, the conservatorio,
the conservatoire de musique, the Hochschule für Musik,
the private local studio, and in the provincial opera house,
rather than in those international houses chiefly inhabited by
the "stars." The listener finds national tendencies most
distinctly in evidence in the individual voice studio where
the groundwork of most prominent artists takes place.

In dealing with national cultural tendencies in singing,
we must also consider literature specialists. Immediately
to mind come those persons who specialize in the works of
a given period, or of a single composer such as Bach,
Mozart, Verdi or Wagner. Some of these singers bind themselves to technical practices which make it nearly impossible to find acceptance outside the confines of a limited repertory. Seldom are such limitations actually due to native
vocal characteristics.

For example, the Duftigkeit which some listeners find
appropriate for singing Bach, finally becomes the permanent
timbre of the instrument so that the singer can perform little
else. Or the technique which results in a constant application of more spinto character of quality closes the door for
a particular singer to any literature other than that of the
Italian verismo. How must it strike such a limited specialist
when he or she sees some colleague in the same vocal Fach
who sings a wide range of vocal literature and styles, including Bach, Mozart and Verdi, not because the other singer
is musically better equipped but because the vocal technique
permits it?

Anyone familiar with the performance scene in a
musically active country such as Germany, is aware of the
number of natively-admired artists who have great success
within the boundaries of their own country and little outside
it. Although some of these singers may be the victims of
managerial manipulations, the experiences of most underscore the necessity for a vocal production which provides
that kind of vocalism equally acceptable in New York, Paris,
London, Vienna, Milan and Berlin. The same can be said
with regard to some singers who perform almost exclusively
in England, France or Italy.

In the case of the Italian singer, he or she is often
restricted by the lack of training in foreign languages and by
a general chauvinistic approach to literature. It is interesting to contrast the Italian-born singer with the large number
of non-native singers trained by Italian-schooled teachers,
who perform a wide range of languages and literatures.

Throughout this study it has been noted that with the exception of the Italian, there exist several main strands of vocalism within each national school. It has been postulated that most individual pedagogical variants, stemming from some imaginative pedagogue, can be recognized as relating to one of the main national streams.

Especially deserving of mention is the phenomenon of atypical methods within the non-Italianate schools which obviously have their sources in the Italian School. These pedagogies run alongside technical systems geared to special national taste in vocal sound; it is often from this Italianate school that artists on the international scene emerge. Most emphatically, it should be noted that not all those who reach international prominence from whatever national source adhere to an Italianate technique of singing; our ears quickly assure us otherwise. Each typical national technical approach to singing has produced artists of great stature. However, international artists who emerge from such origins must modify those aspects of singing which most narrowly identify them with such cultural limitations.

Italian-schooled singers are by no means assured of universal acceptance; certain excesses of the typical Italian singer make recognition outside of Italy problematic. To a large extent, these excesses are matters of musical taste and style, but some are clearly vocal. For example, the appoggio concept is not always kept in proportion; the application of breath becomes so intense that lyrical quality is replaced by driven tone, dynamic variation is impossible, and we tire of the loud, monotonously energetic sound. Luigi Ricci, who has helped shape many international careers over so many decades, was recently reported to have said, "I don't want Italian pupils. They think only of making their voices heard; they always sing at the top of their lungs. Bel canto with crescendos, diminuendos and pianissimos no longer exists here."[1]

Unfortunately, the Italian School seems to be full of young singers who pour forth exciting vocal tone but who do little else when they sing. The answer for this condition is not for the singer trained in the Italianate method (and he or she may be Australian, Dutch, Greek, American, Swedish or Japanese) to look for a new method, but to learn to incorporate into the Italianate technique some of the vocal refinements which may actually be the plague of some other schools. Even if the beauty of the instrument propels a singer into world-wide notoriety in spite of these excesses, the singer will always face critical chastisement for an inability to eliminate them.

Singers trained by Germanic methods, which may just as easily take place in San Francisco, Brussels or London as in Hamburg, Vienna or Zürich, must recognize that nothing is more expressive than the continuous flow of well-balanced vocal sound; these singers must give up some of their introspective, coloristic concerns in favor of the constantly flowing, well-supported, vital legato of the Italian School.

Singers of prominence who have been trained in the French School soon recognize the need to find more body in the sound; they must become aware of the cultural tendency to sacrifice tone to text, understanding that it is possible to expressively communicate text and execute a high level of vocalism simultaneously. For such singers it is often a difficult lesson to learn that singing need be neither precious nor mannered in order to be expressive.

The English artist who wishes to fulfil artistic potential on the international scene must overcome most of the distinctly British tonal characteristics. Admittedly, there are exceptions to be found in a few British singers of note who are utilized the world over in the English vocal literature precisely because of their very Britishness. But the most successful English singers of international stature have largely dropped their Briticisms in singing, joining that group of singers who universally delight.

In several centuries precursive to our own, the international art of singing was based upon vocal techniques as practiced in the Italian School (always excepting provincial situations, of course). As nationalism became a predominant political reality in the nineteenth century, regional cultural awareness in singing seems also to have increased. Vocal literature, geared to the poetry of the new cultural consciousnesses, seemed to require new vocal styles and sounds. Later, especially in Germany, some of the reservoir of accumulating scientific information was turned to vocalism as well as to other topics. Out of this convergence of influences, nationalistic tendencies began to encroach upon the vocalism stemming out of the Italian tradition.

In spite of the technological shrinkage of the modern world, no one should rush to the conclusion that national tendencies in singing are now moribund or that one interna-

tional ideal is about to emerge. The major pedagogical directions found in most important vocal studios are still dictated by national tonal aesthetics. It would be foolish to
predict their disappearance within some specified period of
time. In all probability, they will continue to produce singers who do certain things which please at a national or regional level; certain other singers will transcend those imposed technical limitations to join an international group of
performers.

No doubt distinct national schools will continue until
the aesthetic ideals of those cultural areas have undergone
marked change. Technical devices in singing, within each
school, have arisen in answer to demands of language and
the ear. These demands, we have attempted to show, relate
to a complex cultural milieu, comprising language, literature
and national temperament. It is doubtful that national vocal
tendencies will ever become amalgamated into one universal
school of vocalism, unless cultural distinctions themselves
are to be eradicated. Surely no one would look forward to
such a hypothetical condition with much enthusiasm.

However, it is impossible not to conclude that certain
technical approaches associated with some schools are the
result of actual malfunction, imposed by a false aesthetic
and by misinformation as to the actual physical function of
the vocal instrument. In these cases, the ear has learned
to demand a specific sound because the intellect has convinced
the ear that it is desirable. The disappearance of these
regionally-oriented technical devices need not be lamented.

Chapter XX

THE NORTH AMERICAN SINGER
AND THE NATIONAL SCHOOLS

Where does the North American singer fit into the
major national schools of singing, or are there indications
of a separate school? Certainly American English has more
affinity with British English than do some regional dialects
of Germany and Italy with the "high" languages of those two
countries. Does this commonality of language, and to some
extent, of culture, place the North American singer within
the English School of vocalism?

The answer is a negative one; the American singer
does not share in the total set of cultural circumstances which
shape the English singer's vocal art. The "melting pot,"
on the other hand, which popularly is supposed to characterize some aspects of North American culture, might be assumed to have produced a uniquely American vocal ideal.
Such is not the case, for the melting process is even less
complete in this area than in other cultural fields; coexistent
threads of vocal pedagogy are clearly visible. There is no
American national school of singing because teachers trained
in each of the national vocal traditions have continued to go
their diverse ways; within American pedagogy there is less
unity of approach than in any of the major countries of Western Europe.

In the early years of this century, the most important
impact upon professional American vocal training stemmed
from the Italian School. Numbers of Americans went to Italy
to study the art of singing and Italian teachers were prominent in New York City, where one went to study with an
Italian _maestro di canto_ if one couldn't afford the trip to
Europe. On the other hand, the great American choral soci-
eties were founded mostly by German and English-schooled
musicians. Their concept of good vocal tone produced a

second stream representing the choral-vocal traditions of those two countries. An amazing number of amateur singers were involved in choral groups in this country, while Italianate schooling was directed almost entirely toward the professional solo singer. These two orientations existed, and to some extent continue to exist, side-by-side in North America.

As the century progressed, Paris and Berlin began to draw the American singer, and prominent French and German artists began to settle and teach in New York, Toronto, Philadelphia and Boston, generally at the close of their own performance careers.

In the twenties, "voice science," much of it based on German investigative work, produced a number of prominent teachers who introduced new methods of voice production, often accompanied by gadgetry and devices for direct physical manipulation. This was an important movement with a lasting impact on American vocal pedagogy.

The great influx of teachers from the German School came about with the advent of Nazism, when a large number of vocal coaches and teachers of singing left Austria and Germany to take up residence in the United States. The hegemony of the Italian School as the natural orbit for the solo singer was decisively reduced by these events. Since the forties, one can find the widest possible spread of vocal approaches in North America. The student who decides to change voice teachers in America may discover a directly opposing vocal method just across the street or, indeed, across the hallway; by shopping around a bit, the student may come to represent within his or her person a living compendium of national tendencies in singing.

More frequently in America than elsewhere, one hears that "every teacher has a unique method." This is not the case; as was previously pointed out, all methods of vocal instruction can be fitted rather neatly into established approaches which derive from ideals propounded within the national schools. It goes without saying, one conceivably could encounter a teacher who practices Stauprinzip in Paris, one who advocates Gallic approaches in Berlin, or another giving counter-tenor instruction in Rome; indeed, in New York City the singer may encounter them all within the confines of the same building, one of those hives of vocal industry inhabited by ex-opera luminaries who compete for the questing student of singing.

It should come as no surprise that an American-
trained student of voice may produce a vocal timbre which
is more verdeutscht than any sound to be heard within the
city limits of Münich or Frankfurt, although the teacher may
not label the production specifically a Germanic one. His
or her friend, studying in the studio next door, may sound
more Italianate than someone diplomato from a major Italian
conservatory. (Both teachers probably claim they teach the
old bel canto method!) The impact of French pedagogical approaches in America is more difficult to substantiate. However, probably because of the number of books authored by
British pedagogues in the English language and because of
the impact from the choral-vocal tradition of the English
School, the costal arrest and fixed-diaphragmatic techniques
of the English School are frequently to be met with in North
America as well as in the British Isles. In addition, North
America is second only to Great Britain in the number of
hung-jaw practitioners, this technical shibboleth being the
most obvious symptom of the impact of English vocal methodology.

Canada, a country which produces a greater number of
professional singers than its relatively small population would
indicate, presents the same kind of kaleidoscopic possibilities
as does the United States. There exists an open rivalry in
some regions of Canada between the Italian and the German
techniques. (Indeed, as a result of the popularity among Canadians of one particular segment of the German School,
there are more transplanted Canadians in the Gesangsabteil
of a certain German Hochschule für Musik than there are
native Germans!). The historical accident which established
the French language as the mother tongue of an important
part of the country has also influenced vocal orientation as
part of the general cultural milieu.

It has been a premise of this work that the extremes
of nationalism in vocal pedagogy often are based upon the
distortion of physical function. It can further be stated with
some degree of substantiation that American singers are
subject to any and all of these techniques. However, it is
noteworthy that as a result of this proliferation of vocal offerings, most American singers, by the time they have
reached professional maturity, have been subjected to a
variety of vocal approaches and are therefore less committed
to any single one.

Less kindly, it could be said that the North American

singer does not come out of a cultural heritage which imbues him or her with well-defined vocal concepts. The young Italian baritone has a very different set of vocal influences about him, narrower in character, much better formulated, more distinct. A young singer in a provincial town in Germany can go to the opera nightly (twice on Sundays and holidays); the American student of singing turns on the stereo and knows only the electronically-perfected international "stars," or the Saturday Metropolitan broadcasts. (For the live event, even the cost of seats in the balconies may be prohibitive for the American student.)

It is, however, partly due to this locally deprived cultural circumstance that the American student may just be in a potentially more advantageous position than is the European. The American has no great heritage of song or operatic literature and no actual native vocal tradition to which he or she is bound. Musical life in America has always been somewhat eclectic, and the American habit of assimilation may in matters vocal be to the singer's advantage. American students of singing simply do not have those built-in national and regional responses to tonal concepts held by most of their European counterparts.

Perhaps the biggest detriment to the artistic development of the European singer is his or her trust in the personal inheritance of the cultural tradition. On the opposite pole, the American, showing the general rootlessness of the national culture, strives to acquire style and tradition through analysis and assimilation; precious little has been handed down. The European student who believes one naturally breathes the same cultural air which surrounded Schubert, Brahms or Wolf (or Rossini, Verdi and Puccini), is easily led to assume the automatic possession of certain abilities; he or she hopes vocal traditions occur through a kind of subconscious process. Although any person can "inherit" cultural attitudes toward vocal ideals, the actual techniques of execution and the artistic skills of communication in singing remain to be acquired through personal perseverance.

The ability to assimilate, to consciously work at the process of artistic development and communication, has been typical of the American singer in Europe. Sometimes the belief in the existence of styles and vocal techniques which lie about, to be acquired by the diligent, approaches the naive; it is perhaps not too unkind to cite the example of one young American who confided that he had gotten his

<u>Lieder</u> voice in Germany and was now going to Italy to pick
up his <u>bel</u> <u>canto</u> voice.

The position of the American-trained singer in Europe
is of considerable interest to the professional European colleague.   (Is it true that the American Embassy doubles your
salary?   Are you also in the employ of American govern-
mental agencies?   Were you trained specifically to represent
American culture in Europe?)   Political considerations aside,
an American in a European opera house is observed with increasing admiration on account of his or her technical prowess.   The American singer has found a major outlet in the
German Theater, especially after World War II.   It is by now
common knowledge that for over a quarter of a century some
of the most active singers in German opera houses have been
the Americans.   (No wonder that one American observer
thought that "a. G." [als Gast] meant American guest!)

It is partly due to economics rather than to pedagogical superiority that the American-born singer is in a favorable position vis-à-vis the native German singer.   But, whatever the contributive causes, the Americans often arrive
musically better equipped and vocally more secure than many
of their European counterparts.   A matter not overlooked by
those who hire them, American singers often have a vocal
technique which permits them to sing a wider scope of
literature than many native singers no matter how polished.
As one German agent expressed it, "We prefer Americans to
sing the Italian repertory because they have the right technical approach to the sound which so many of our singers
lack, without the stylistic excess and the language limitations
of the Italians."

Throughout Europe today, one finds general agreement
that the Americans and the Canadians are producing excep-
tionally fine singers.   To a large extent, this is due to lack
of the narrow national tendencies which still figure so prominently within Western European pedagogies.

Of equal interest to many European teachers is the
situation of the Japanese voice student in European conservatories and professional performance situations.   Many teachers in German conservatories of music will frankly admit
that their most motivated and productive students are the
Americans and the Japanese.   In some major German conservatories the Japanese comprise nearly ten per cent of the
enrollment in the vocal departments.   The Japanese student

arrives with vocal maturity, good musical training, and
often with an exceptional gift for languages. He or she, in
the same fashion as the American colleague, has not trusted
to osmosis or to general transmission of a racial culture.
With discipline and incentive evident, there is little reason
to doubt that the Japanese singer will eventually have an impact similar to that made by the American singer abroad.

In summary, the North American singer, it is clear,
need not go to Italy to find an Italian-schooled teacher, nor
to Germany to find a German-trained one. The singer's current teacher probably recognizably relates to one or the
other of these two major schools, though possibly without
acknowledging a specific allegiance. However, there is less
probability that the American-trained student will encounter
a teacher who advocates the French-schooled approach to
singing, because that school has had far less general impact
on American pedagogy than any other. The influence of the
English School on American voice teaching (as noted above)
especially in matters of breath-technique and vowel formation, is greater than that of the French, but probably less
than that of the German and Italian Schools. This may be
the case because of the somewhat eclectic nature of the English School itself.

A number of technical systems as regards the production of vocal sound have been examined in this work. Some
of them are indisputably more efficient from the standpoint of
physical function than are others. The young singer, European, North or South American, or Asiatic, should look for
a technique which will equip him or her to sing expressively
without violating physical function; such a technique should
avoid the over-specialized vocal production which often results from the aesthetic demands of regional schools of singing. A wise singer will look for that internationalization of
technique which closely corresponds to the best elements of
the historical tradition of the Italian School.

CHAPTER NOTES

CHAPTER I

1. Emanuele [i. e., Manuel] Garcia, Trattato completo dell'arte del canto, part I (Milan: G. Ricordi and Co., n. d.), p. 9.

CHAPTER II

1. Henry Gray, Gray's Anatomy, 35th British ed., ed. by Robert Warwick and Peter Williams (London: Longmans, 1973), p. 515.
2. Ibid.
3. E. J. M. Campbell, E. Agostoni, and J. Newsom Davis, The Respiratory Muscles, 2d. ed., (London: Lloyd-Luke Medical Books Ltd., 1970), p. 170.
4. Gray, op. cit., p. 518.
5. Ibid.
6. Campbell, op. cit., p. 149.
7. A. A. Viljanen, "Motor Activity in Breathing," Breathing: Hering-Breuer Centenary Symposium, ed. by Ruth Porter (London: J. & A. Churchill, 1970), p. 189.
8. Campbell, op. cit., pp. 178-179.
9. Ibid., pp. 181-193.
10. Ibid., p. 181.
11. Ibid., p. 187.
12. Herbert Witherspoon, Singing (New York: G. Schirmer, 1925), p. 55.

CHAPTER III

1. Elizabeth Rado (trans. and rev. by Martha Mehta),

"Breath Crisis in Relation to Breath and Resonance Control:
I," American Music Teacher, vol. 23, no. 5 (April-May
1974), 33-34.
    2. Frederick Husler and Yvonne Rodd-Marling, Sing-
ing: The Physical Nature of the Vocal Organs (London: Faber and Faber, 1965), p. 36.
    3. Ibid., p. 38.
    4. Gray, op. cit., p. 529.
    5. Ibid., p. 1294.
    6. George Armin, Von der Urkraft der Stimme, 3d.
ed. (Lippstadt: Kistner & Siegel & Co., n.d.).
    7. Husler and Rodd-Marling, op. cit., pp. 44-46.

CHAPTER IV

    1. William Shakespeare, The Art of Singing, rev.
ed. (Bryn Mawr, Pa.: Oliver Ditson Co., 1921), p. 15.
    2. Ibid., p. 16.
    3. William Vennard, Singing: The Mechanism and
the Technic, 3d ed. (Ann Arbor, Mich.: Edwards Brothers,
1964), p. 33.
    4. Campbell, op. cit., p. 186.
    5. John Newburn Levien, Some Notes for Singers
(London: Novello Co., 1940), p. 12.
    6. Campbell, op. cit., p. 188.
    7. David D. Slater, Vocal Physiology and the Teach-
ing of Singing: A Complete Guide to Teachers, Students and
Candidates for the A.R.C.M., L.R.A.M., and All Similar
Examinations (London: J. H. Harway, n.d.), pp. 31-32.

CHAPTER V

    1. Pierre Bonnier, La voix professionnelle (Paris:
Bibliothèque Larousse, 1908), pp. 138-139. My translation.
    2. Franceso Lamperti, A Treatise on the Art of
Singing (London: G. Ricordi and Co., n.d.), p. 33.
    3. Giovanni Battista Lamperti, Vocal Wisdom, ed. by
William Earl Brown (N.Y.: Hudson Offset Co., 1953), p. 36.

CHAPTER VI

    1. Peter E. Denes and Elliot N. Pinson, The Speech

Chain (Bell Telephone Laboratories, 1963), p. 40.

2. John S. Kenyon, "Pronunciation," in Introduction to Webster's New International Dictionary of the English Language, 2d ed., unabridged (Springfield, Mass.: G. and C. Merriam Co., 1961 printing), p. xxviii.

3. Josef Kemper, Stimmpflege (Mainz: B. Schott's Söhne, 1951), p. 41.

4. Harry Plunket Greene, Interpretation in Song (London: Macmillan Co., and Stainer and Bell, 1934), p. 312.

5. Charles Kennedy Scott, The Fundamentals of Singing (London: Cassell and Co., 1954), pp. 31-32.

6. W. A. Aikin, The Voice (London: Longmans, Green & Co., 1963 printing), p. 51.

7. Ibid., p. 82.

8. Arnold Rose, The Singer and the Voice, 2d ed., Faber and Faber, 1971), pp. 184-185.

9. The Musical Times, May 1972, p. 480.

10. Percy Judd, Vocal Technique (London: Sylvan Press, 1951), p. 69.

11. Francesco Lamperti, op. cit., p. 13 (quoting Pacchiarotti).

CHAPTER VII

1. Richard Paget, Human Speech (New York: Harcourt, Brace & Co.; London: Kegan Paul, Trench, Trubner & Co., 1930), pp. 303-309.

2. V. E. Negus, The Comparative Anatomy and Physiology of the Larynx (London: Hafner Pub. Co., 1962 reprinting), p. 199.

3. H. Lowery, A Guide to Musical Acoustics (New York: Dover Publications, 1966), p. 83.

4. Vennard, op. cit., pp. 80-105.

5. Adolf Rüdiger, Was ich über meine Stimme wissen sollte, 3d ed. (Basal: Bärenreiter-Verlag, 1956), p. 14. My translation.

6. Robert M. Taylor, "Acoustics for the Singer," The Emporia [Kansas] State Research Studies, vol. 6, no. 4, (June 1958), 30-31.

7. Heinrich Egenolf, Die menschliche Stimme (Stuttgart: Paracelsus-Verlag, 1959), p. 35-36. My translation.

8. Franziska Martienssen-Lohmann, Der Opernsänger (Mainz: B. Schott's Söhne, 1943), pp. 51-52. My translation.

9. Interview given John Higgins, The Times (London), June 21, 1972.
10. Giovanni B. Lamperti, op. cit., p. 70.
11. Francesco Lamperti, op. cit., p. 27.
12. Carlo Meano, La voce umana nella parola e nel canto (Milan: Casa Editrice Ambrosiana, 1964), p. 156. My translation.

CHAPTER VIII

1. Manuel Garcia, Complete School of Singing (London: Cramer, Beale and Chappell, n.d.), pp. iv-vi.
2. Manuel Garcia, Hints on Singing (London: Ascherberg, Hopwood and Crew, 1894), pp. iii-iv.
3. Wilhelm Nagel, "Physiologie der Stimmwerkzeuge," Handbuch der Physiologie (Braunschweig), vol. IV, 1909, p. 745. My translation.
4. Raoul Husson, La voix chantée (Paris: Gaultier-Villars, 1960), pp. 151-155.
5. Georges Loiseau, Notes sur le chant (Paris: Durand, n.d.), pp. 102-146 and passim.
6. John Simpson et al., A Synopsis on Otorhino-laryngology (Bristol: John Wright & Sons, 1957), p. 297.

CHAPTER IX

1. Carl E. Seashore, "Psychology of the Vibrato in Voice and Instrument," University of Iowa Studies in the Psychology of Music, vol. 3 (1936), 7.
2. Michael Smith, "The Effect of Straight-tone Feedback on the Vibrato," NATS [National Association of Teachers of Singing] Bulletin, vol. 23, no. 4 (May/June 1972), 28-32.

CHAPTER X

1. John Large, "Towards an Integrated Physiologic-Acoustic Theory of Vocal Registers," National Association of Teachers of Singing Bulletin, vol. 28, no. 3 (Feb./March 1972), 18-36.
2. Ibid., p. 34.
3. Victor A. Fields, "Review of the Literature on

Vocal Registers," National Association of Teachers of Singing Bulletin, vol. 26, no. 3 (Feb. /March 1970), 39.

4. W. J. Henderson, Early History of Singing (London: Longmans, Green & Co., 1921), pp. 28-29.

5. Gray, op. cit., p. 1181.

6. Vennard, op. cit., pp. 53-57.

7. Ibid., pp. 60-69.

8. Philip Duey, Bel Canto in Its Golden Age (New York: King's Crown Press, Columbia University, 1951), pp. 112-125.

9. Pietro Francesco Tosi, Observations on the Florid Song, transl. by Galliard (London: J. Wilcox, 1743).

10. Giovanni Battista Mancini, Practical Reflections on the Art of Singing, transl. by Pietro Buzzi (Boston: Gorham Press, 1912).

11. Emanuele [i.e., Manuel] Garcia op. cit., pp. x-xi.

12. F. Lamperti, op. cit., p. 17.

13. Emil Behnke, The Mechanism of the Human Voice (London: J. Curwen and Sons, 1881), pp. 5-6.

14. Henry Pleasants, The Great Singers (New York: Simon and Schuster, 1966), p. 120.

15. Ibid., p. 124.

16. Herman Klein, The Bel Canto (London: Humphrey Milford, Oxford University Press, 1923), pp. 28-29.

CHAPTER XVI

1. F. Martienssen-Lohmann, op. cit., p. 47.

CHAPTER XVII

1. Giulio Bertoni and Francesco Ugolini, "Firenze e Roma," Prontuario di pronunzia e di ortografia (Turin: Istituto del Libro Italiano, 1949), pp. xi-xviii.

2. Pierre Bernac, The Interpretation of French Song (New York: Praeger Publishers, 1970), pp. 34-35.

3. Martin Cooper, French Music from the Death of Berlioz to the Death of Fauré (London: Oxford University Press, 1951), p. 97.

4. Ibid.

5. Helmut de Boor, Hugo Moser, and Christian Winkler, Siebs deutsche Aussprache (Berlin: Walter de Gruyter & Co., 1969).

6. R. K. Webb, Modern England from the Eighteenth Century to the Present (New York: Dodd, Mead & Co., 1968), p. 2.

7. George Baker, The Common Sense of Singing (London: Pergamon Press, 1973), p. 7.

CHAPTER XVIII

1. H. Egenolf, op. cit., p. 14. My translation.
2. Ibid. My translation.
3. P. Bernac, op. cit., p. 35.
4. Ibid., p. 34.

CHAPTER XIX

1. Cleveland Plain Dealer, 6 Dec. 1975, p. B-8.

Appendix I

INSTITUTIONS VISITED
in Connection with This Study

L'accademia di Santa Cecilia, Rome

Akademie für Musik, "Mozarteum," Salzburg

Conservatoire de musique de Genève

Conservatoire de musique, Marseilles

Conservatoire de musique, Montpellier

Conservatoire de musique de Strasbourg

Conservatoire national de musique de Paris

Conservatoire royal de musique de Bruxelles

Conservatorio di musica "Gioacchino Rossini," Pesaro

Conservatorio di musica "Giuseppe Verdi," Milan

Conservatorio di musica "San Pietro a Maiella," Naples

Conservatorio di musica "Santa Cecilia," Rome

Conservatorio di musica "Vincenzo Bellini," Palermo

Conservatorio di musica "Benedetto Marcello," Venice

Conservatorio statale di musica "G. B. Martini," Bologna

Conservatorio statale di musica "Giuseppe Verdi," Turin

Ecole normale de musique de Paris

Guildhall School of Music and Drama, London

Istituto musicale Niccolò Paganini, Genoa

Konigliche Musikconserv. von Brussel (Flemish Division)

London Opera Center

Royal Academy of Music, London

Royal College of Church Music, Croydon

Royal College of Music, London

Royal College of Music, Manchester

Koninklijk Conservatorium, Amsterdam

Royal Scottish Academy of Music and Drama, Glasgow

Staatliche Hochschule für Musik, Detmold

Staatliche Hochschule für Musik, Cologne

Staatliche Hochschule für Musik, Munich

Staatliche Hochschule für Musik, und darstellende Kunst, Berlin

Staatliche Hochschule für Musik und darstellende Kunst, Hamburg

Staatliche Hochschule für Musik und darstellende Kunst, Stuttgart

Staatliche Hochschule für Musik und darstellende Kunst, Vienna

Staatliche Hochschule für Musik und Theater, Hannover

Trinity College of Music, London

Appendix II

IPA SYMBOLS USED IN THIS VOLUME

IPA symbols	English	German	Italian	French
(i)	keen	Liebe	prima	lis, dire
(ɪ)	thin	ich		
(e)	chaotic	Leben	sete	été, gai
(ɛ)	bet	Bett, Gäste, Apfel	sette	êtes, père crayon, mais, est, Neige, objet
(a)	task (American)			parle, partir
(ɑ)	father	Stadt, Staat	camera	âme, classe, pas
(ɔ)	horse	Sonne	morto	sommes, joli, votre
(o)	note	Sohn	non	beaux, pauvre, gros
(U)	nook	Mutter		
(u)	gnu, fool	Mut	uso	ou
(ə) (schwa)	ahead	getan		demain
(y)	(approximates (i) plus (u))	müde		vaincu, une, volume, sur
(Y)	(approximates (ɪ) plus (U))	Glück		
(ø)	(approximates (e) plus (u))	schön		neveu, peu, vieux, Meuse
(oe)	(approximates (ɛ) plus (ɔ))	Köpfe		neuf, heure, feuilleton
(ʔ)	(stroked glottal) uh-oh!	der Unteroffizier		
(h)	(glottal aspirate) house	Haus		
(ç)	(palatal fricative)	ich		
(x)	(velar fricative)	ach		
(ʃ)	(linguo-alveolar) Sh!	Stunde		
(ʁ)	(velar (r))			roi
(ɜ) (ɚ)	(mid-western r) mother, rare (stressed and unstressed)			
(:)	(indicates that the preceding vowel is of longer than usual duration)			
(~)	(indicates nasality)			

BIBLIOGRAPHY

BOOKS

Adams, Frederic A. The Singer's Manual: For Teachers, Pupils and Private Students. New York: John Wiley, 1849.

Adler, Kurt. Phonetics and Diction in Singing. Minneapolis: The University of Minnesota Press, 1965.

Aikin, W. A. The Voice: Introduction to Practical Phonology (1910). Reprint. London: Longmans, Green and Co., 1951.

American Academy of Teachers of Singing. Classification of the Singing Voice. Forest Hills, N.Y.: American Assoc. of Teachers of Singing, 1956.

_____. Terminology in the Field of Singing. New York: G. Schirmer, 1969.

Appelman, Ralph. The Science of Vocal Pedagogy. Bloomington: Indiana University Press, 1967.

Armin, George. Von der Urkraft der Stimme, 3d ed. Lippstadt: Kistner & Siegel & Co., n.d.

Arnold, William Harkness. French Diction for Singers and Speakers. Philadelphia: Oliver Ditson Co., 1912.

Bach, Alberto B. The Art of Singing. London: William Blackwood and Sons, 1886.

Bachner, Louis. Dynamic Singing. New York: L. B. Fischer, 1944.

Bacilly, Bénique de. A Commentary upon the Art of Proper Singing, transl. and ed. by Austin B. Caswell.

Brooklyn, N.Y.: Institute of Medieval Music, 1968.

Bacon, Richard Mackenzie. Elements of Vocal Science. Reprint. Champaigne, Ill.: Pro Musica Press, 1966.

Baker, George. The Common Sense of Singing. London: Pergamon Press, 1963.

Bartholomew, Wilmer T. Acoustics of Music. New York: Prentice-Hall, 1942.

Bartoschek, Walter. Gesangstechnik im Lichte neuerer Erkenntnisse. Berlin: Privately published, n.d.

Baum, Günther. Die Stimmbildungslehre des Dr. Jean Nadolovitch. Hamburg: Hüllenhagen & Griehl Verlag, 1955.

Bechman, Gertrude Wheeler. Tools for Speaking and Singing. New York: G. Schirmer, 1955.

Behnke, Emil. The Mechanism of the Human Voice. London: J. Curwen & Sons, 1880.

Bérard, Jean-Baptiste. L'art du chant, transl. by Sidney Murray. 1775. Reprint. Milwaukee: Pro Musica Press, 1968.

Bernac, Pierre. The Interpretation of French Song. New York: Praeger Publishers, 1970.

Bertoni, Giulio, and Ugolini, Francesco. Prontuario di pronunzia e di ortografia. Turin: Istituto del Libro Italiano, 1949.

Bloch, Bernard, and Trager, George L. Outline of Linguistic Analysis. Ann Arbor, Mich.: Edwards Brothers, 1949.

Bonnier, Pierre. La Voix professionnelle. Paris: Bibliothèque Larrousse, 1908.

Brewer, David W., ed. Research Potentials in Voice Physiology. From International Conference on Research Potentials ... New York: State Univ. of N.Y., 1964.

Brodnitz, Friedrich S. Vocal Rehabilitation, 2d ed. Rochester, Minn: Whiting Press, 1961. (American

Academy of Ophthalmology and Otolaryngology.)

Brook, Donald. Singers of Today, 2d rev. ed. London: Rockliff, 1958.

Brown, William Earl. Vocal Wisdom: Maxims of Giovanni Battista Lamperti. Reprint. Boston: Crescendo Pub. Co., 1973.

Browne, Lennox, and Behnke, Emil. Voice, Song and Speech. New York: G. P. Putnam's Sons, n. d.

Brunelli, M. D., and Pittola, E. Guida per l'insegnamento pratica della fonetica italiana. Perugia: Regia Università per Stranieri, 1940.

Burgin, John Carroll. Teaching Singing. Metuchen, N. J.: Scarecrow Press, 1973.

Buzzi-Peccia, A. How to Succeed in Singing. Philadelphia: Theodore Presser Co., 1925.

Campbell, Moran; Agostoni, Emilio; and Newsom Davis, John. The Respiratory Muscles, Mechanics and Neural Control. London: Lloyd-Luke (Medical Books), 1970.

Cappiani, Luisa. Practical Hints and Helps for Perfection in Singing. New York: Leo Feist, 1908.

Christy, Van A. Expressive Singing. Dubuque, Iowa: Wm. C. Brown Co., 1961. 2 vols.

Clippinger, D. A. Fundamentals of Voice Training. New York: Oliver Ditson Co., 1929.

_____. The Head Voice and Other Problems. Philadelphia: Oliver Ditson Co., 1917.

Cooper, Martin. French Music from the Death of Berlioz to the Death of Fauré. London: Oxford University Press, 1951.

Cox, Richard G. The Singer's Manual of German and French Diction. New York: G. Schirmer, 1970.

Cranmer, Arthur. The Art of Singing. London: Dennis Dobson, 1957.

Culver, Charles A. Musical Acoustics. New York: McGraw-
Hill Book Co., 1956.

Curry, Robert. The Mechanism of the Human Voice. New
York: Longmans, Green and Co., 1940.

Curtis, H. Holbrook. Voice Building and Tone Placing.
New York: D. Appleton and Co., 1901.

Davies, David Ffrangcon. The Singing of the Future (1905).
Reprint. Champaigne, Ill.: Pro Musica Press,
1968.

Dawson, John J. The Voice of the Boy. New York: A.
S. Barnes Co., 1902.

de Boor, Helmut; Moser, Hugo; and Winkler, Christian.
Siebs Deutsche Aussprache. Berlin: Walter de
Gruyter & Co., 1969.

Deferrari, Harry A. A Phonology of Italian, Spanish and
French. Ann Arbor, Mich.: Edwards Brothers, 1954.

Denes, Peter B., and Pinson, Elliot N. The Speech Chain:
The Physics and Biology of Spoken Language. Baltimore: Waverly Press, 1963. (Bell Telephone Laboratories.)

DeYoung, Richard. The Singer's Art. Chicago: DePaul
University, 1958.

Downing, William B. Vocal Pedagogy. New York: Carl
Fischer, 1927.

Duey, Philip. Bel Canto in Its Golden Age. New York:
King's Crown Press, Columbia University, 1950.

Dunkley, Ferdinand. The Buoyant Voice Acquired by Correct
Pitch-Control. Boston: C. C. Birchard and Co.,
1942.

Egenolf, Heinrich. Die menschliche Stimme; Ihre Erziehung,
Erhaltung und Heilung, 2d ed. Stuttgart: Paracelsus-
Verlag, 1959.

Ellis, Alexander. Speech in Song. London: Novello and
Co., 1898.

Emil-Behnke, Kate. The Technique of Singing. London: Williams and Norgate, 1945.

Errolle, Ralph. Italian Diction for Singers, 3d ed. Boulder: Pruett Press, 1963.

Field-Hyde, Frederick C. Vocal Vibrato, Tremolo and Judder. London: Oxford University Press, 1946.

Fields, Victor Alexander. Training the Singing Voice. New York: King's Crown Press, Columbia University, 1947.

Fillebrown, Thomas. Resonance in Singing and Speaking. Bryn Mawr, Pa.: Oliver Ditson Co., 1911.

Forman, Edward, ed. The Porpora Tradition. Milwaukee: Pro Musica Press, 1968.

Forneberg, Erich. Stimmbildungsfibel. Frankfurt: Verlag Moritz Diesterweg, 1964.

Franca, Ida. Manual of Bel Canto. New York: Coward-McCann, 1959.

Frisell, Anthony. The Baritone Voice. Reprint. Boston: Crescendo Pub. Co., 1970.

_____. The Tenor Voice. Boston: Bruce Humphries, 1964.

Fuchs, Viktor. The Art of Singing and Voice Technique. London: Calder and Boyars, 1963.

Fucito, Salvatore and Beyer, Barnet. Caruso, Gesangskunst und Methode, transl. by Curt Thesing. Berlin: Bote & Bock, 1924.

Fugère, Lucien, and Duhamel, Raoul. Nouvelle Méthode pratique de chant français par l'articulation. Paris: Enoch & Cie., 1929.

Garcia, Manuel. Garcia's Complete School of Singing. London: Cramer, Beale and Chappell, n.d.

_____. Hints on Singing, transl. by Beata Garcia. London: Ascherberg, Hopwood and Crew, 1894.

Gardiner, Julian. A Guide to Good Singing and Speech. London: Cassell, 1968.

Gescheidt, Adelaide. Make Singing a Joy. New York: R. L. Huntzinger, 1930.

Ghislanzoni, Alberto. Melodia e polifonia. Rome: Edizioni Musicali "Ortipe," 1959.

Gib, Charles. Vocal Science and Art. London: William Reeves, 1911.

Goldschmidt, Hugo. Die italienische Gesangsmethode des XVII. Jahrhunderts und ihre Bedeutung für die Gegenwart. Breslau: Schlesische Buchdruckerei, Kunst und Verlags Anstalt., 1892.

Grant, J. C. Boileau. An Atlas of Anatomy. London: Bailliere, Tindall & Cox, 1962.

Gray, Henry. Gray's Anatomy, 35th British ed., ed. by Robert Warwick and Peter Williams. London: Longmans, 1973.

Greene, Harry Plunket. Interpretation in Song (1912). Reprint. London: Macmillan and Co., 1956.

Gümmer, Paul. Erziehung der menschlichen Stimme. Kassel: Bärenreiter-Verlag, 1970.

Haywood, Frederick H. Universal Song: A Voice-Culture Course in Three Volumes for the Studio and the Class Room. New York: G. Schirmer, 1932.

Heaton, Wallace, and Hargens, C. W. An Interdisciplinary Index of Studies in Physics, Medicine and Music Related to the Human Voice. Bryn Mawr, Pa.: Theodore Presser Co., 1968.

Heizler, Sister Louise Marie. Basic Techniques for Voice Production. New York: Exposition Press, 1973.

Helmholtz, Herman L. F. On the Sensations of Tone, transl. by Alexander J. Ellis (1875). Reprint. London: Longmans, Green & Co., 1930.

Henderson, William James. The Art of Singing. New York: Dial Press, 1937. Reprint.

222 / Bibliography

_____. Early History of Singing. London: Longmans,
Green and Co., 1921.

Herbert-Caesari, E. The Alchemy of Voice. London:
Robert Hale, 1965.

_____. The Science and Sensations of Vocal Tone, 2d
ed., rev. Boston: Crescendo Pub. Co., 1968.

_____. Vocal Truth. London: Robert Hale, 1969.

Heriot, Angus. The Castrati in Opera. New York: Da
Capo Press, 1964.

Hinman, Florence Lamont. Slogans for Singers. New York:
G. Schirmer, 1934.

Huls, Helen Steen. The Adolescent Voice. New York:
Vantage Press, 1957.

Husler, Frederick. Das vollkommene Instrument. Stuttgart:
Belsar Verlag, 1970.

_____, and Rodd-Marling, Yvonne. Singing: The Physi-
cal Nature of the Vocal Organ. London: Faber &
Faber, 1965.

Husson, Raoul. La Voix chantée. Paris: Gauthier-Villars,
Editeur, 1960.

Jones, D. Lautzeichen und ihre Anwendung in verschiedenen
Sprachgebieten. Das System des Association Phoné-
tique Internationale (Weltlautschriftverein). Berlin:
Die Reichsdruckerei, 1928.

Jones, Dora Duty. Lyric Diction for Singers, Actors and
Public Speakers. London: Harper & Brothers, 1913.

Judd, Percy. Vocal Techniques. London: Sylvan Press,
1951.

Kagen, Sergius. On Studying Singing. New York: Dover
Publications, 1960.

Kaiser, L. Manual of Phonetics. Amsterdam: North Hol-
land Pub. Co., for the Permanent Council for the
International Congress of Phonetic Sciences, 1957.

Kantner, Claude E., and West, Robert. Phonetics: An
Introduction to the Principles of Phonetic Science from
the Point of View of English Speech. New York:
Harper & Brothers Publishers, 1960.

Kay, Elster. Bel Canto and the Sixth Sense. London:
Dennis Dobson, 1963.

Kelsey, Franklyn. The Foundations of Singing. London:
Williams and Northgate, 1950.

Kemper, Josef. Stimmpflege: Eine Handwerkslehre im
Grundriss. Mainz: B. Schott's Söhne, 1951.

Klein, Herman. An Essay on the Bel Canto. London:
Oxford University Press, 1923.

_____. The Golden Age of Opera. London: George
Routledge & Sons, 1933.

_____. Great Women-Singers of My Time. London:
George Routledge & Sons, 1931.

Klein, Joseph J. Singing Technique. Princeton, N. J.:
D. Van Nostrand Co., 1967.

Knudson, Charles A. and Chapard, Louis. Introduction to
French Pronunciation, 2d ed. Urbana, Ill.: Privately
Published, 1966.

Kockritz, Hubert. Language Orientation--An Introduction
to the Pronunciation of Foreign Languages Based
Upon the International Phonetic Alphabet. Cincinnati:
Privately Published, 1965.

Kofler, Leo. The Art of Breathing As the Basis of Tone-
Production, 6th rev. ed. New York: Edward S.
Weaver, 1902.

Lablache, Louis. Lablache's Complete Method of Singing;
or A Rational Analysis of the Principles According
to Which the Studies Should Be Directed for Developing the Voice and Rendering It Flexible, and for
Forming the Voice. Boston: Oliver Ditson & Co.,
n. d.

Lamperti, Francesco. The Art of Singing, transl. by J. C.
Griffith. New York: G. Schirmer, n. d.

Lamperti, Giovanni Battista see Brown, William Earl.

Lang, Paul Henry. Music in Western Civilization. New
    York: W. W. Norton and Co., 1941.

Lawson, James Terry. Full-Throated Ease. New York:
    Mills Music Co., 1955.

Lefort, Jules. L'Emission de la voix chantée. Paris:
    Lemoine & Fils, 1892.

Lehmann, Lilli. How to Sing. New York: Macmillan Co.,
    1903.

Lehmann, Lotte. More Than Singing. London: Boosey and
    Hawkes, 1946.

Lemaire, Théophile, and Favoix, Henri (Fils). Le Chant;
    Ses principes et son histoire. Paris: Heugel et
    Fils, 1881.

Lerche, William. The Esophagus and Pharynx in Action.
    Oxford, England: Blackwell Scientific Publications,
    1950.

Levien, John Newburn. Some Notes for Singers. London:
    Novello and Co., n.d.

Lewis, Joseph. Singing Without Tears. London: Ascher-
    berg, Hopwood & Crew, 1940.

Lohmann, Paul. Die sängerische Einstellung. Lindau: C.
    F. Kahnt, 1929.

_____. Stimmfehler--Stimmberatung. Mainz: B. Schott's
    Söhne, 1933.

Loiseau, Georges. Notes sur le chant. Paris: Durand,
    n.d.

Lowery, H. A Guide to Musical Acoustics. New York:
    Dover Publications, 1966.

Luchsinger, Richard, and Arnold, Godfrey E. Voice--Speech
    --Language, transl. by Godfrey E. Arnold and Evelyn
    Robe Finkbeiner. Belmont, Calif.: Wadsworth Pub.
    Co., 1965.

McKensie, Duncan. Training the Boy's Changing Voice. New Brunswick, N.J.: Rutgers University Press, 1956.

Mackenzie, Sir Morell. Hygiene of the Vocal Organs. London: Macmillan and Co., 1890.

McKerrow, Janet. The Vocal Movements. London: Kegan Paul, Trench, Trubner & Co., 1925.

MacKinlay, M. Sterling. The Singing Voice and Its Training. London: George Routledge & Sons, 1910.

Magrini, Gustavo. Il canto, arte e tecnica. Milan: Ulrico Hoepli, 1918.

Manchester, Arthur L. Twelve Lessons in the Fundamentals of Voice Production. Boston: Oliver Ditson Co., 1907.

Mancini, Giovanni Battista. Practical Reflections on the Art of Singing, transl. by Pietro Buzzi. Boston: Gorham Press, 1912.

Manén, Lucie. The Art of Singing. London: Faber Music, 1974.

Marafioti, P. Mario. Caruso's Method of Voice Production. New York: D. Appleton-Century Co., 1937.

Marchesi, Mathilde. Ten Singing Lessons. New York: Harper & Brothers, 1901.

_____. Theoretical and Practical Vocal Method. Reprint. New York: Dover Publications, 1970.

Mari, Nanda. Canto e voce. Milan: G. Ricordi, 1959.

Marshall, Madeleine. The Singer's Manual of English Diction. New York: G. Schirmer, 1953.

Martienssen[-Lohmann], Franziska. Das bewusste Singen. Leipzig: C. F. Kahnt, 1923.

_____. Der Opernsänger. Mainz: B. Schott's Söhne, 1943.

_____. Der wissende Sänger. Zürich: Atlantis-Verlag, 1963.

Meano, Carlo. La voce umana nella parola e nel canto.
    Milan: Casa Editrice Ambrosiana, 1964.

Melba, Nellie. Melba Method. London: Chappell & Co.,
    1926.

Mellalieu, W. Norman. The Boy's Changing Voice (1905).
    Reprint. London: Oxford University Press, 1966.

Messinger, Henry. Langenscheidt's New College German
    Dictionary. Berlin: Langenscheidt, 1973.

Metzger, Zerline Muhlman. Individual Voice Patterns. New
    York: Carlton Press, 1966.

Miller, Dayton Clarence. The Science of Musical Sounds.
    New York: Macmillan Co., 1916.

Miller, Frank E. The Voice; Its Production, Care and
    Preservation. New York: G. Schirmer, 1913.

Mills, Wesley. Voice Production in Singing and Speaking.
    3d ed. Philadelphia: J. P. Lippincott Co., 1908.

Moore, Gerald. Am I Too Loud? New York: Macmillan
    Co., 1962.

Moriarty, John. Diction. Boston: E. C. Schirmer Music
    Co., 1975.

Muret, E., and D. Sanders. German and English Encyclo-
    pedic Dictionary. New York: Frederick Ungar Pub.
    Co., n.d.

Myer, Edmund J. The Voice from a Practical Stand-Point.
    New York: Wm. A. Pond & Co., 1886.

Nagel, Wilhelm. Handbuch der Physiologie, vol. 4. Braun-
    schweig: Vieweg, 1909.

National Association of Teachers of Singing. Training the
    Vocal Instrument. New York: National Assoc. of
    Teachers of Singing, 1957.

Negus, V. E. The Comparative Anatomy and Physiology of
    the Larynx (1949). Reprint. London: Hafner Pub.
    Co., 1962.

Neidlinger, W. H. A Primer on Voice and Singing. Chicago: Rand, McNally & Co., 1903.

Nicolaus, Gertrud. Die Gesetzmässigkeit der richtigen Vokalbildung jeder Tonhöhe als Vorbedingung für Schönheit und Dauer der Stimme. Berlin, Privately Published, 1963.

Nouveau Larousse universel. Paris: Larousse, 1948-9. 2 vols.

O'Brien, Grace. The Golden Age of Italian Music. London: Jarrolds Publishers, n. d.

Paget, Richard. Human Speech. New York: Harcourt, Brace & Co., 1930.

Panzèra, Charles. L'Amour de chanter. Paris: Henry Lemoine et Cie., Editeurs, 1957.

_____. Mélodies Françaises; Lessons in Style and Interpretation. Brussels: Schott Frères, 1964.

Peterson, Paul W. Natural Singing and Expressive Conducting, rev. ed. Winston-Salem: John F. Blair Publisher, 1966.

Peyrollaz, Marguerite, and Bara de Trovar, M. -L. Manuel de phonétique et de diction françaises. Paris: Librairie Larousse, 1954.

Pfautsch, Lloyd. English Diction for the Singer. New York: Lawson-Gould Music Publishers, 1971.

Pleasants, Henry. The Great Singers. New York: Simon and Schuster, 1966.

Pleasants, Jeanne Varney. Pronunciation in French, transl. by Esther Egerton. Ann Arbor, Mich.: Edwards Brothers, 1962.

Porter, Ruth. Breathing: Hering-Breuer Centenary Symposium. London: J. & A. Churchill, 1970.

Proschowsky, Frantz. The Way to Sing. Boston: C. C. Birchard & Co., 1923.

Quiring, Daniel P., and Warfel, John H. The Head, Neck and Trunk. Philadelphia: Lea & Febiger, 1967.

Randegger, Alberto. Singing. London: Novello, Ewer and Co., n. d.

Reid, Cornelius L. Bel Canto: Principles and Practices. New York: Coleman-Ross Co., 1950.

_____. The Free Voice. New York: Coleman-Ross Co., 1965.

Reusch, Fritz. Der kleine Hey--Die Kunst des Sprechens. Mainz: B. Schott's Söhne, 1956.

Rogers, Clara Kathleen. Clearcut Speech in Song. Boston: Oliver Ditson Co., 1927.

Romanes, G. J., ed. Cunningham's Manual of Practical Anatomy. Vol. III, Head and Neck and Brain. London: Oxford University Press, 1967.

Root, Frederic W. The Polychrome Lessons in Voice Culture. New York: Fillmore Bros. Co., 1896.

Rose, Arnold. The Singer and the Voice. London: Faber and Faber, 1962.

Rosenthal, Harold. Great Singers of Today. London: Calder and Boyars, 1966.

Rosewall, Richard B. Handbook of Singing. Evanston, Ill.: Summy-Birchard Co., 1961.

Ross, William Ernest. Secrets of Singing. Bloomington, Ind.: Privately Published, 1959.

Rosvaenge, Helge. Leitfaden für Gesangsbeflissene. Munich: Obpacher, 1969.

Rüdiger, Adolf. Was ich über meine Stimme wissen sollte! Kassel: Bärenreiter-Verlag, 1954.

Rushmore, Robert. The Singing Voice. New York: Dodd, Mead & Co., 1971.

Russell, William. Orthophony, or Vocal Culture. Boston: Houghton Mifflin Co., 1882.

Samoiloff, Lazar S. The Singer's Handbook. Philadelphia: Theodore Presser Co., 1942.

Schiøtz, Aksel. The Singer and His Art. New York: Harper & Bros., 1953.

Schlaffhorst, Clara, and Anderson, Hedwig. Atmung und Stimme. Wolfenbüttel: Möseler Verlag, 1928.

Schmauk, Theodore E. The Voice in Speech and Song. New York: John B. Alden, 1890.

Seiler, Emma. The Voice in Singing. Philadelphia: J. B. Lippincott and Co., 1875.

Shakespeare, William. The Art of Singing. Bryn Mawr, Pa.: Oliver Ditson Co., 1921.

_____. Plain Words on Singing. Bryn Mawr, Pa.: Oliver Ditson Co., 1921.

Shaw, W. Warren. Authentic Voice Production. Philadelphia: J. B. Lippincott Co., 1930.

Sieber, Ferdinand. The Art of Singing, transl. by Seeger. New York: William A. Pond & Co., 1872.

Siebs, Th. see de Boor et al.

Simpson, John F.; Ballantyne, J.; Chalmers, J.; Robert, Ian G.; and Evans, Charles Harold. A Synopsis of Otorhinolaryngology. Bristol: John Wright & Sons, 1957.

Slater, David D. Vocal Physiology and the Technique of Singing. London: J. H. Harway, n. d.

Spinelli, Nicola. Dizionario scolastico. Turin: Società Editrice Internazionale, 1965.

Stampa, Aribert. Atem, Sprache und Gesang. Kassel: Bärenreiter Verlag, 1956.

Stanley, Douglas. The Science of Voice. New York: Carl Fischer, 1929.

_____. Your Voice, Its Production and Reproduction. New York: Pitman Pub. Co., 1933.

_____. Your Voice--Applied Science of Vocal Art. New York: Pitman Pub. Co., 1945.

Stein, Jack M. Poem and Music in the German Lied from Gluck to Hugo Wolf. Cambridge, Mass.: Harvard University Press, 1971.

Stevens, Denis. A History of Song. New York: W. W. Norton & Co., 1961.

Stubbs, G. Edward. The Adult Male Alto or Counter-Tenor Voice. London: Novello & Co., 1908.

Sunderman, Lloyd F. Artistic Singing: Its Tone Production and Basic Understandings. Metuchen, N.J.: Scarecrow Press, 1970.

Tarneaud, Jean. Le Chant: Sa construction, sa destruction. Paris: Librarie Maloine, 1957.

Thomas, Franz. Die Lehre des Kunstgesanges nach der altitalienischen Schule. Berlin: George Achterberg Verlag, 1968.

Tosi, Pier Francesco. Observations on the Florid Song, transl. by J. E. Galliard. London: J. Wilcox, 1743.

Ulrich, Bernhardt. Concerning the Principles of Vocal Training in the A Cappella Period, 1474-1640, transl. by John Seale. Milwaukee: Pro Musica Press, 1968.

Uris, Dorothy. To Sing in English. New York: Boosey & Hawkes, 1971.

Vaccai, Nicola. Practical Method of Italian Singing. Reprint. New York: G. Schirmer, 1975.

Vale, Walter S. Tone Production in the Human Voice. London: The Faith Press, 1934.

van Borre, Thooris. Le chant humain. Paris: Madédée Legrand, 1927.

Vannini, Vincenzo. Della voce umana. Florence: Tipografia Barbera, 1924.

Vennard, William. Singing; The Mechanism and the Technic. 3d ed. Ann Arbor, Mich.: Edwards Brothers, 1964.

Voorhees, Irving Wilson. Hygiene of the Voice. New York: Macmillan Co., 1923.

Warman, E. B. The Voice: How to Train It and How to Care for It. Boston: Lee and Shepard, 1889.

Waters, Crystal. Song; The Substance of Vocal Study. New York: G. Schirmer, 1930.

Webb, R. K. Modern England from the Eighteenth Century to the Present. New York: Dodd, Mead and Co., 1968.

Weer, Robert Lawrence. Your Voice. Los Angeles: Privately Published, 1948.

Westerman, Kenneth N. Emergent Voice. Ann Arbor, Mich.: Privately Published, 1947.

White, Ernest G. Science and Singing (London: J. M. Dent and Sons, 1909). Reprint. Boston: Crescendo Publishers, 1969.

_____. Sinus Tone Production (1938). Reprint. Boston: Crescendo Publishers, 1970.

Whitlock, Weldon. Bel Canto for Twentieth Century. Champaign, Ill.: Pro Musica Press, 1961.

_____. Facets of the Singing Art. Champaign, Ill.: Pro Musica Press, 1967.

Wilcke, Eva. German Diction in Singing, transl. by Arthur E. Smith, New York: Dutton & Co., 1930.

Wilcox, John C. The Living Voice. New York: Carl Fischer, 1945.

Witherspoon, Herbert. Singing. New York: G. Schirmer, 1925.

Wolf, Artur. Criticism of One-Sided Singing Methods: Problems of Voice-Building and Their Solution, trans. by Bert Jahr. New York: Irene Tauber, n.d.

Wood, Alexander. The Physics of Music (1944). Rev. by J. M. Bowsher. London: Methuen & Co., 1961.

Woodbury, Isaac Baker. The Cultivation of the Voice Without a Master. New York: F. J. Huntington, 1853.

Young, Gerald M. What Happens in Singing. New York: Pitman Pub. Corp., 1956.

Zingarelli, Nicola. Vocabolario della lingua italiana, 10th ed. Bologna: Nicola Zanichelli, 1970.

Zuckerman, Solly. A New System of Anatomy. London: Oxford University Press, 1961.

ARTICLES

Alberti, Helen. "Facts Concerning the Art of Bel Canto or the Basis of Bel Canto." NATS Bulletin 4 (1947): 4.

Brodnitz, Friedrich S. "The Singing Teacher and the Laryngologist." NATS Bulletin, 13 (1957): 2-3.

Carhart, Paul W. and Kenyon, John S. "A Guide to Pronunciation." Webster's New International Dictionary of the English Language. 2d ed., unabridged. Springfield, Mass. Pp. xxii-lxxx.

Coffin, Berton. "The Instrumental Resonance of the Singing Voice." NATS Bulletin, 31 (1974): 26-39.

_____. "The Relationship of the Breath, Phonation and Resonance in Singing." NATS Bulletin, 31 (1975): 18-24.

Conley, Eugene. "An X-Ray Study of the Larynx Position of Good and Poor Speakers." NATS Bulletin, 24 (1967): 4-5.

De Bidoli, Emi. "Old Methods of Voice Teaching versus New Ones." NATS Bulletin, 3 (1947): 3.

Draper, M. A.; Ladefoged, Peter; and Whitredge, D. "Respiratory Muscles in Speech." Journal of Speech and Hearing Research, 2 (1959): 19-27.

Duey, Philip A. "Science and Voice." Music Journal, 16 (1958): 29-30.

Dwyer, Edward J. "Concepts of Breathing in Singing."
NATS Bulletin, 24 (1967): 40-43.

Faaborg-Andersen, K. "Electromyographic Investigation of
Intrinsic Laryngeal Muscles in Humans. Acta Physi-
ologica Scandinavica, Supplement 140 (1957): 1-149.

Fields, Victor A. "Review of the Literature on Vocal Registers." NATS Bulletin, 14 (1957): 6-7.

Flanagan, J. L. "Some Properties of the Glottal Sound
Source." Journal of Speech and Hearing Research,
1 (1958): 99-116.

Fletchner, Adlene Smith. "Low Formant in Soprano Voices."
NATS Bulletin, 26 (1969): 23-26.

Garlinghouse, Burton. "Dialogue on Vocal Pedagogy."
NATS Bulletin, 27 (1970): 25.

_____. "Rhythm and Relaxation in Breathing." NATS
Bulletin, 7 (1951): 2.

Gigli, Beniamino. "Breathing and Vowels: An Interview."
Choral and Organ Guide, 18 (1945): 13.

Hisey, Philip D. "Head Quality versus Nasality: A Review
of Some Pertinent Literature." NATS Bulletin, 28
(1971): 4.

Hollien, Henry. "Some Laryngeal Correlates of Vocal
Pitch." Journal of Speech and Hearing Research, 3
(1960): 4-11.

_____, and Curtis, James F. "Elevation and Tilting of
the Vocal Folds as a Function of Vocal Pitch."
Folia Phoniatica, 4 (1962): 23-26.

_____, and Moore, G. Paul. "Measurements of the
Vocal Folds during Changes in Pitch." Journal of
Speech and Hearing Research, 3 (1960): 157-165.

Husson, Raoul. "The Classification of Human Voices."
NATS Bulletin, 4 (1957): 6-11.

_____. "The Pharyngo-Buccal Cavity and Its Phonatory
Physiology." NATS Bulletin, 16 (1960): 4-11.

Landeau, Michel. "Voice Classification," transl. by Harold C. Luckstone. NATS Bulletin, 20 (1963): 4-31.

Large, John. "Acoustic-Perceptual Evaluation of Register Equalization." NATS Bulletin, 32 (1974): 20-24.

_____. "An Acoustical Study of Isoparametric Tones in the Female Chest and Middle Registers in Singing." NATS Bulletin, 25 (1968): 12-15.

_____. "A Method for the Selection of Samples for Acoustical and Perceptual Studies of Voice Registers." NATS Bulletin, 25 (1969): 40-42.

_____. "Toward an Integrated Physiologic-Acoustic Theory of Vocal Registers." NATS Bulletin, 28 (1973): 18-36.

_____, and Iwata, Schigenbu. "The Significance of Air Flow Modulations in Vocal Vibrato." NATS Bulletin, 32 (1976): 42-46.

_____, and Shipp, T. "The Effect of Certain Parameters on the Perception of Vocal Registers." NATS Bulletin, 26 (1969): 12-15.

Lester, John L. "Breathing Related to Phonation." NATS Bulletin, 14 (1957): 26.

Lewis, Don. "Vocal Resonators." Journal of the Acoustical Society of America, 7 (1935): 74.

McGinnis, C. S.; Elnick, M.; and Kraichman, M. "A Study of the Vowel Formants of Well-Known Male Operatic Singers." Journal of the Acoustical Society of America, 23 (1951): 440-446.

Mason, R. M., and Zemlin, W. R. "The Phenomenon of Vocal Vibrato." NATS Bulletin, 22 (1966): 12.

Miller, Richard. "Diction in Relation to the Vocal Legato." NATS Bulletin, 4 (1966): 12-123.

_____. "Vibrato in Relation to Vocal Legato." NATS Bulletin, 3 (1966): 10-21.

Milner, Anthony. "The Sacred Capons." The Musical Times, 114 (1973): 150-252.

Oncley, Paul B. "Acoustics of the Singing Voice." Journal of the Acoustical Society of America, 26 (1954): 932.

_____. "Research and the Singing Voice." Journal of the Acoustical Society of America, 28 (1956): 790.

Phemister, V. "A New Look into the Singer's Throat." Music Journal, 16 (1958): 34.

Potter, Ralph K., and Peterson, Gordon E. "The Representation of Vowels and Their Movements." Journal of the Acoustical Society of America, 20 (1948): 118-135.

Rado, Elizabeth. "Breath Crisis in Relation to Breath and Resonance Control: I," transl. by Martha Mehta, American Music Teacher, 23 (1974): 33-34.

Raskin, Judith. "American Bel Canto." Opera News, 30 (1966): 6.

Ringel, Harvey. "Consonantal Deterrence." NATS Bulletin, 5 (1948): 8.

_____. "Vowel Vanish--A Vocal Deterrent." NATS Bulletin, 4 (1947): 3.

Roman, Stella. "The Italian and German Approach to Singing." Music Journal, 7 (1949): 22.

Rose, Arnold. "The Italian Method and the English Singer." Musical Times, 96 (1955): 637-638.

Rushmore, Robert. "The Singing Voice: National Types." Opera News, 31 (1967): 22.

Ruth, Wilhelm. "The Registers of the Singing Voice." NATS Bulletin, 19 (1963): 2-5.

Scott, Anthony. "Acoustical Peculiarities of Head Tone and Falsetto." NATS Bulletin, 33 (1974): 32-35.

Seashore, Carl E. "Psychology of the Vibrato in Voice and Instrument." University of Iowa Studies in the Psychology of Music, 3 (1936): 7.

Sharnova, Sonia. "Breath Control--Foundation of Singing

and Acting Technique," Music Journal, 7 (1949):   36.

Simmions, Louis.   "The Two Points of View in Teaching the
Control of the Human Voice in Speech and Song."
Journal of the Acoustical Society of America, 2 (1930):
6

Smith, Ethel.   "An Electromyographic Investigation of the
Relationship between Abdominal Muscular Effort and
the Rate of Vocal Vibrato."   NATS Bulletin, 26
(1970):   2.

Smith, Michael.   "The Effect of Straight-Tone Feedback on
the Vibrato."   NATS Bulletin, 28 (1972):   28-33.

Sonninen, A.   "The Role of the External Laryngeal Muscles
in Length-Adjustment of the Vocal Cords in Singing."
Acta Oto-Laryngologica, Supplement 130 (1956):   1-102.

_____.   "The Role of the External Laryngeal Muscles in
the Adjustment of the Length of the Vocal Cords during Singing."   Folia Phoniatica, 10 (1958):   5-29.

Stevens, Kenneth N., and House, A. S.   "Development of a
Quantitative Description of Vowel Articulation."
Journal of the Acoustical Society of America, 27
(1955):   488-493.

Strongin, Lillian.   "What Is Bel Canto?"   NATS Bulletin,
22 (1965):   14-15.

Taff, Merle E.   "An Acoustic Study of Vowel Modification
and Register Transition in the Male Singing Voice."
NATS Bulletin, 22 (1965):   8-35.

Tarneau, Jean.   "Psychological and Clinical Study of the
Pneumophonic Synergy."   NATS Bulletin, 14 (1958):
12-15.

Taylor, Robert M.   "Acoustics for the Singer."   Emporia
State Research Studies, 6 (1958):   5-35.

Treash, Leonard.   "The Importance of Vowel Sounds and
Their Modification in Producing Good Tone."   NATS
Bulletin, 4 (1943):   3.

Truby, H. M.   "Contribution of the Pharyngeal Cavity to
Vowel Resonance and in General."   Journal of the

Acoustical Society of America, 34 (1912): 1978.

Wadsworth, Stephen. "Bonynge on Bel Canto: Interpreting the Early 19th Century." Opera News, 40 (1976): 18-22.

Waengler, Hans-Heinrich. "Some Remarks and Observations on the Function of the Soft Palate." NATS Bulletin, 25 (1968): 24.

Wooldridge, Warren B. "Is There Nasal Resonance?" NATS Bulletin, 13 (1953): 25.

Zemlin, W. R.; Mason, Robert M.; and Holstead, Lisa. "Notes on the Mechanics of Vocal Vibrato." NATS Bulletin, 28 (1971): 22-26.

Zerffi, William A. "Male and Female Voices." Archives of Otolaryngology, 65 (1957): 7-10.

INDEX

Abdomen
    action of, in appoggio, 41-43
    anatomy of, 11-13 (plate 8), 14
    in coughing, 13
    in sitting and standing, 41
    inward movement of, 30, 35-37
    outward and downward movement of, 9, 21, 22, 26-29,
      30
Acoustical properties of the vocal tract, 45-46, 50, 53, 55,
    59, 70, 73, 139, 174, 181
"Adam's apple", 127, 165
Agostoni, Emilio, The Respiratory Muscles, 11
Aikin, W. A. "Singing," Grove's Dictionary of Music and
    Musicians, 51-52
Anal orifice, 26
Anterolateral muscles, 14
appoggiare (appoggiarsi in petto, in testa), 41, 79, 80, 81
appoggio, 41-44, 79, 80, 146, 198
Armin, George, Von der Urkraft der Stimme, 28
Arytenoid cartilages, movements of, 4 (plate 3), 118
Arytenoid muscles, 3 (plate 2), 4 (plate 3), 5
Atemstütze, 21
attacco (l'attacco della voce, l'attacco del suono), 6
Attack
    aspirated, 2, 5, 6
    Garcia and the, 2, 4, 6
    glottal, 2, 4, 6
    hard, 4-5
    light cough as, 5
    physical action in, 1, 4 (plate 3)
    precise, 6
    soft, 2, 5, 6, 73
    stylistic influences on, 6
    vibrato excluded from, 145
    whispered, 73
ausgeglichene Vokale, 48

"cantare come si parla," 175
Cantilena, 110, 169, 177
Caruso, 5, 78, 91
Castrati, 106, 107, 109, 110, 115, 122, 123
"Cathedral tone," 77-78, 148, 163
"chanter dans le masque," 76
Character alto, 133, 154-155
Charakter-bariton, 170
Chest (thoracic cage)
    anatomy of, 7-8, 10 (plate 5), 11, 19 (plate 12)
    calculated collapse of, 28
    elevation of, 33, 36-37, 158
    heaving, 18
    in lifting, 37
    lowered posture of, 21, 26, 29, 31, 158
    muscular connection of, with pelvis, 14, 25
    muscular resistance in, 44
    recoil of wall of, during expiration 11
    stabilization of, in appoggio, 43
    sternocleidomastoidal action with the, 89
Chest mixture, 131, 132, 133, 145, 147, 150, 154, 171
Chest voice, 104, 116, 118, 120, 121, 122, 123, 124, 129,
        131, 133, 134, 135, 145, 147, 150, 152, 153, 154,
        159, 162, 170, 171
chiaroscuro, 78, 79, 82, 96, 142, 159
Chin
    elevation of, 84, 85, 158
    pressure upon larynx, 87
"chi pronuncia bene, canta bene," 177
Chondroglossus, 89
Choral singing, 148-149, 191, 201, 202, 203
Clavicles
    as auxiliary muscles of breathing, 18, 33, 85
    in action with shoulder muscles, 33-35, 40, 89
Coccygeus
    in relation to levatores ani, 25-26
    opposition to intra-abdominal pressures, 26
Coloratura soprano, 83, 135, 143, 145, 146, 147, 149
colpo della glottide (colpo di glottide), 2, 6
"come si parla," 56
"comme on parle," 76
Constrictor pharyngis inferior, 62, 64 (plates 15 & 16),
        68 (plate 18)
Constrictor pharyngis medius, 62, 64 (plate 15 & 16), 68
        (plate 18), 89
Constrictor pharyngis superior, 62, 64 (plates 15 & 16),
        68 (plate 18)

Physics, Medicine and Music Related to the Human
Voice, 31
harter Einsatz, 2, 4
Head mixture, 131, 132
Head posture, 40, 84, 90, 158
Head sensation, 44, 118, 119, 121, 135
Head voice, 5, 70, 71, 81, 113, 114, 118, 120, 121, 122,
123, 125, 134, 135, 147, 150, 152, 153
Heaton, Wallace. An Interdisciplinary Index of Studies in
Physics, Medicine and Music Related to the Human
Voice, 31.
Heavy mechanism, 103, 118, 124, 132, 133, 134, 159, 162
Heldenbariton, 170
Heldentenor, 29, 129, 157, 160
Henderson, W. J., Early History of Singing, 101
heroic technique, 5, 6, 29
Higgins, John, Interview of Nicolai Gedda in The Times
(London), 76
hochdramatische Sopran, 144, 145
hohe Quinta, 120
Humeris, in relation to latissimus dorsi, 34
Husson, Raoul, La voix chantée, 87
influence on French pedagogy, 190
low laryngeal position considered by, 87
phonation in absence of air currents investigated by,
30-31
Hyoid bone, 3 (plate 2), 66 (plate 17), 68 (plate 18), 77,
85, 89
Hypoglossus, 19 (plate 13), 64 (plate 15), 66 (plate 17), 89

Ibos, Guilliaume, 87, 91
l'impostazione della voce, 79, 80
l'impostazione dell'organo fonatore, 79
Imposto, 79; see also Placement
Infrahyoid muscles, 87
ingolato, 160
Intercostal muscles
action of, 8-9, 11, 23, 24, 26, 36, 38
anatomy of, 8, 9, 10 (plate 6), 17 (plate 11)
Internal Congress for the Training of Musicians, 22
Internal oblique, 10 (plate 6), 12-13 (plate 8), 16 (plate 10),
17 (plate 11)
Internal thyroarytenoids, 134
Interosseus internal intercostals, 9
Irish tenor, 129, 155

Pharynx see also Buccopharynx
    anatomy of, 61 (plate 14), 64 (plate 15 & 16), 66
        (plate 17), 68 (plate 18)
    as resonator, 60
    cavity of, 46
    enlargement of, 63, 64, 65, 67, 69, 70, 75, 139, 144,
        152
    low jaw posture and, 52-53
    muscular action in shaping of, 62, 63
    narrowed, 49, 97-98
    spread, 72, 137, 160, 162, 168
piano allemand, 71
piano tedesco, 71, 74
Piccolo range, 120; see also Bell register
Pitch, 53, 59
    buccal position in ascending, 138, 139
    fluctuation of, as corrective mechanism, 95
    frequencies of fixed, 73
    in "cathedral" tone, 148
    intrinsic laryngeal action in ascending, 118, 120
    upper partials in ascending, 137, 140
Placement see also l'imposto; Resonance
    and appoggio technique, 79
    coordination of breath and, 80
    facial, 77, 144, 147
    forehead, 72
    forward, 59, 76, 77, 78, 110, 144, 147
    head, 119
    Hinterkopf, 72
    imagery of, 58, 59, 71, 72, 101
    in Kopfstimme, 70
    in lowered laryngeal position, 88
    pedagogic controversy regarding, 59-60
    pharyngeal, 63, 65
    posterior, 67, 69-70
    sensation, 58, 147
Platysma, 89
Pleasants, Henry, The Great Singers, 115
"plus en avant," 76, 147
Posterior cricoarytenoids, 3 (plate 2), 4 (plate 3)
Posture, 21, 24, 25, 28, 33, 37, 38, 39, 41, 43, 44, 85
Primitive cry, 28, 134
primo passaggio, 104, 117, 123, 128, 129, 138, 139, 164;
      see also passaggio
Prinzip des Nach-hinten-Singens, 67, 71
pronuncia aperta, 176
Puberty, developmental aspects of, 116, 120, 122, 123,
    164